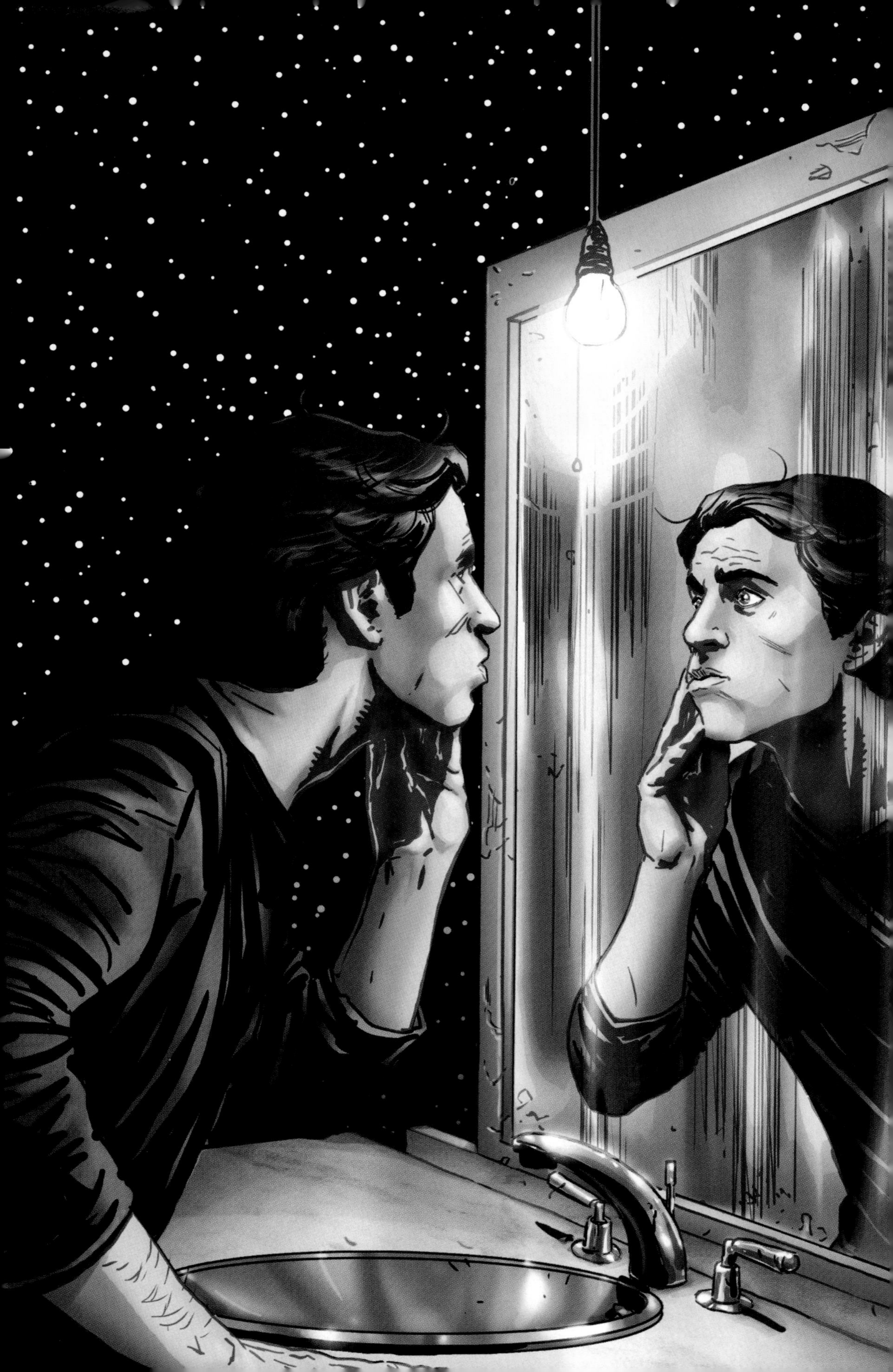

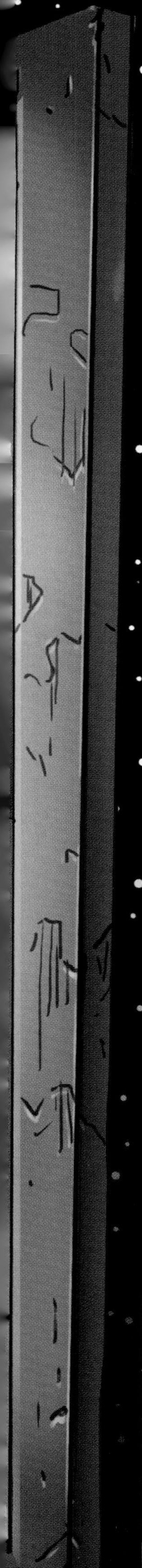

The TWILIGHT ZONE

VOLUME ONE: THE WAY OUT

WRITTEN BY
J. MICHAEL STRACZYNSKI

ILLUSTRATED BY
GUIU VILANOVA

COLORED BY
VINICIUS ANDRADE

LETTERED BY
ROB STEEN

COVER BY
FRANCESCO FRANCAVILLA

DYNAMITE®

Nick Barrucci, CEO / Publisher
Juan Collado, President / COO
Rich Young, Director Business Development
Keith Davidsen, Marketing Manager

Joe Rybandt, Senior Editor
Hannah Gorfinkel, Associate Editor
Josh Green, Traffic Coordinator
Molly Mahan, Assistant Editor

Josh Johnson, Art Director
Jason Ullmeyer, Senior Graphic Designer
Katie Hidalgo, Graphic Designer
Chris Caniano, Production Assistant

ISBN-10: 1-60690-505-8
ISBN-13: 978-1-60690-505-0
First Printing
10 9 8 7 6 5 4 3 2 1

Certified Chain of Custody
Promoting Sustainable Forestry
SUSTAINABLE FORESTRY INITIATIVE
www.sfiprogram.org
This label only applies to the text section.

Visit us online at **www.DYNAMITE.com**
Follow us on Twitter **@dynamitecomics**
Like us on Facebook **/Dynamitecomics**
Watch us on YouTube **/Dynamitecomics**

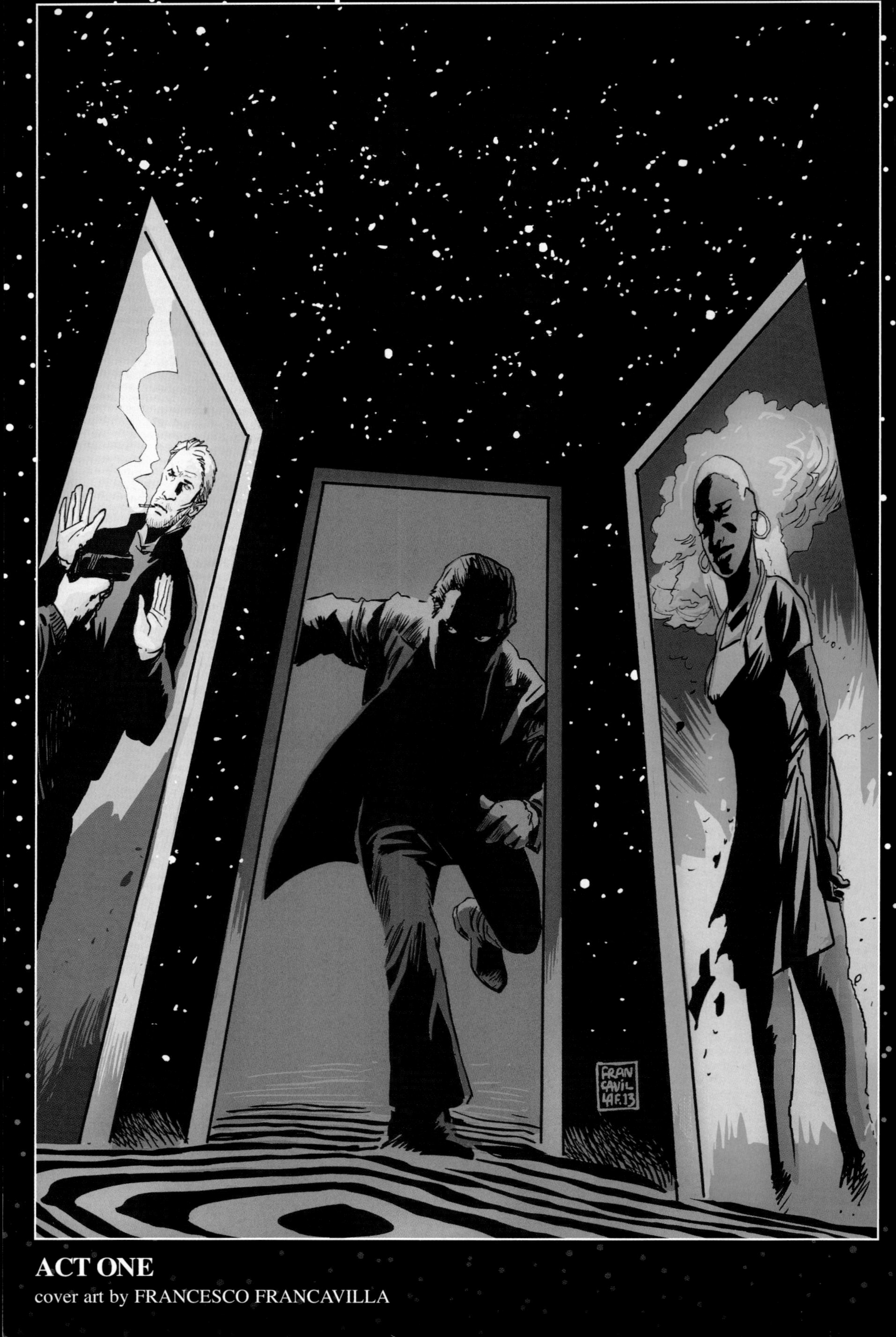
FRAN
CAVIL
LA F.13

ACT ONE

cover art by FRANCESCO FRANCAVILLA

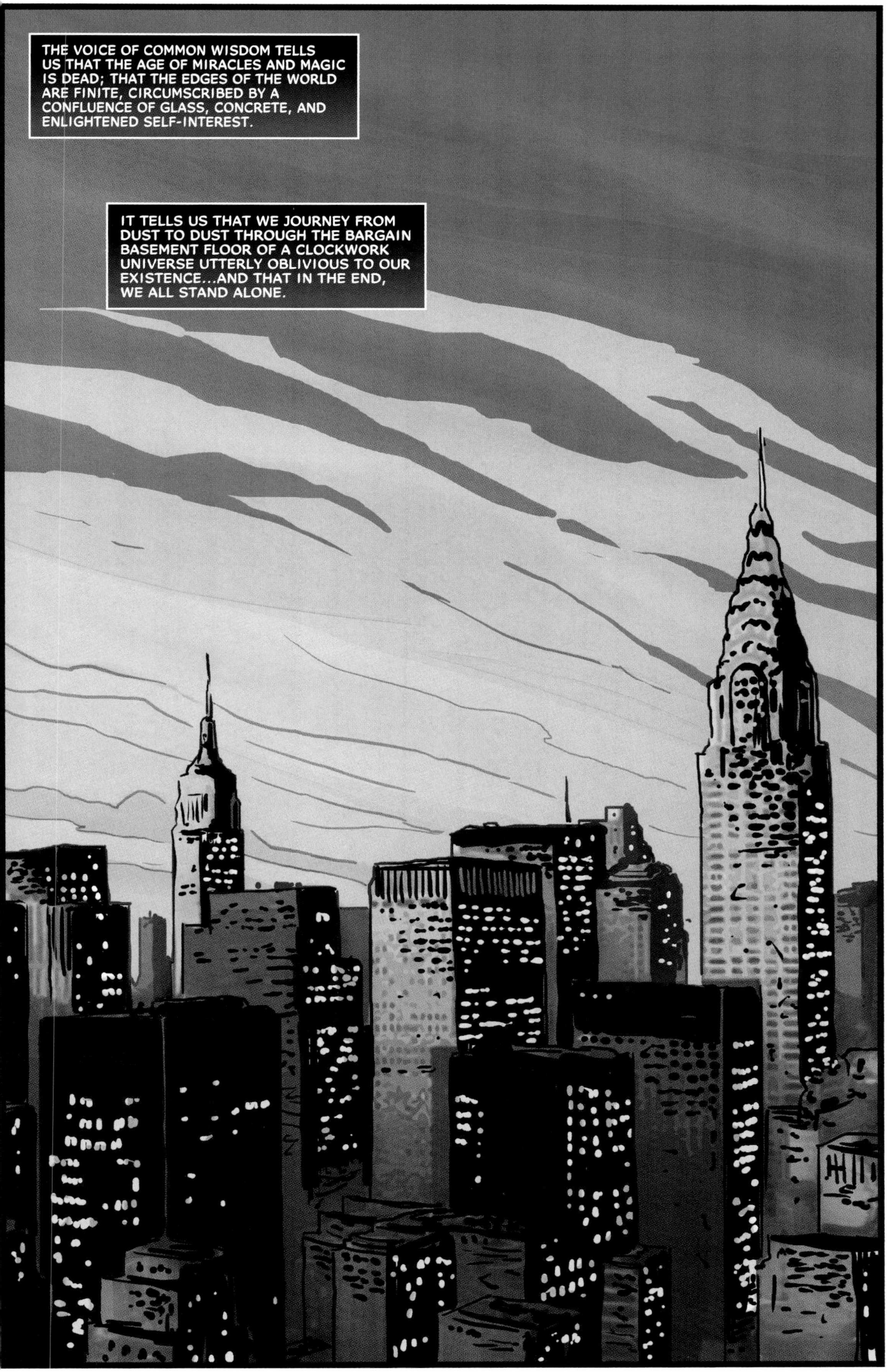
THE VOICE OF COMMON WISDOM TELLS US THAT THE AGE OF MIRACLES AND MAGIC IS DEAD; THAT THE EDGES OF THE WORLD ARE FINITE, CIRCUMSCRIBED BY A CONFLUENCE OF GLASS, CONCRETE, AND ENLIGHTENED SELF-INTEREST.
IT TELLS US THAT WE JOURNEY FROM DUST TO DUST THROUGH THE BARGAIN BASEMENT FLOOR OF A CLOCKWORK UNIVERSE UTTERLY OBLIVIOUS TO OUR EXISTENCE...AND THAT IN THE END, WE ALL STAND ALONE.

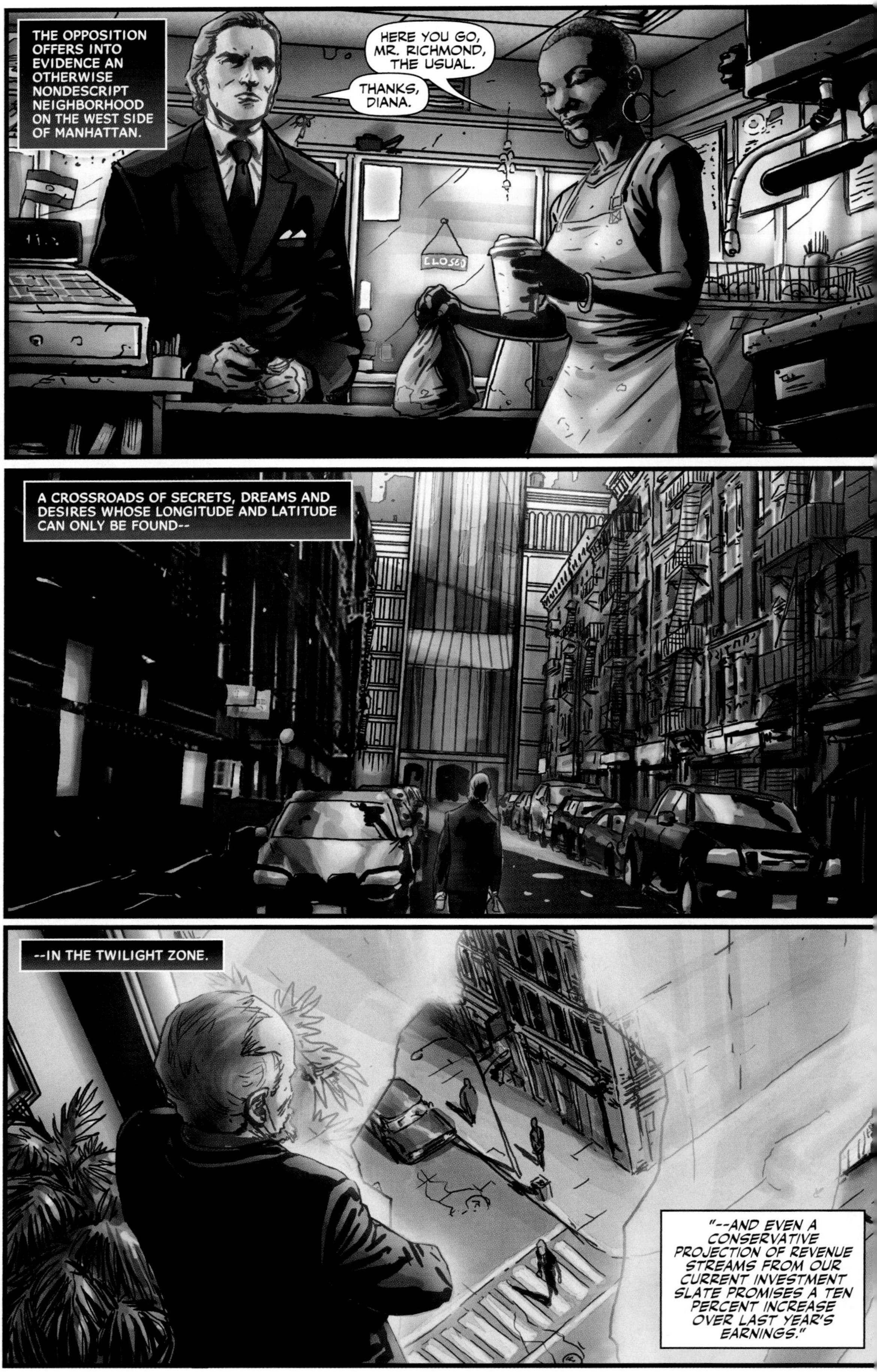
THE OPPOSITION OFFERS INTO EVIDENCE AN OTHERWISE NONDESCRIPT NEIGHBORHOOD ON THE WEST SIDE OF MANHATTAN.
HERE YOU GO, MR. RICHMOND, THE USUAL.
THANKS, DIANA.
A CROSSROADS OF SECRETS, DREAMS AND DESIRES WHOSE LONGITUDE AND LATITUDE CAN ONLY BE FOUND--
--IN THE TWILIGHT ZONE.
"--AND EVEN A CONSERVATIVE PROJECTION OF REVENUE STREAMS FROM OUR CURRENT INVESTMENT SLATE PROMISES A TEN PERCENT INCREASE OVER LAST YEAR'S EARNINGS."

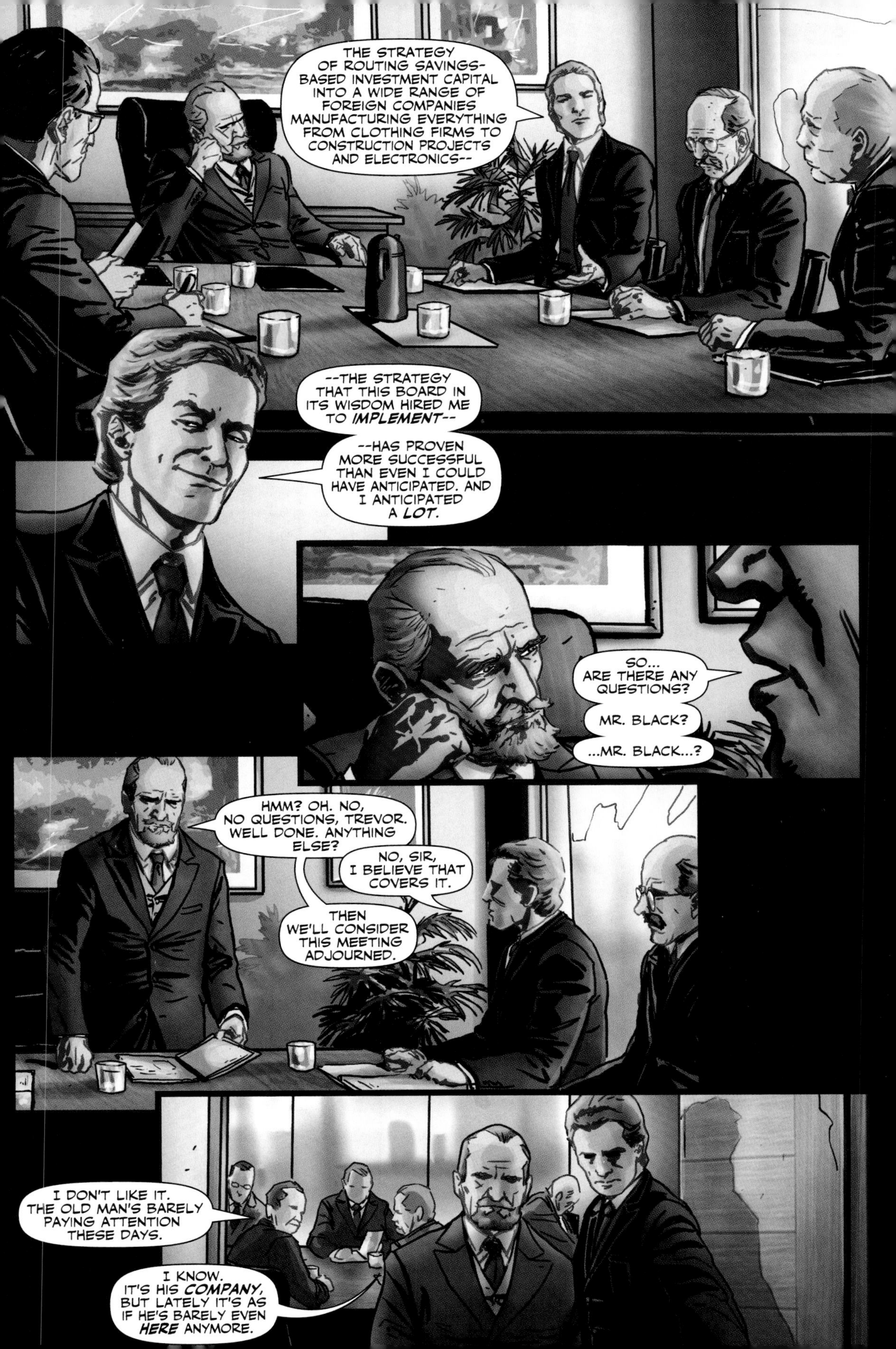
THE STRATEGY OF ROUTING SAVINGS-BASED INVESTMENT CAPITAL INTO A WIDE RANGE OF FOREIGN COMPANIES MANUFACTURING EVERYTHING FROM CLOTHING FIRMS TO CONSTRUCTION PROJECTS AND ELECTRONICS--
--THE STRATEGY THAT THIS BOARD IN ITS WISDOM HIRED ME TO *IMPLEMENT*--
--HAS PROVEN MORE SUCCESSFUL THAN EVEN I COULD HAVE ANTICIPATED. AND I ANTICIPATED A *LOT*.
SO... ARE THERE ANY QUESTIONS?
MR. BLACK?
...MR. BLACK...?
HMM? OH. NO, NO QUESTIONS, TREVOR. WELL DONE. ANYTHING ELSE?
NO, SIR, I BELIEVE THAT COVERS IT.
THEN WE'LL CONSIDER THIS MEETING ADJOURNED.
I DON'T LIKE IT. THE OLD MAN'S BARELY PAYING ATTENTION THESE DAYS.
I KNOW. IT'S HIS *COMPANY*, BUT LATELY IT'S AS IF HE'S BARELY EVEN *HERE* ANYMORE.

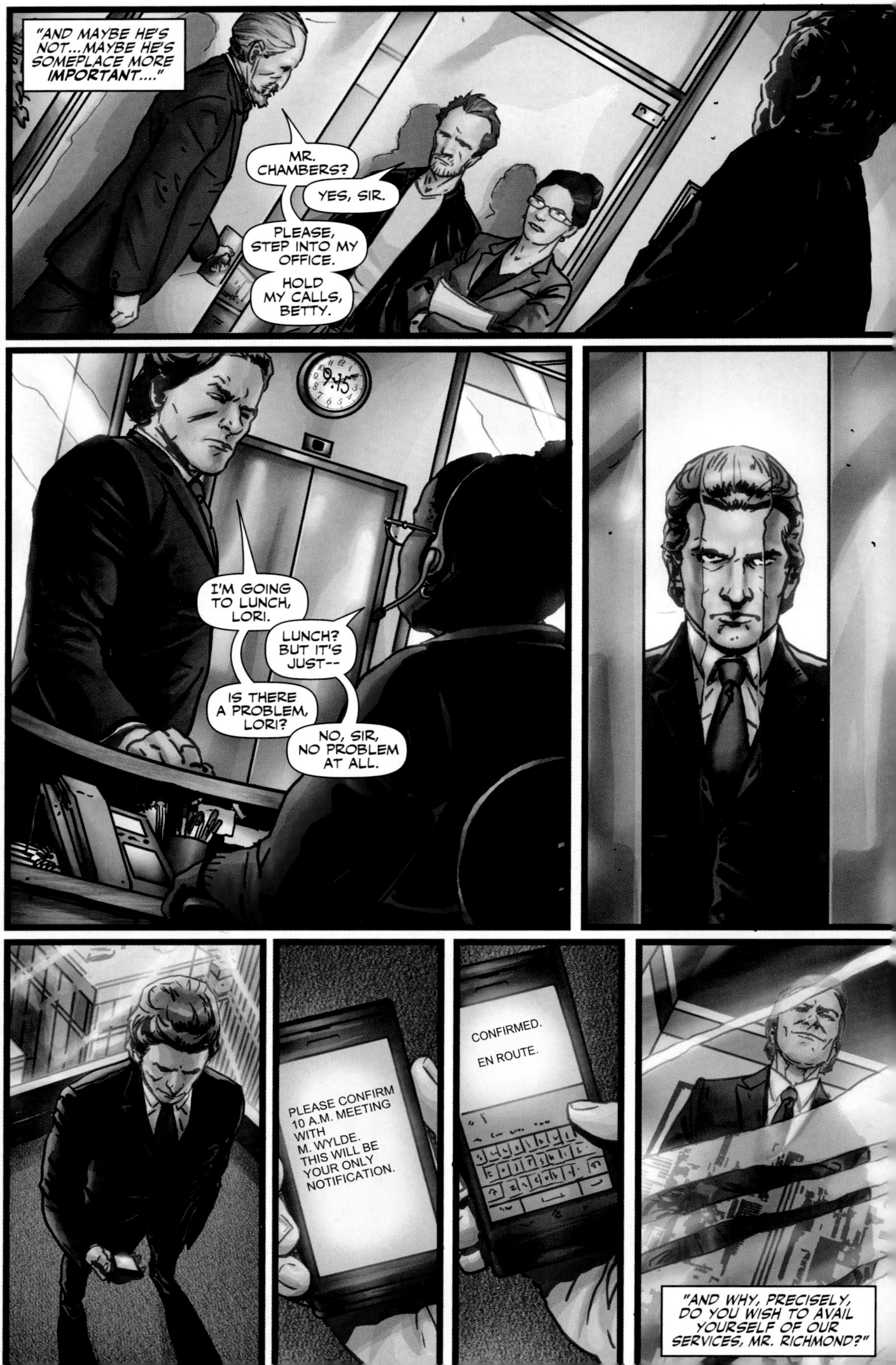
"AND MAYBE HE'S NOT...MAYBE HE'S SOMEPLACE MORE IMPORTANT...."
MR. CHAMBERS?
YES, SIR.
PLEASE, STEP INTO MY OFFICE.
HOLD MY CALLS, BETTY.
I'M GOING TO LUNCH, LORI.
LUNCH? BUT IT'S JUST--
IS THERE A PROBLEM, LORI?
NO, SIR, NO PROBLEM AT ALL.
PLEASE CONFIRM 10 A.M. MEETING WITH M. WYLDE. THIS WILL BE YOUR ONLY NOTIFICATION.
CONFIRMED.
EN ROUTE.
"AND WHY, PRECISELY, DO YOU WISH TO AVAIL YOURSELF OF OUR SERVICES, MR. RICHMOND?"

I'M A MAN WHO LIKES CHALLENGES, MR. WYLDE. I'VE GONE ABOUT AS FAR AS I CAN IN MY CURRENT SITUATION, AND I'D LIKE TO START FRESH, START *OVER* WITH A NEW SET OF CHALLENGES.

AND A NEW NAME, A NEW IDENTITY--

OF COURSE.

MMMMM.

STARTING OVER IN THE WAY OUR FIRM CAN ARRANGE IS NOT SOMETHING TO BE DONE OUT OF BOREDOM, ONLY AS A LAST RESORT. SURELY THERE ARE NEW CHALLENGES STILL BEFORE YOU?

NOT REALLY....

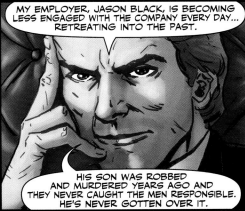

MY EMPLOYER, JASON BLACK, IS BECOMING LESS ENGAGED WITH THE COMPANY EVERY DAY... RETREATING INTO THE PAST.

HIS SON WAS ROBBED AND MURDERED YEARS AGO AND THEY NEVER CAUGHT THE MEN RESPONSIBLE. HE'S NEVER GOTTEN OVER IT.

"NOW THAT HE'S APPROACHING DEATH HIMSELF, THAT LOSS IS PULLING HIM DOWN. HE CAN'T MOVE FORWARD AND HE WON'T LET ANYONE ELSE--ME, FOR INSTANCE--STEP IN TO TAKE OVER."

PROMISE A DYING MAN THAT YOU WILL GO WHEREVER THE TRUTH TAKES YOU, NO MATTER WHERE IT LEADS.

YOU HAVE MY WORD, MR. BLACK.

"I'M DROWNING IN ROUTINE. I EVEN PICK UP THE SAME EGG SANDWICH EVERY MORNING ON MY WAY TO THE OFFICE."

WHAT'S THAT?

I DON'T KNOW...A COIN OF SOME KIND. LOOKS REALLY OLD.

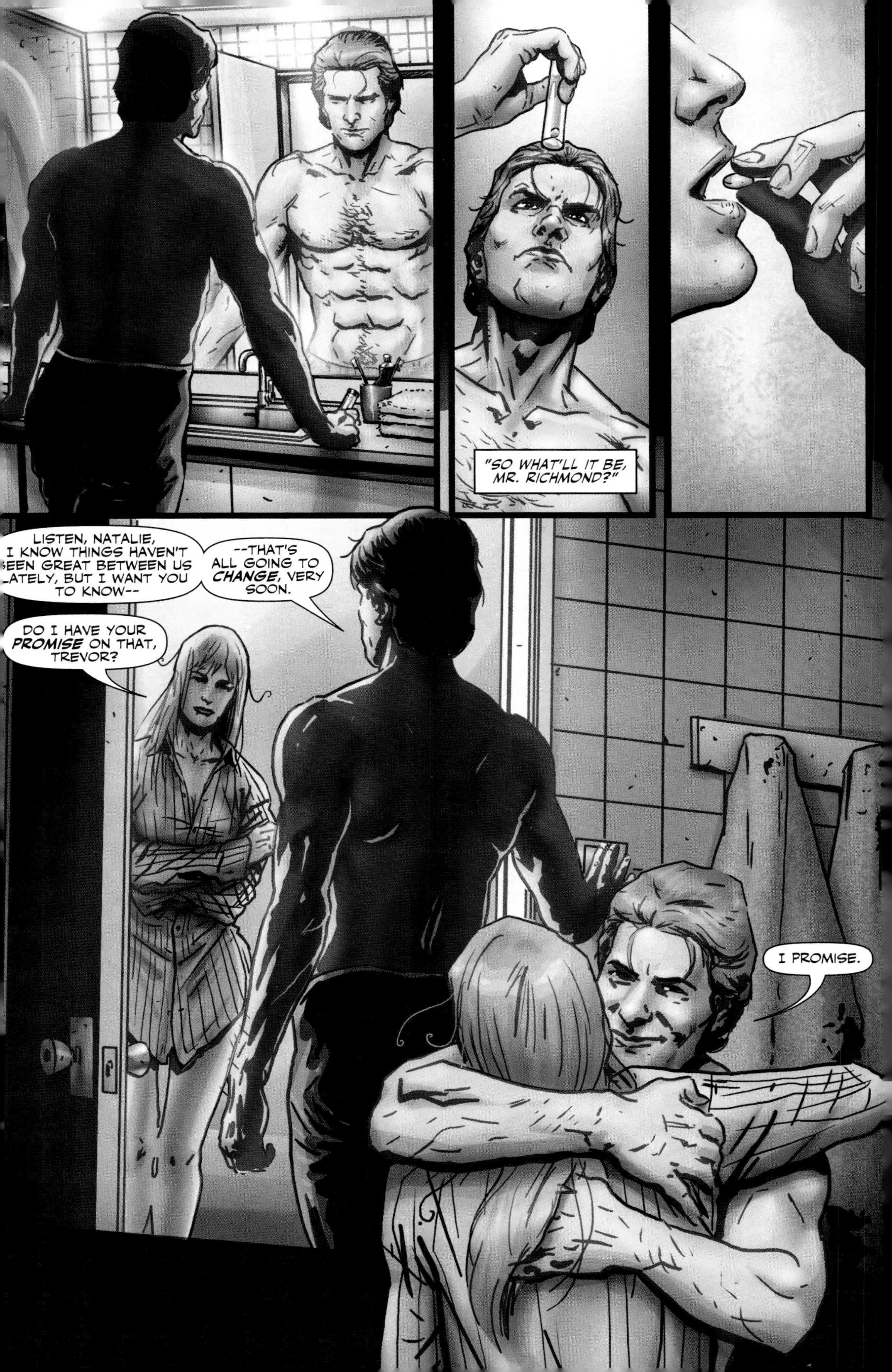
"SO WHAT'LL IT BE, MR. RICHMOND?"
LISTEN, NATALIE, I KNOW THINGS HAVEN'T BEEN GREAT BETWEEN US LATELY, BUT I WANT YOU TO KNOW--
--THAT'S ALL GOING TO CHANGE, VERY SOON.
DO I HAVE YOUR PROMISE ON THAT, TREVOR?
I PROMISE.

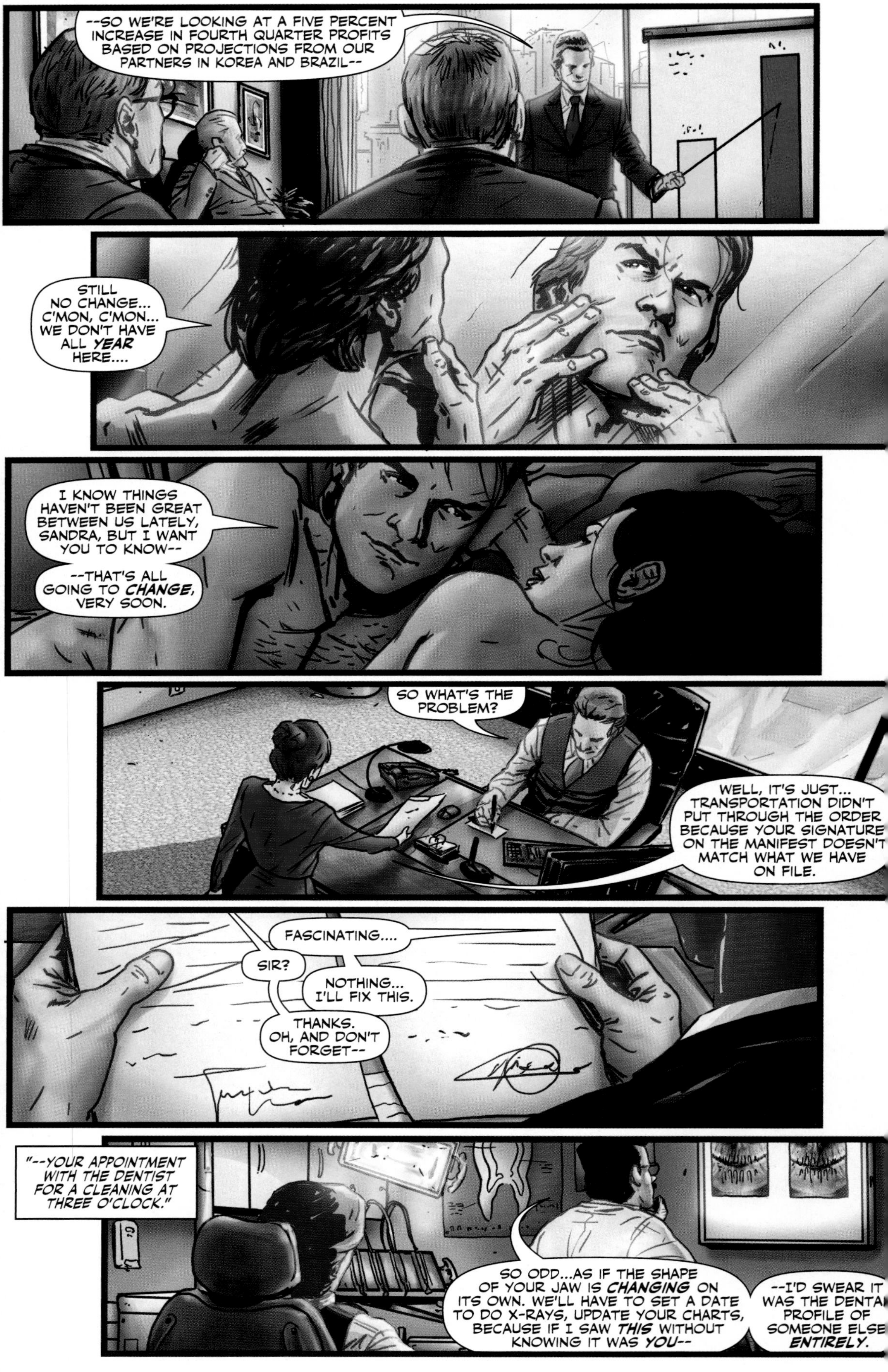
--SO WE'RE LOOKING AT A FIVE PERCENT INCREASE IN FOURTH QUARTER PROFITS BASED ON PROJECTIONS FROM OUR PARTNERS IN KOREA AND BRAZIL--
STILL NO CHANGE... C'MON, C'MON... WE DON'T HAVE ALL YEAR HERE....
I KNOW THINGS HAVEN'T BEEN GREAT BETWEEN US LATELY, SANDRA, BUT I WANT YOU TO KNOW--
--THAT'S ALL GOING TO CHANGE, VERY SOON.
SO WHAT'S THE PROBLEM?
WELL, IT'S JUST... TRANSPORTATION DIDN'T PUT THROUGH THE ORDER BECAUSE YOUR SIGNATURE ON THE MANIFEST DOESN'T MATCH WHAT WE HAVE ON FILE.
FASCINATING....
SIR?
NOTHING... I'LL FIX THIS.
THANKS. OH, AND DON'T FORGET--
"--YOUR APPOINTMENT WITH THE DENTIST FOR A CLEANING AT THREE O'CLOCK."
SO ODD...AS IF THE SHAPE OF YOUR JAW IS CHANGING ON ITS OWN. WE'LL HAVE TO SET A DATE TO DO X-RAYS, UPDATE YOUR CHARTS, BECAUSE IF I SAW THIS WITHOUT KNOWING IT WAS YOU--
--I'D SWEAR IT WAS THE DENTAL PROFILE OF SOMEONE ELSE ENTIRELY.

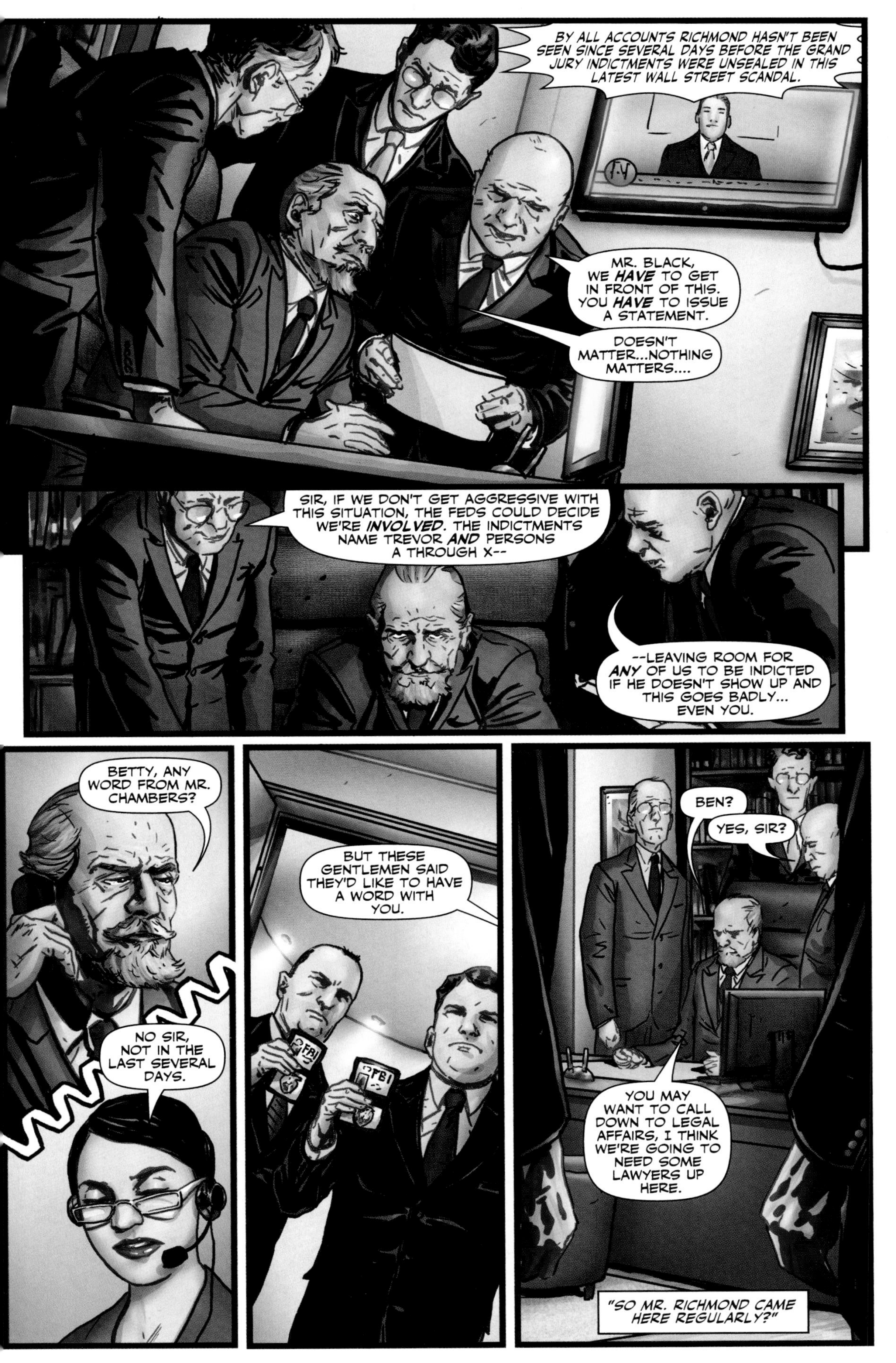
BY ALL ACCOUNTS RICHMOND HASN'T BEEN SEEN SINCE SEVERAL DAYS BEFORE THE GRAND JURY INDICTMENTS WERE UNSEALED IN THIS LATEST WALL STREET SCANDAL.
MR. BLACK, WE *HAVE* TO GET IN FRONT OF THIS. YOU *HAVE* TO ISSUE A STATEMENT.
DOESN'T MATTER...NOTHING MATTERS....
SIR, IF WE DON'T GET AGGRESSIVE WITH THIS SITUATION, THE FEDS COULD DECIDE WE'RE *INVOLVED*. THE INDICTMENTS NAME TREVOR *AND* PERSONS A THROUGH X--
--LEAVING ROOM FOR *ANY* OF US TO BE INDICTED IF HE DOESN'T SHOW UP AND THIS GOES BADLY... EVEN YOU.
BETTY, ANY WORD FROM MR. CHAMBERS?
NO SIR, NOT IN THE LAST SEVERAL DAYS.
BUT THESE GENTLEMEN SAID THEY'D LIKE TO HAVE A WORD WITH YOU.
FBI
FBI
BEN?
YES, SIR?
YOU MAY WANT TO CALL DOWN TO LEGAL AFFAIRS, I THINK WE'RE GOING TO NEED SOME LAWYERS UP HERE.
"SO MR. RICHMOND CAME HERE REGULARLY?"

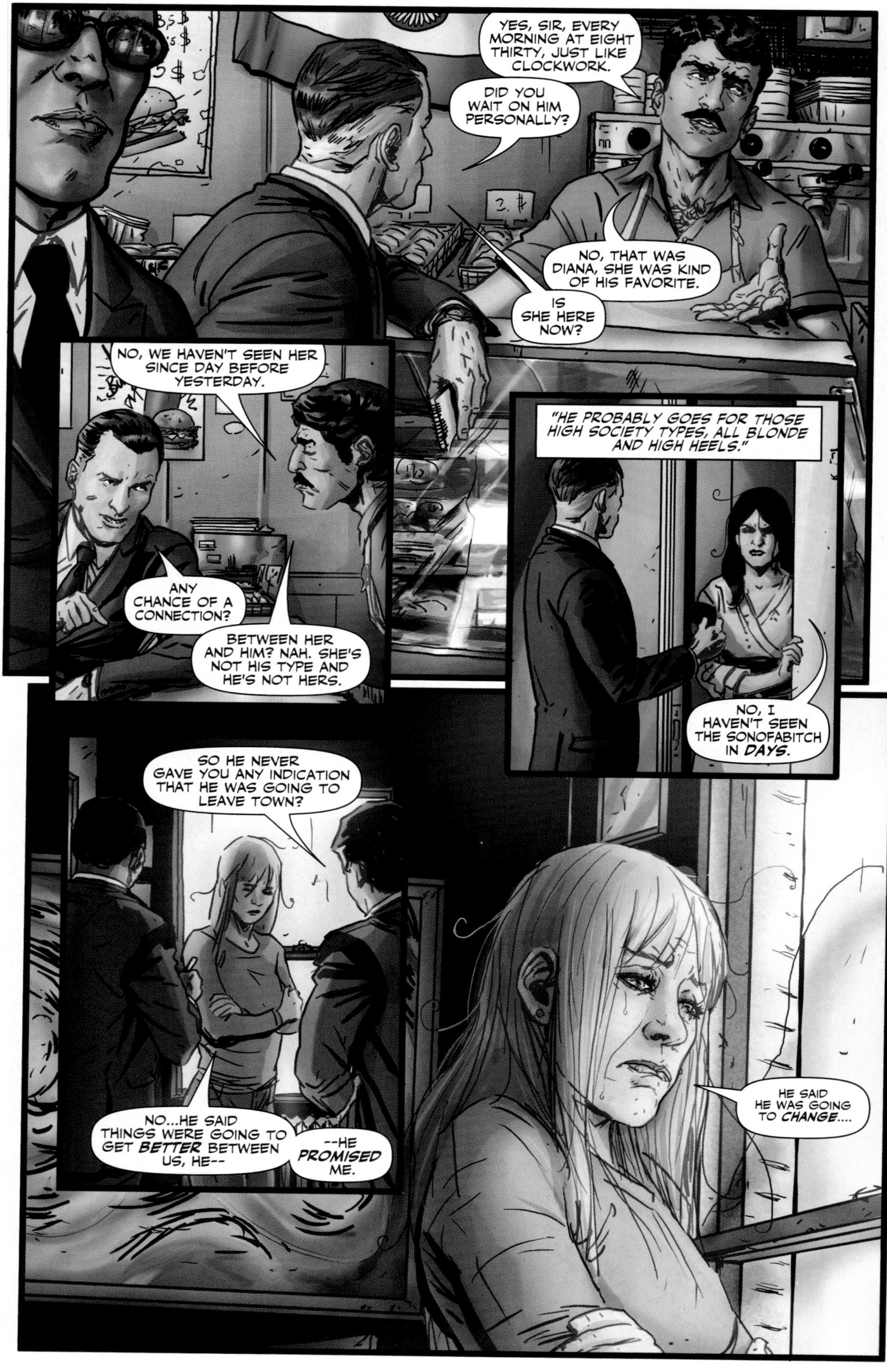

YES, SIR, EVERY MORNING AT EIGHT THIRTY, JUST LIKE CLOCKWORK.
DID YOU WAIT ON HIM PERSONALLY?
NO, THAT WAS DIANA, SHE WAS KIND OF HIS FAVORITE.
IS SHE HERE NOW?
NO, WE HAVEN'T SEEN HER SINCE DAY BEFORE YESTERDAY.
ANY CHANCE OF A CONNECTION?
BETWEEN HER AND HIM? NAH. SHE'S NOT HIS TYPE AND HE'S NOT HERS.
"HE PROBABLY GOES FOR THOSE HIGH SOCIETY TYPES, ALL BLONDE AND HIGH HEELS."
NO, I HAVEN'T SEEN THE SONOFABITCH IN *DAYS*.
SO HE NEVER GAVE YOU ANY INDICATION THAT HE WAS GOING TO LEAVE TOWN?
NO...HE SAID THINGS WERE GOING TO GET **BETTER** BETWEEN US, HE--
--HE ***PROMISED*** ME.
HE SAID HE WAS GOING TO ***CHANGE***....

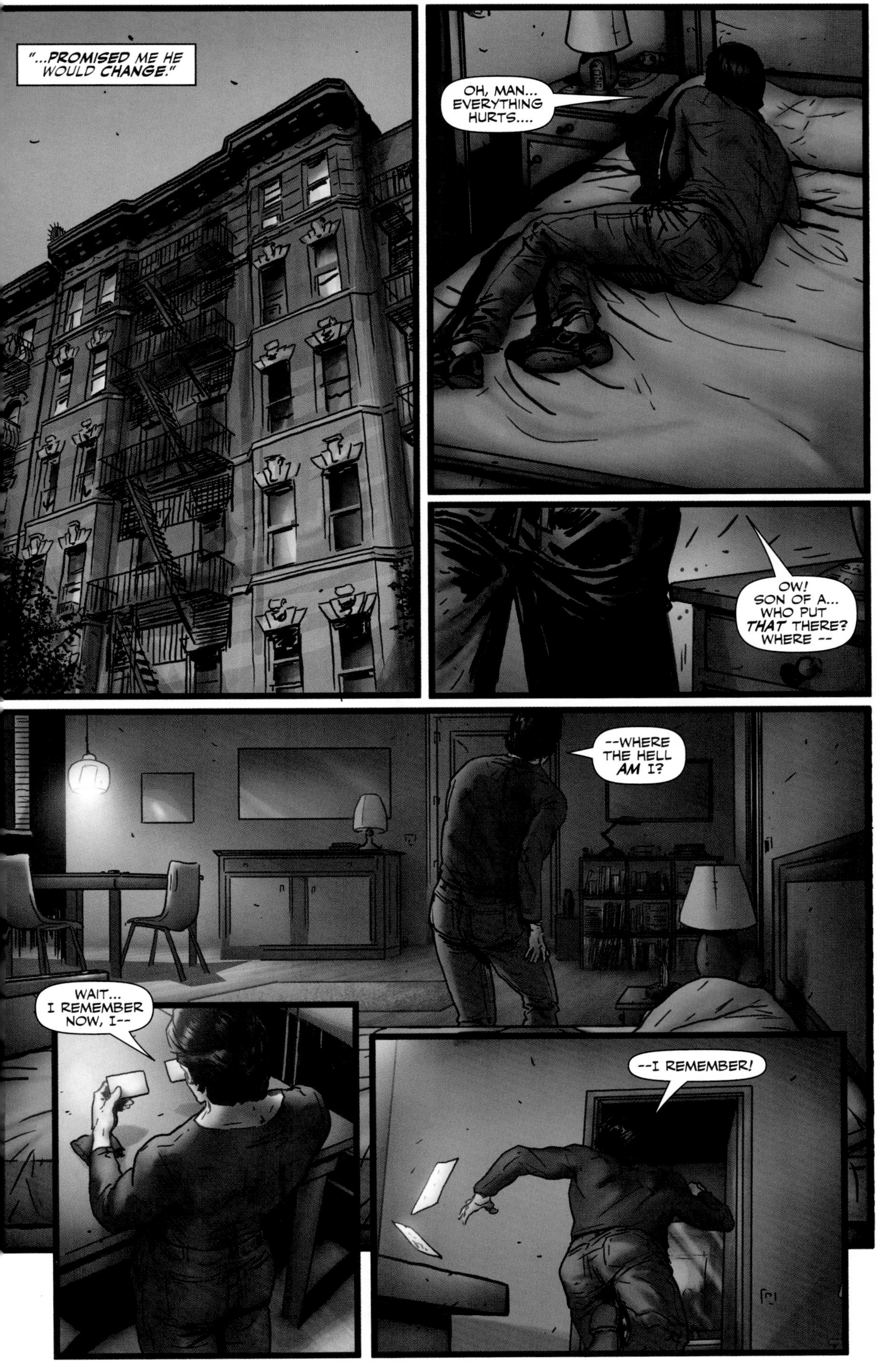
"...PROMISED ME HE WOULD CHANGE."
OH, MAN... EVERYTHING HURTS....
OW! SON OF A... WHO PUT THAT THERE? WHERE --
--WHERE THE HELL AM I?
WAIT... I REMEMBER NOW, I--
--I REMEMBER!

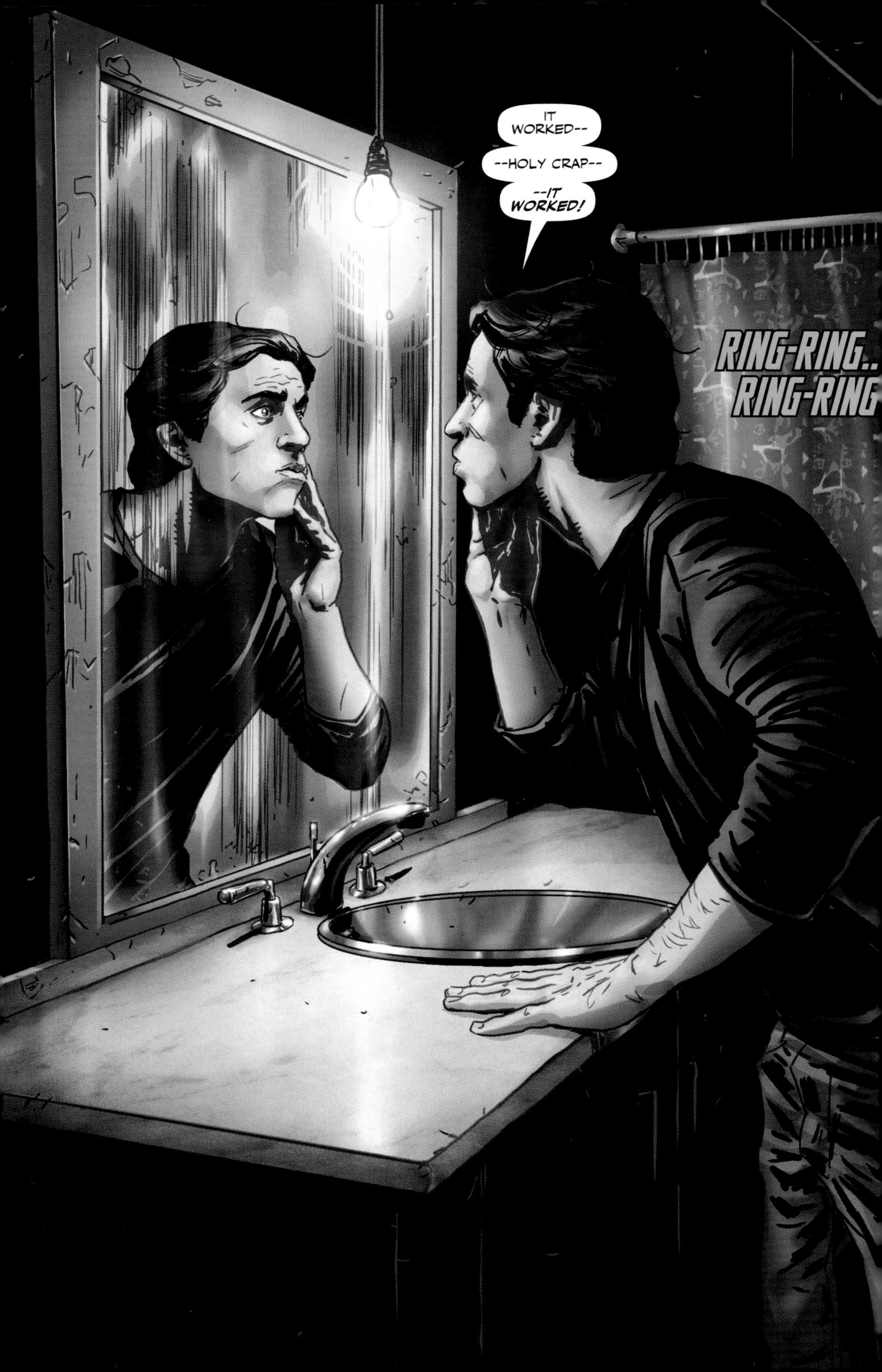
IT WORKED--
--HOLY CRAP--
--IT WORKED!
RING-RING.. RING-RING

RING-RING...
RING-RING....

HELLO?

WELCOME TO YOUR NEW LIFE, THOMAS.

THOMAS?

THOMAS RILEY. PUCKISH, I SUPPOSE, BUT I GAVE YOU THE SAME INITIALS IN CASE YOU LOVED THE LOOK IN A MONOGRAM.

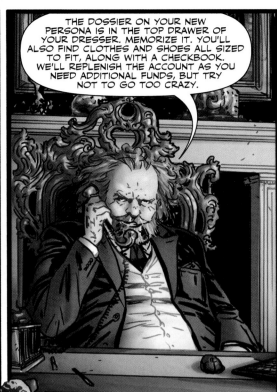

THE DOSSIER ON YOUR NEW PERSONA IS IN THE TOP DRAWER OF YOUR DRESSER. MEMORIZE IT. YOU'LL ALSO FIND CLOTHES AND SHOES ALL SIZED TO FIT, ALONG WITH A CHECKBOOK. WE'LL REPLENISH THE ACCOUNT AS YOU NEED ADDITIONAL FUNDS, BUT TRY NOT TO GO TOO CRAZY.

THESE LOOK USED--

A CAREFUL ILLUSION. NOTHING MORE SUSPICIOUS THAN SOMEONE WHO APPEARS OUT OF NOWHERE WITH AN ALL NEW WARDROBE.

SINCE YOU'VE BEEN OUT OF THE LOOP FOR A WHILE, YOU SHOULD KNOW THAT THE HAMMER HAS FALLEN, AS PREDICTED. BUT BECAUSE OF YOUR FORESIGHT, IT'S GOING TO HIT EVERYONE BUT YOU. YOU SHOULD BE MOST PROUD.

THAT SAID: NEVER CONTACT US AGAIN EXCEPT IN AN EMERGENCY. GOODBYE, MR. RILEY.

YES! I DID IT! I GOT AWAY WITH IT!

YES!

CLICK

"AS AFTERSHOCKS OF THE LATEST WALL STREET SCANDAL CONTINUE TO RIPPLE OUT ACROSS THE FINANCIAL COMMUNITY."

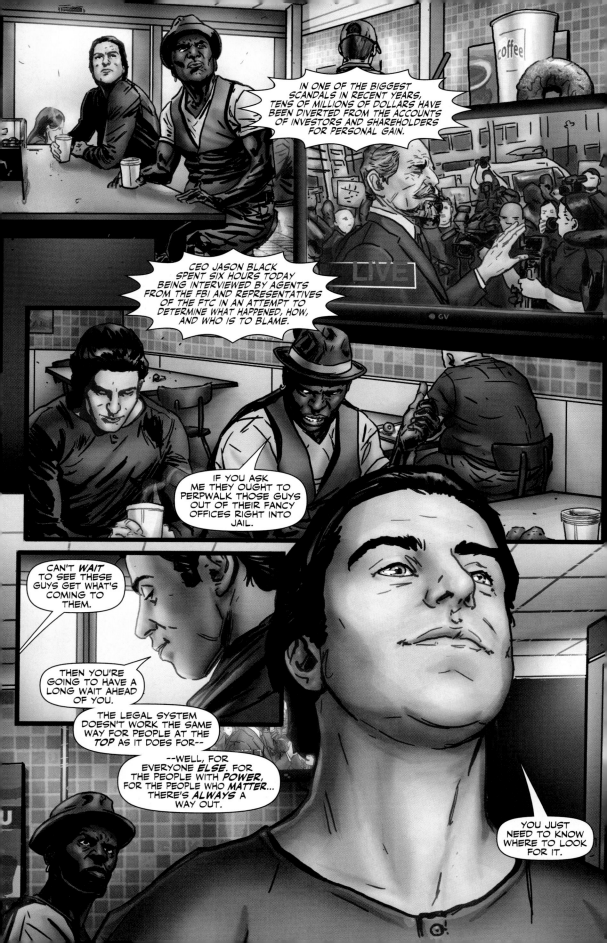

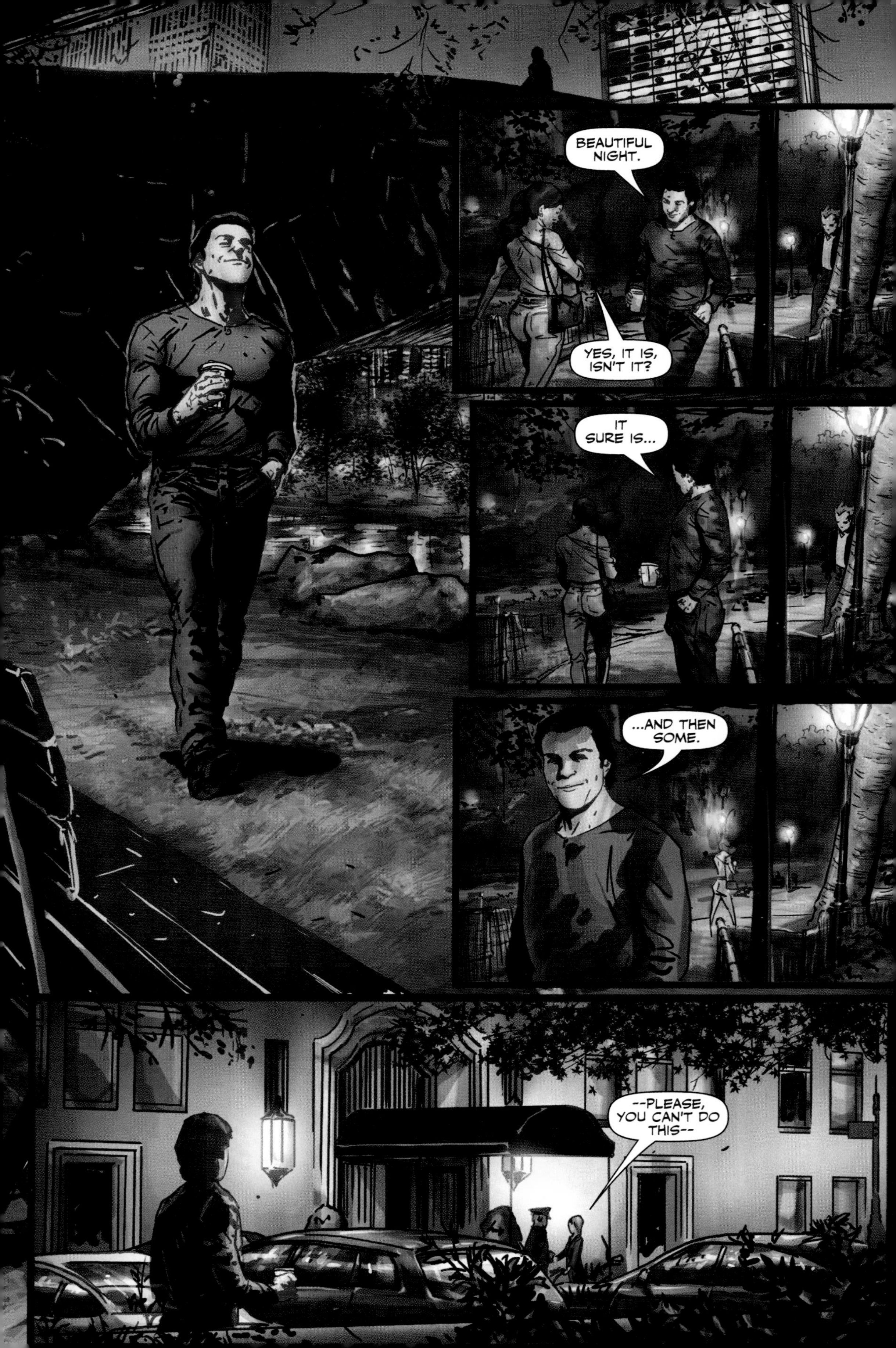
BEAUTIFUL NIGHT.
YES, IT IS, ISN'T IT?
IT SURE IS...
...AND THEN SOME.
--PLEASE, YOU CAN'T DO THIS--

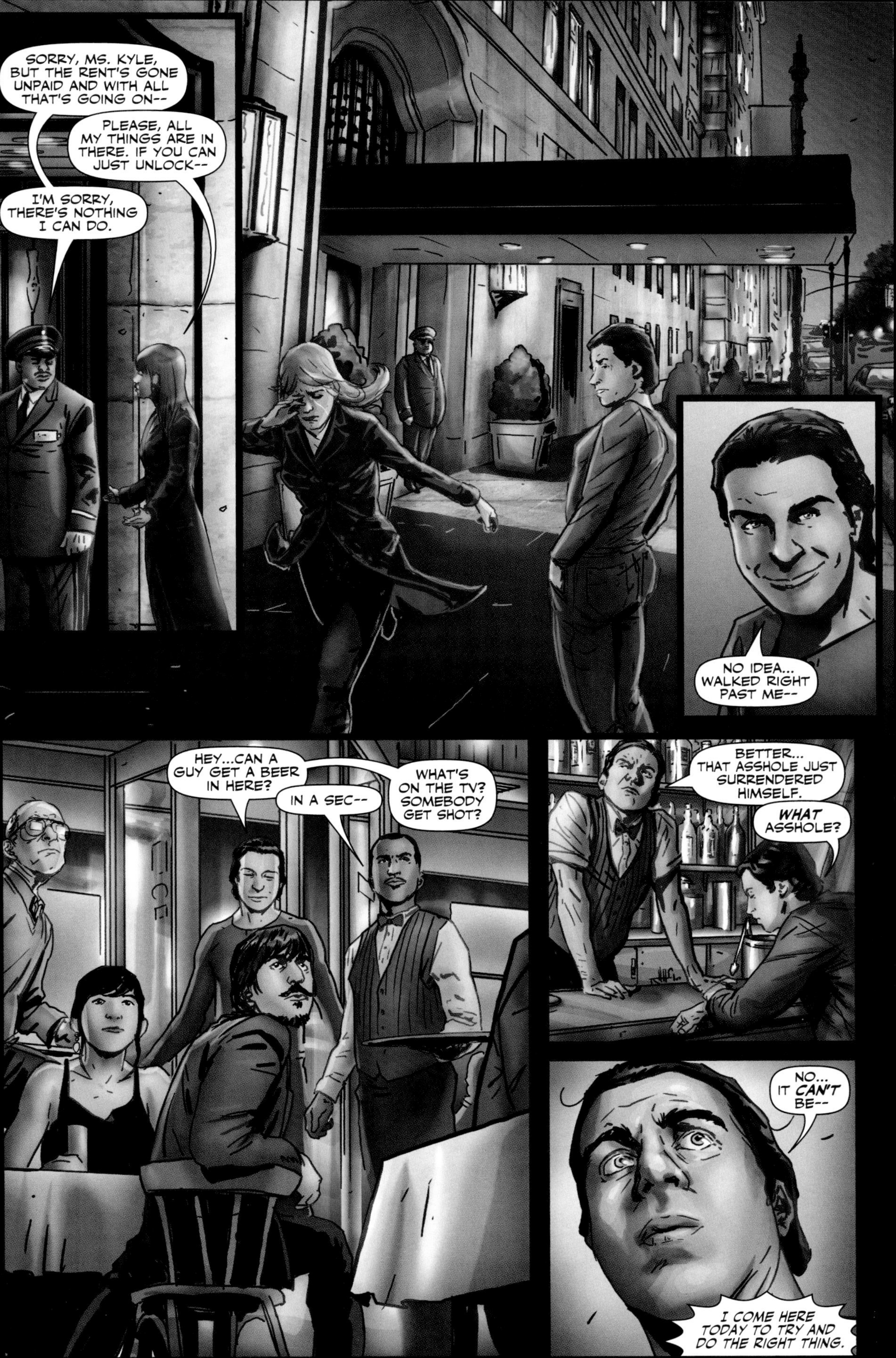
SORRY, MS. KYLE, BUT THE RENT'S GONE UNPAID AND WITH ALL THAT'S GOING ON--
PLEASE, ALL MY THINGS ARE IN THERE. IF YOU CAN JUST UNLOCK--
I'M SORRY, THERE'S NOTHING I CAN DO.
NO IDEA... WALKED RIGHT PAST ME--
HEY...CAN A GUY GET A BEER IN HERE?
IN A SEC--
WHAT'S ON THE TV? SOMEBODY GET SHOT?
BETTER... THAT ASSHOLE JUST SURRENDERED HIMSELF.
WHAT ASSHOLE?
NO... IT CAN'T BE--
I COME HERE TODAY TO TRY AND DO THE RIGHT THING.

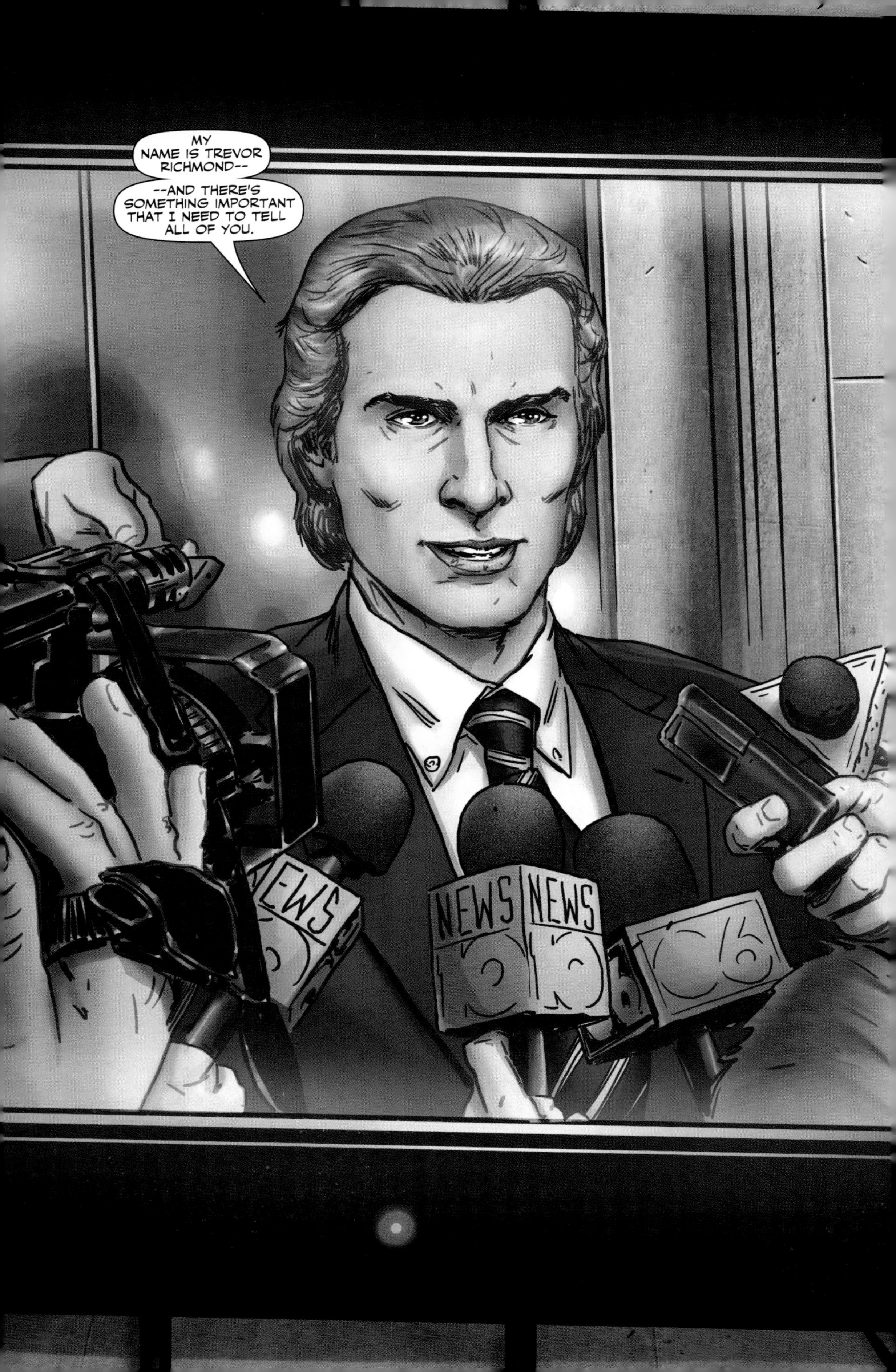
MY NAME IS TREVOR RICHMOND--
--AND THERE'S SOMETHING IMPORTANT THAT I NEED TO TELL ALL OF YOU.
NEWS
NEWS
NEWS

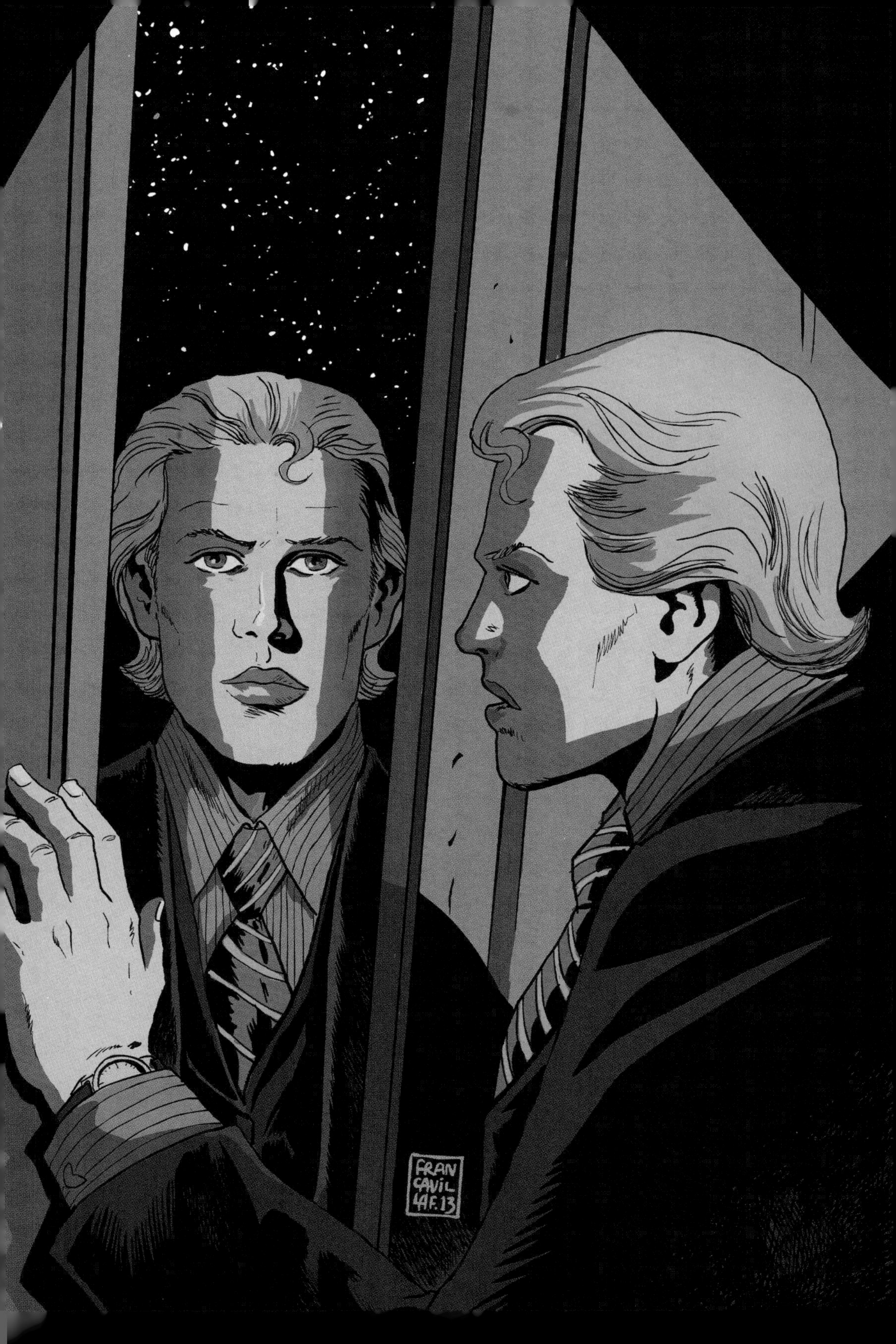
FRAN
GAVIL
4F.13

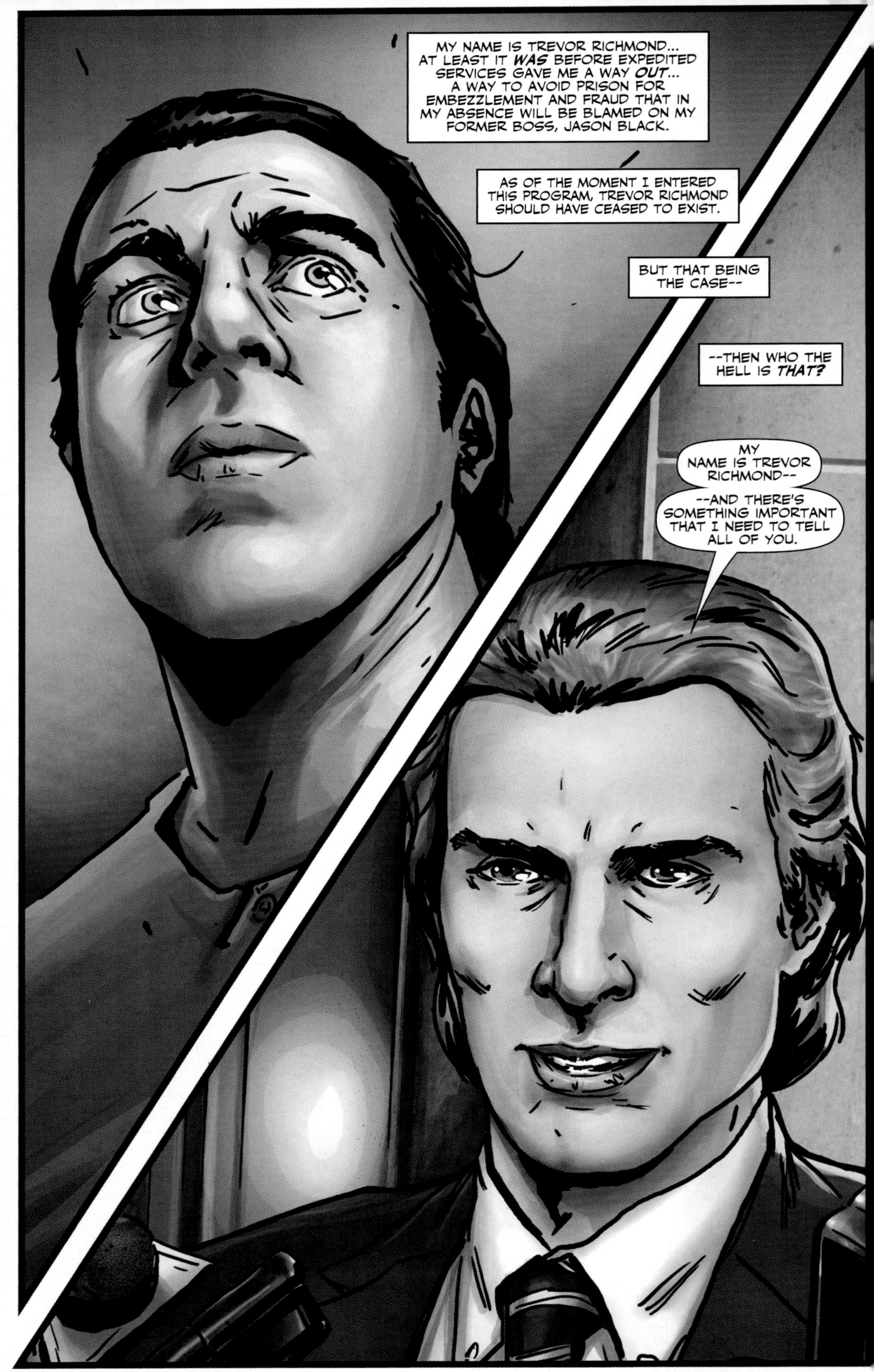
MY NAME IS TREVOR RICHMOND... AT LEAST IT WAS BEFORE EXPEDITED SERVICES GAVE ME A WAY OUT... A WAY TO AVOID PRISON FOR EMBEZZLEMENT AND FRAUD THAT IN MY ABSENCE WILL BE BLAMED ON MY FORMER BOSS, JASON BLACK.
AS OF THE MOMENT I ENTERED THIS PROGRAM, TREVOR RICHMOND SHOULD HAVE CEASED TO EXIST.
BUT THAT BEING THE CASE--
--THEN WHO THE HELL IS THAT?
MY NAME IS TREVOR RICHMOND--
--AND THERE'S SOMETHING IMPORTANT THAT I NEED TO TELL ALL OF YOU.

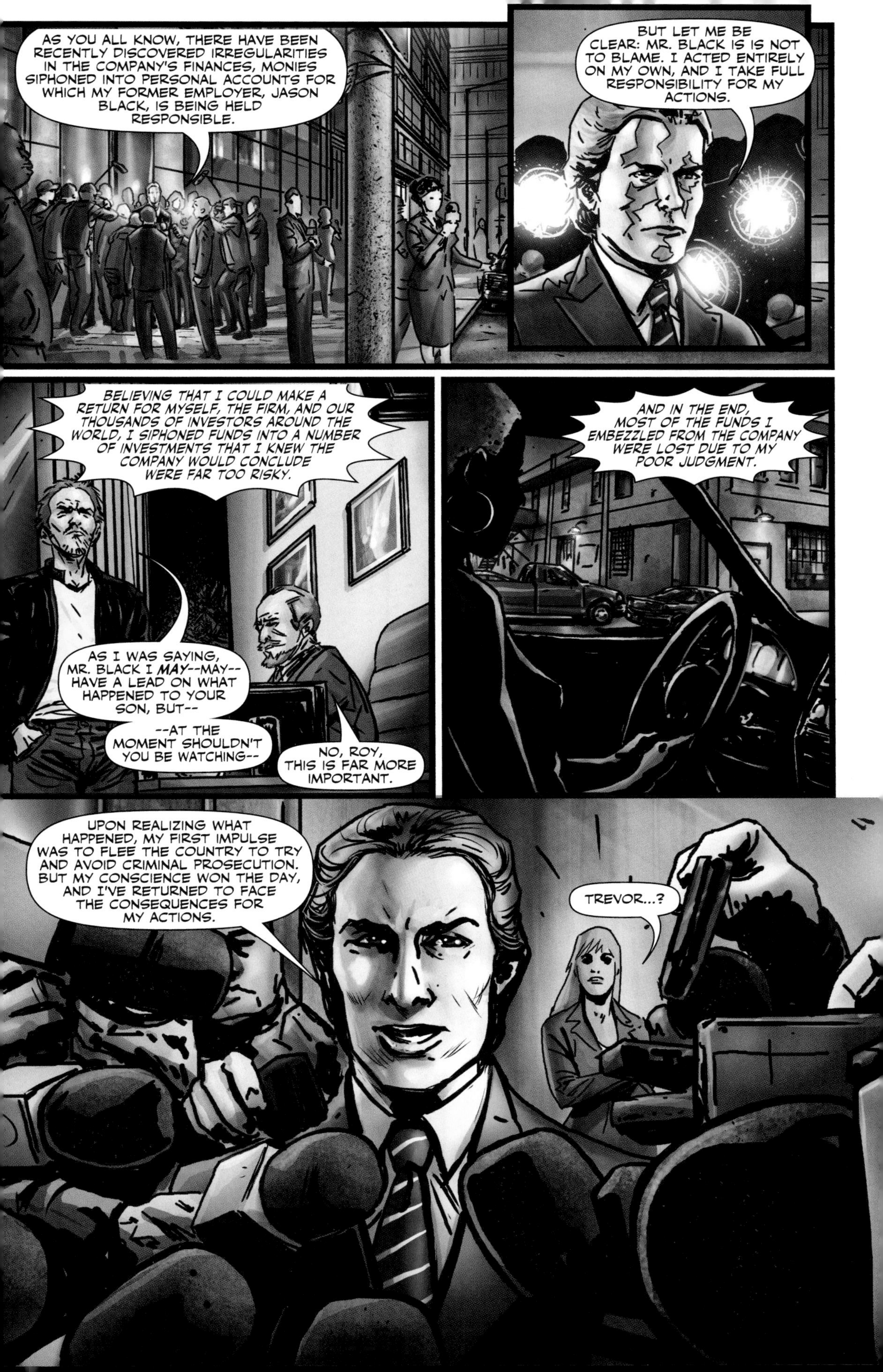
AS YOU ALL KNOW, THERE HAVE BEEN RECENTLY DISCOVERED IRREGULARITIES IN THE COMPANY'S FINANCES, MONIES SIPHONED INTO PERSONAL ACCOUNTS FOR WHICH MY FORMER EMPLOYER, JASON BLACK, IS BEING HELD RESPONSIBLE.
BUT LET ME BE CLEAR: MR. BLACK IS IS NOT TO BLAME. I ACTED ENTIRELY ON MY OWN, AND I TAKE FULL RESPONSIBILITY FOR MY ACTIONS.
BELIEVING THAT I COULD MAKE A RETURN FOR MYSELF, THE FIRM, AND OUR THOUSANDS OF INVESTORS AROUND THE WORLD, I SIPHONED FUNDS INTO A NUMBER OF INVESTMENTS THAT I KNEW THE COMPANY WOULD CONCLUDE WERE FAR TOO RISKY.
AS I WAS SAYING, MR. BLACK I *MAY*--MAY--HAVE A LEAD ON WHAT HAPPENED TO YOUR SON, BUT--
--AT THE MOMENT SHOULDN'T YOU BE WATCHING--
NO, ROY, THIS IS FAR MORE IMPORTANT.
AND IN THE END, MOST OF THE FUNDS I EMBEZZLED FROM THE COMPANY WERE LOST DUE TO MY POOR JUDGMENT.
UPON REALIZING WHAT HAPPENED, MY FIRST IMPULSE WAS TO FLEE THE COUNTRY TO TRY AND AVOID CRIMINAL PROSECUTION. BUT MY CONSCIENCE WON THE DAY, AND I'VE RETURNED TO FACE THE CONSEQUENCES FOR MY ACTIONS.
TREVOR...?

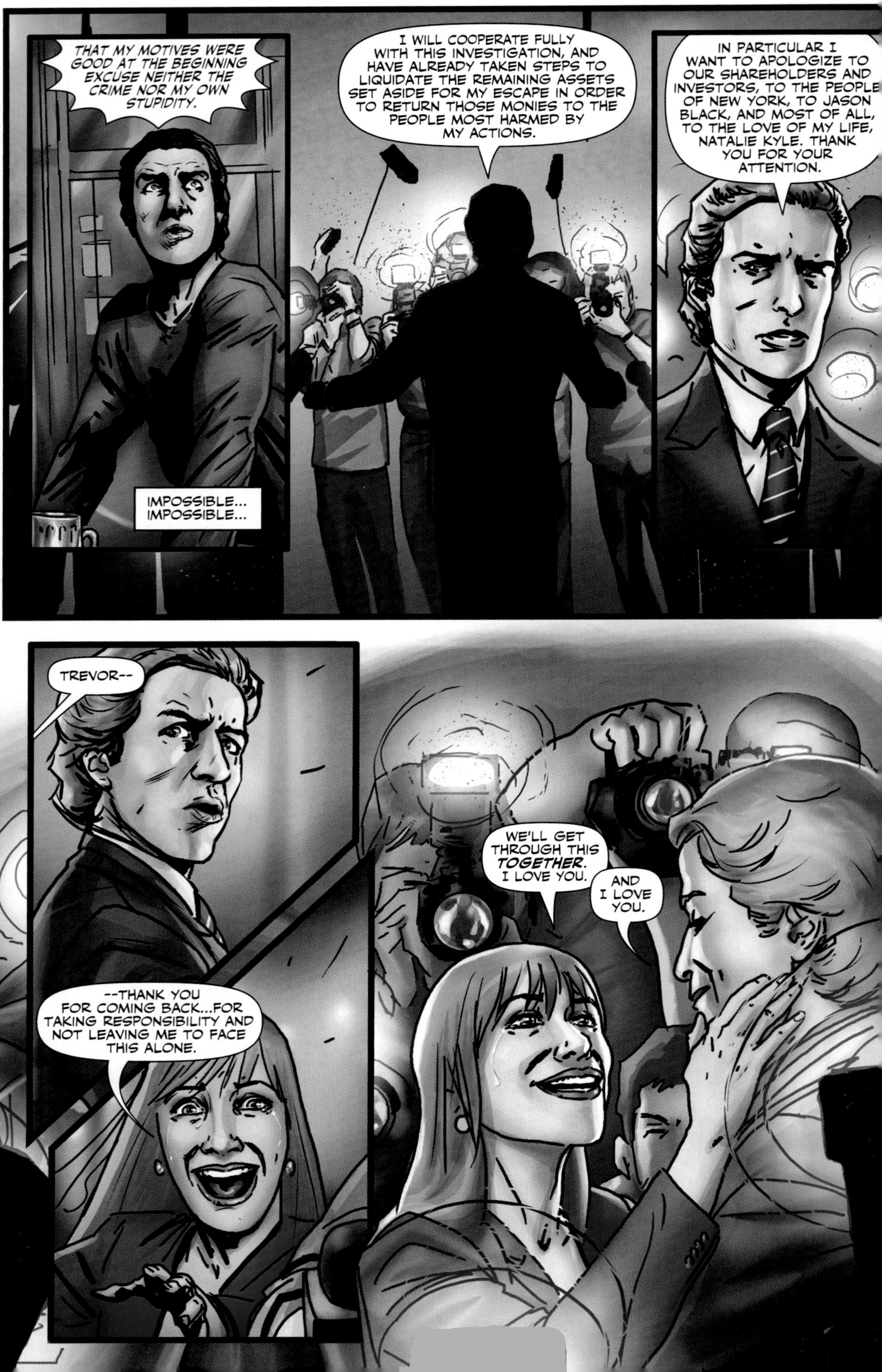
THAT MY MOTIVES WERE GOOD AT THE BEGINNING EXCUSE NEITHER THE CRIME NOR MY OWN STUPIDITY.
IMPOSSIBLE... IMPOSSIBLE...
I WILL COOPERATE FULLY WITH THIS INVESTIGATION, AND HAVE ALREADY TAKEN STEPS TO LIQUIDATE THE REMAINING ASSETS SET ASIDE FOR MY ESCAPE IN ORDER TO RETURN THOSE MONIES TO THE PEOPLE MOST HARMED BY MY ACTIONS.
IN PARTICULAR I WANT TO APOLOGIZE TO OUR SHAREHOLDERS AND INVESTORS, TO THE PEOPLE OF NEW YORK, TO JASON BLACK, AND MOST OF ALL, TO THE LOVE OF MY LIFE, NATALIE KYLE. THANK YOU FOR YOUR ATTENTION.
TREVOR--
--THANK YOU FOR COMING BACK...FOR TAKING RESPONSIBILITY AND NOT LEAVING ME TO FACE THIS ALONE.
WE'LL GET THROUGH THIS *TOGETHER*. I LOVE YOU.
AND I LOVE YOU.

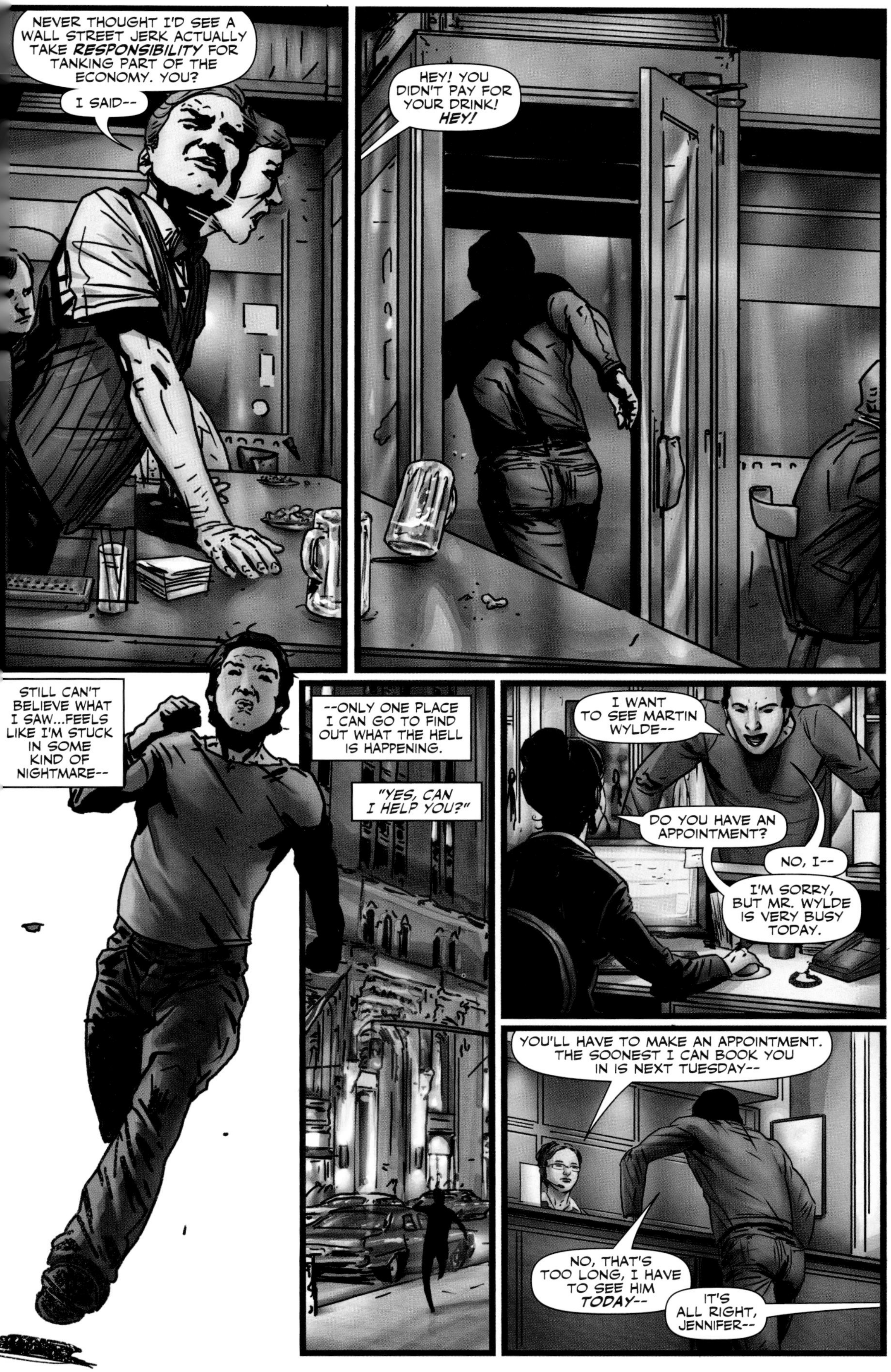
NEVER THOUGHT I'D SEE A WALL STREET JERK ACTUALLY TAKE RESPONSIBILITY FOR TANKING PART OF THE ECONOMY. YOU?
I SAID--
HEY! YOU DIDN'T PAY FOR YOUR DRINK! HEY!
STILL CAN'T BELIEVE WHAT I SAW...FEELS LIKE I'M STUCK IN SOME KIND OF NIGHTMARE--
--ONLY ONE PLACE I CAN GO TO FIND OUT WHAT THE HELL IS HAPPENING.
"YES, CAN I HELP YOU?"
I WANT TO SEE MARTIN WYLDE--
DO YOU HAVE AN APPOINTMENT?
NO, I--
I'M SORRY, BUT MR. WYLDE IS VERY BUSY TODAY.
YOU'LL HAVE TO MAKE AN APPOINTMENT. THE SOONEST I CAN BOOK YOU IN IS NEXT TUESDAY--
NO, THAT'S TOO LONG, I HAVE TO SEE HIM TODAY--
IT'S ALL RIGHT, JENNIFER--

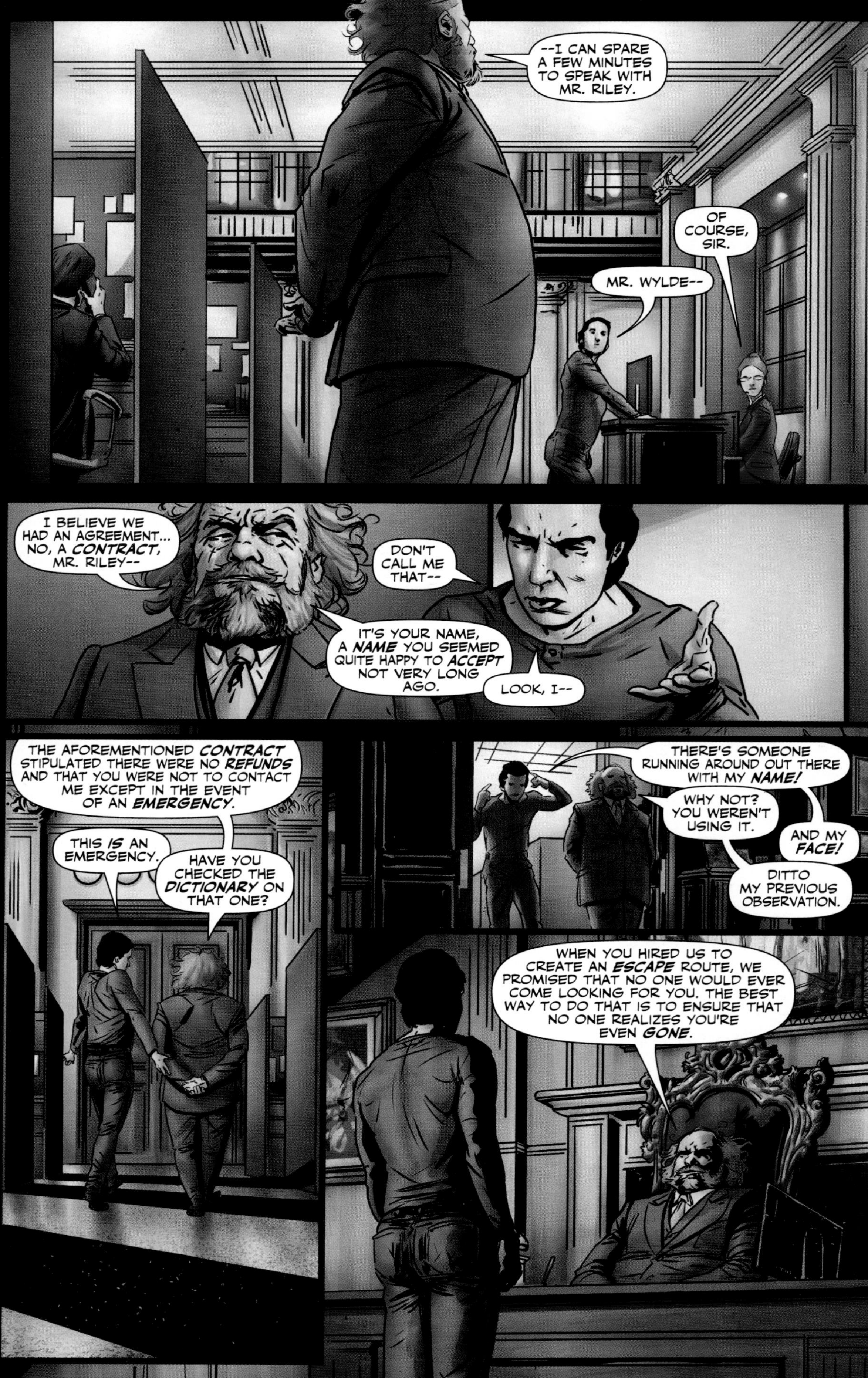

--I CAN SPARE A FEW MINUTES TO SPEAK WITH MR. RILEY.
MR. WYLDE--
OF COURSE, SIR.
I BELIEVE WE HAD AN AGREEMENT... NO, A *CONTRACT,* MR. RILEY--
DON'T CALL ME THAT--
IT'S YOUR NAME, A *NAME* YOU SEEMED QUITE HAPPY TO *ACCEPT* NOT VERY LONG AGO.
LOOK, I--
THE AFOREMENTIONED *CONTRACT* STIPULATED THERE WERE NO *REFUNDS* AND THAT YOU WERE NOT TO CONTACT ME EXCEPT IN THE EVENT OF AN *EMERGENCY*.
THIS *IS* AN EMERGENCY.
HAVE YOU CHECKED THE *DICTIONARY* ON THAT ONE?
THERE'S SOMEONE RUNNING AROUND OUT THERE WITH MY *NAME!*
WHY NOT? YOU WEREN'T USING IT.
AND MY *FACE!*
DITTO MY PREVIOUS OBSERVATION.
WHEN YOU HIRED US TO CREATE AN *ESCAPE* ROUTE, WE PROMISED THAT NO ONE WOULD EVER COME LOOKING FOR YOU. THE BEST WAY TO DO THAT IS TO ENSURE THAT NO ONE REALIZES YOU'RE EVEN *GONE*.

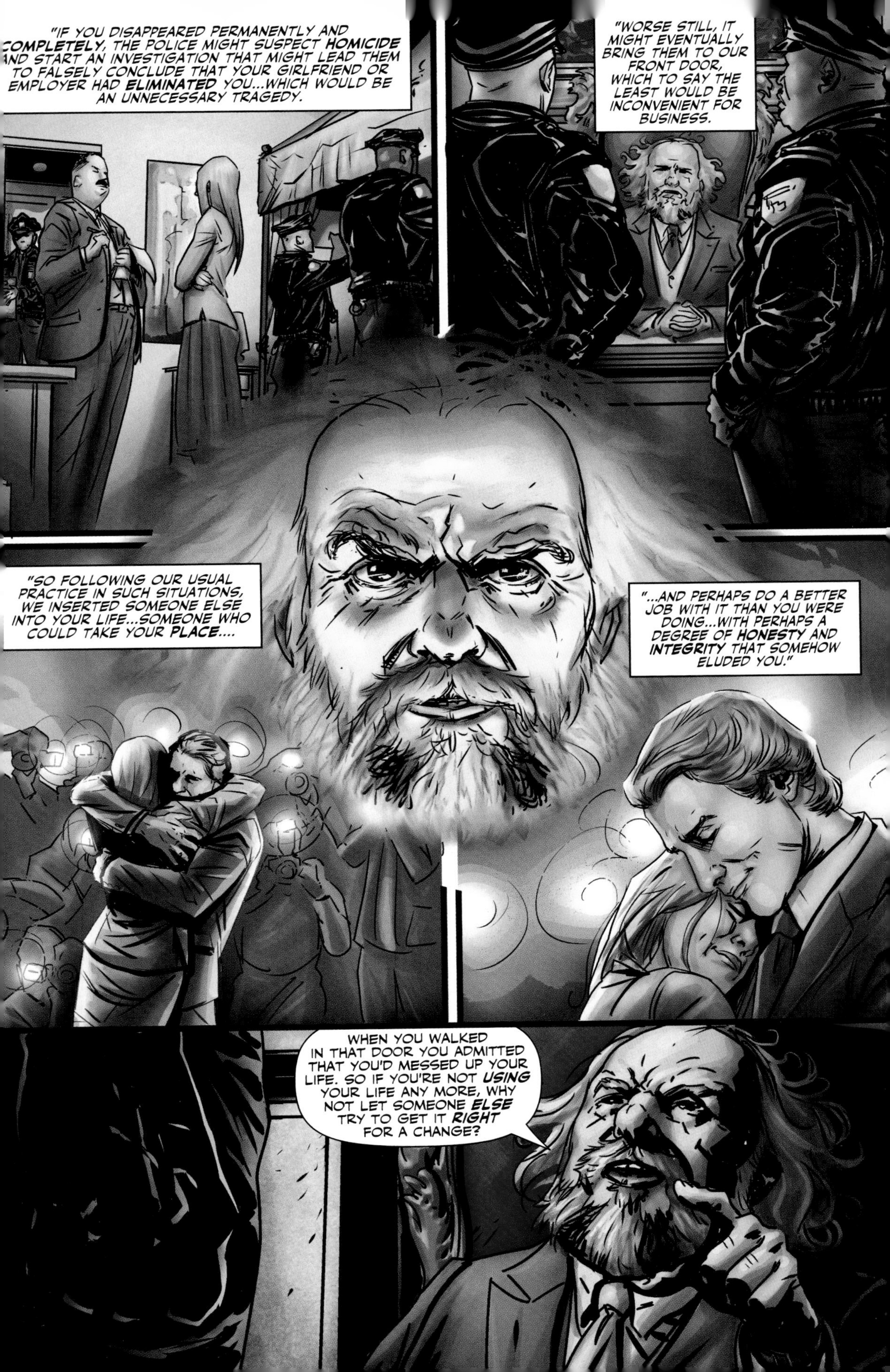
"IF YOU DISAPPEARED PERMANENTLY AND COMPLETELY, THE POLICE MIGHT SUSPECT HOMICIDE AND START AN INVESTIGATION THAT MIGHT LEAD THEM TO FALSELY CONCLUDE THAT YOUR GIRLFRIEND OR EMPLOYER HAD ELIMINATED YOU...WHICH WOULD BE AN UNNECESSARY TRAGEDY.
"WORSE STILL, IT MIGHT EVENTUALLY BRING THEM TO OUR FRONT DOOR, WHICH TO SAY THE LEAST WOULD BE INCONVENIENT FOR BUSINESS.
"SO FOLLOWING OUR USUAL PRACTICE IN SUCH SITUATIONS, WE INSERTED SOMEONE ELSE INTO YOUR LIFE...SOMEONE WHO COULD TAKE YOUR PLACE....
"...AND PERHAPS DO A BETTER JOB WITH IT THAN YOU WERE DOING...WITH PERHAPS A DEGREE OF HONESTY AND INTEGRITY THAT SOMEHOW ELUDED YOU."
WHEN YOU WALKED IN THAT DOOR YOU ADMITTED THAT YOU'D MESSED UP YOUR LIFE. SO IF YOU'RE NOT USING YOUR LIFE ANY MORE, WHY NOT LET SOMEONE ELSE TRY TO GET IT RIGHT FOR A CHANGE?

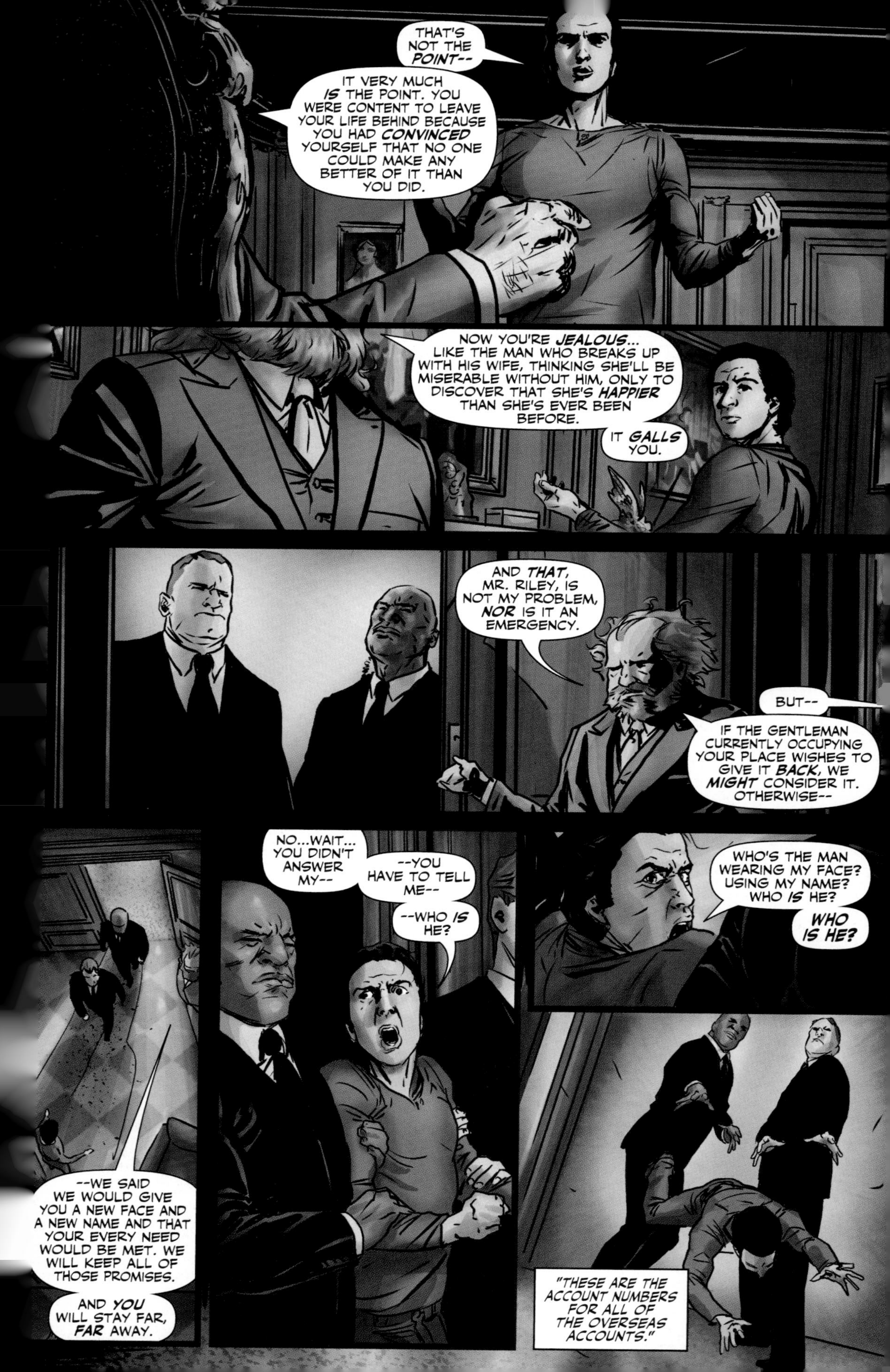
THAT'S NOT THE POINT--
IT VERY MUCH IS THE POINT. YOU WERE CONTENT TO LEAVE YOUR LIFE BEHIND BECAUSE YOU HAD CONVINCED YOURSELF THAT NO ONE COULD MAKE ANY BETTER OF IT THAN YOU DID.
NOW YOU'RE JEALOUS... LIKE THE MAN WHO BREAKS UP WITH HIS WIFE, THINKING SHE'LL BE MISERABLE WITHOUT HIM, ONLY TO DISCOVER THAT SHE'S HAPPIER THAN SHE'S EVER BEEN BEFORE.
IT GALLS YOU.
AND THAT, MR. RILEY, IS NOT MY PROBLEM, NOR IS IT AN EMERGENCY.
BUT--
IF THE GENTLEMAN CURRENTLY OCCUPYING YOUR PLACE WISHES TO GIVE IT BACK, WE MIGHT CONSIDER IT. OTHERWISE--
--WE SAID WE WOULD GIVE YOU A NEW FACE AND A NEW NAME AND THAT YOUR EVERY NEED WOULD BE MET. WE WILL KEEP ALL OF THOSE PROMISES.
AND YOU WILL STAY FAR, FAR AWAY.
NO...WAIT... YOU DIDN'T ANSWER MY--
--YOU HAVE TO TELL ME--
--WHO IS HE?
WHO'S THE MAN WEARING MY FACE? USING MY NAME? WHO IS HE?
WHO IS HE?
"THESE ARE THE ACCOUNT NUMBERS FOR ALL OF THE OVERSEAS ACCOUNTS."

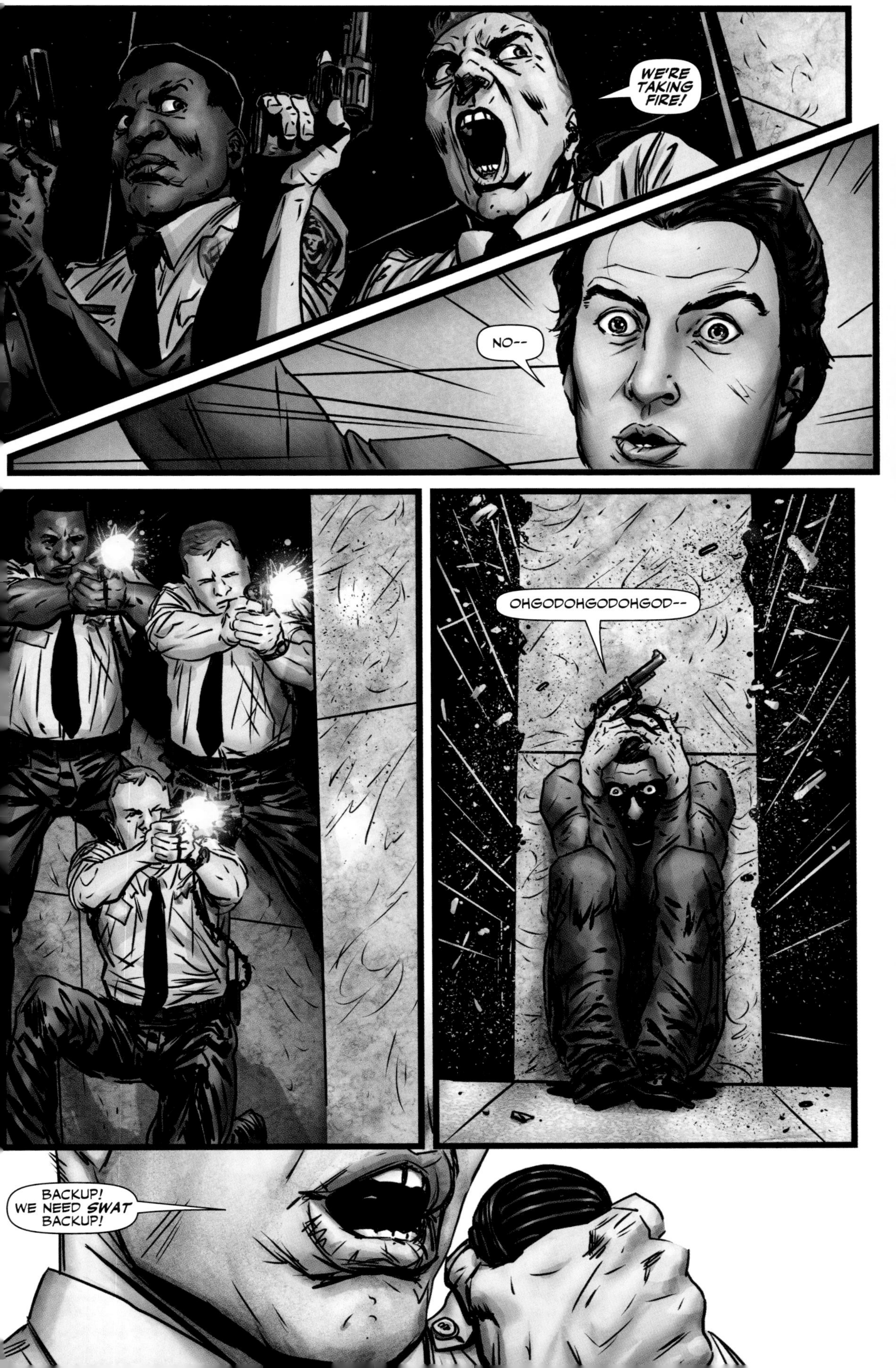
WE'RE TAKING FIRE!
NO--
OHGODOHGODOHGOD--
BACKUP! WE NEED SWAT BACKUP!

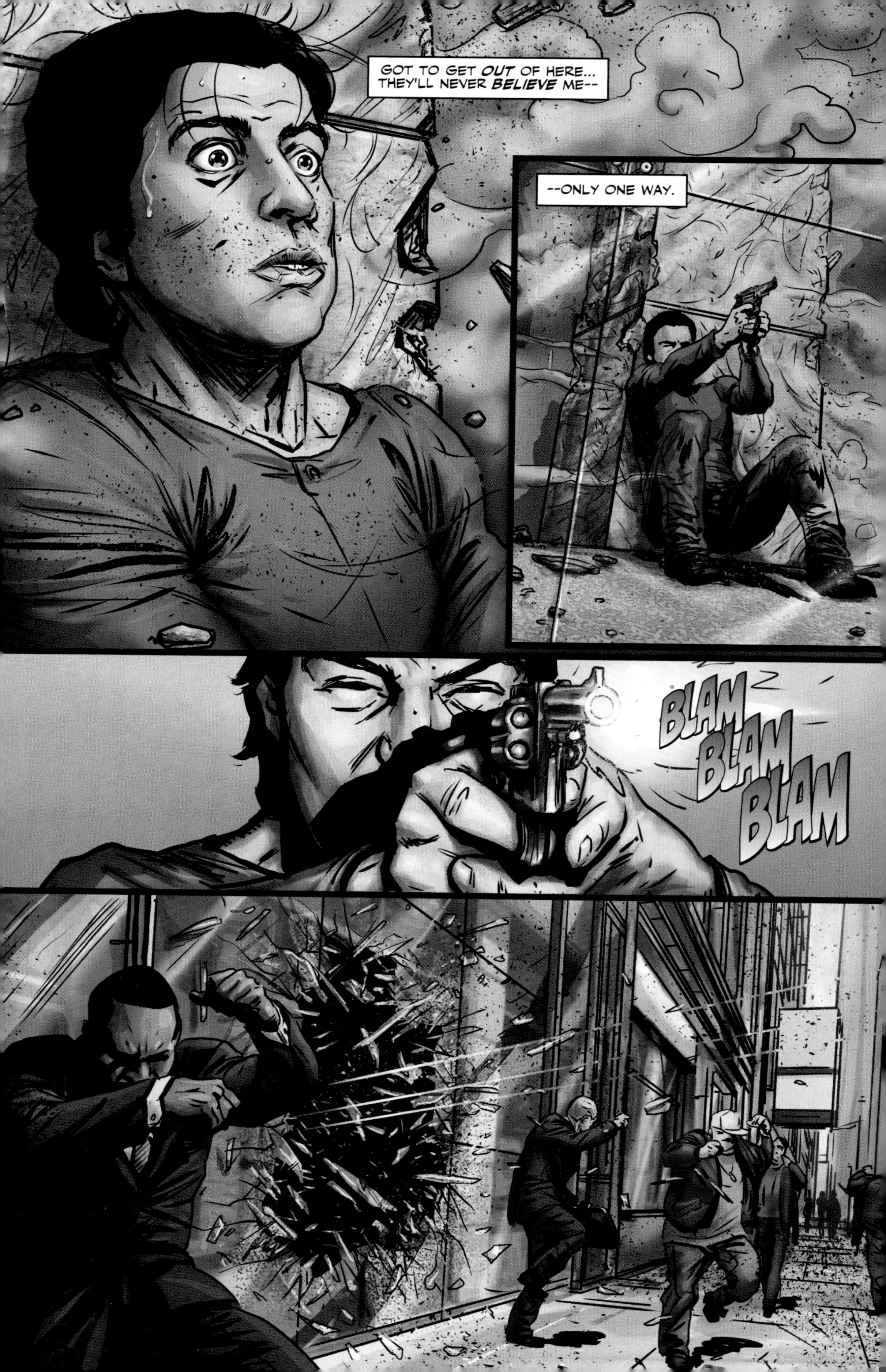
GOT TO GET OUT OF HERE... THEY'LL NEVER BELIEVE ME--
--ONLY ONE WAY.
BLAM
BLAM
BLAM

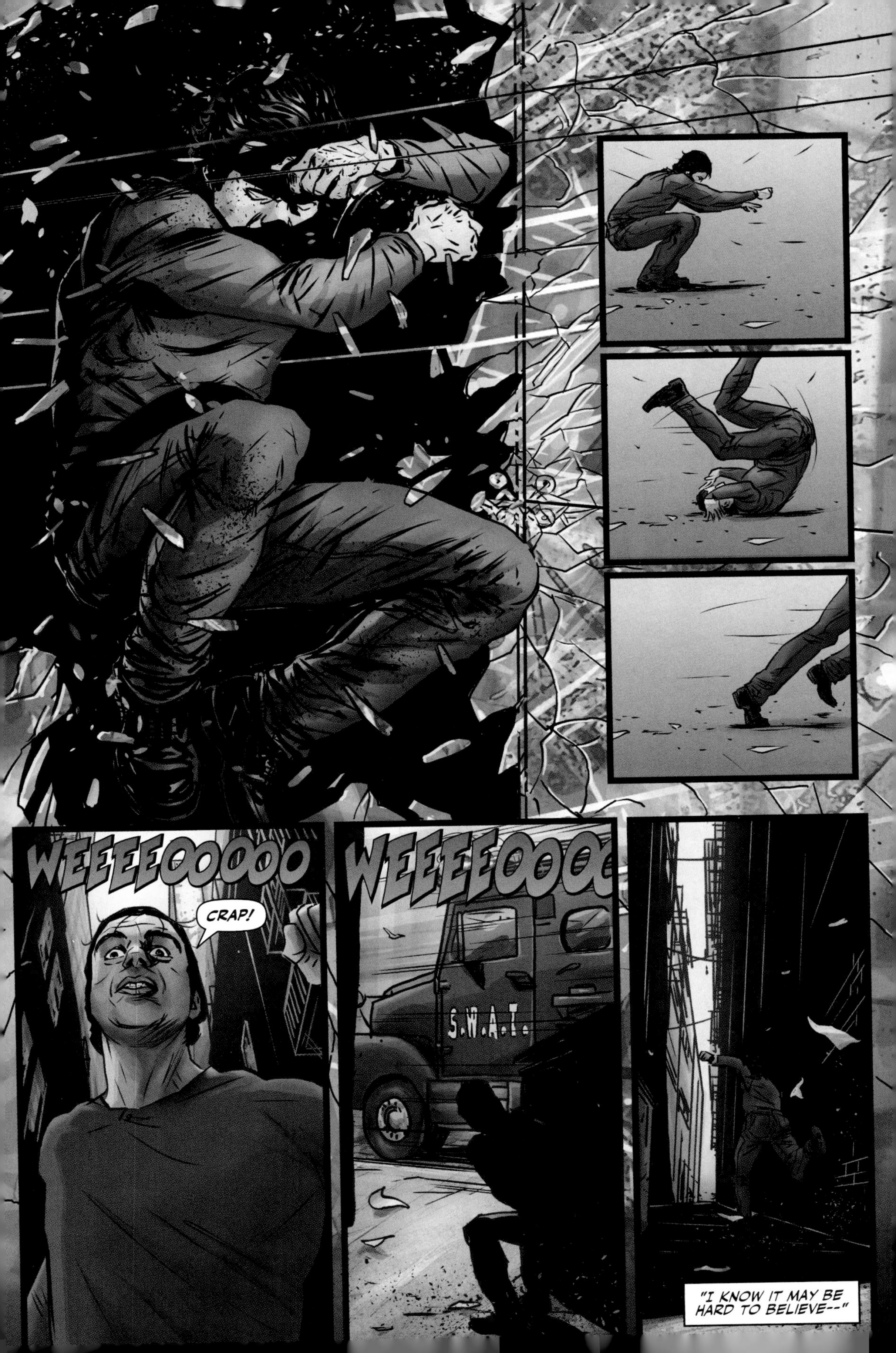
WEEEEOOOOO
CRAP!
WEEEEOOOO
S.W.A.T.
"I KNOW IT MAY BE HARD TO BELIEVE--"

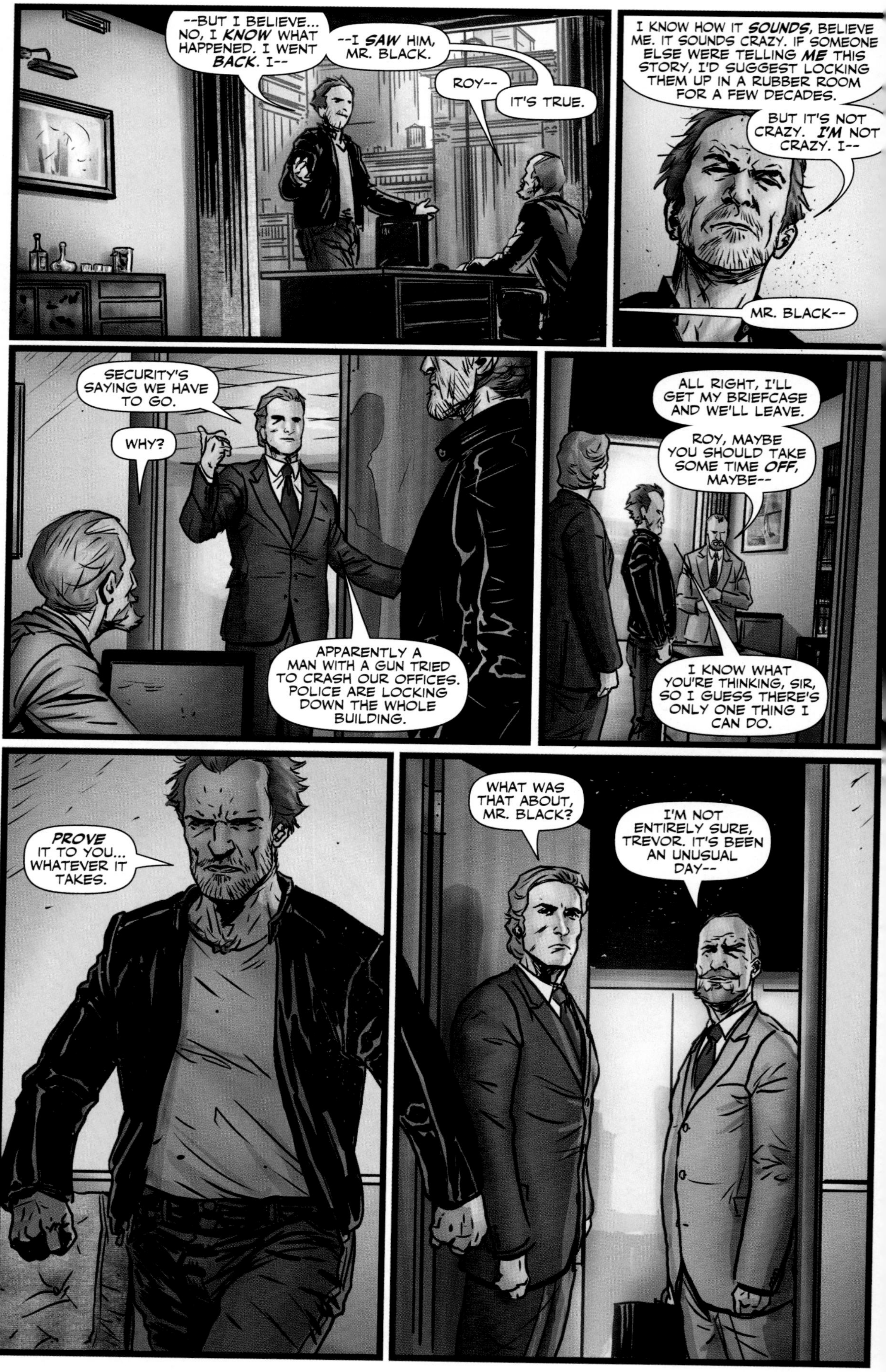
--BUT I BELIEVE... NO, I KNOW WHAT HAPPENED. I WENT BACK. I--
--I SAW HIM, MR. BLACK.
ROY--
IT'S TRUE.
I KNOW HOW IT SOUNDS, BELIEVE ME. IT SOUNDS CRAZY. IF SOMEONE ELSE WERE TELLING ME THIS STORY, I'D SUGGEST LOCKING THEM UP IN A RUBBER ROOM FOR A FEW DECADES.
BUT IT'S NOT CRAZY. I'M NOT CRAZY. I--
MR. BLACK--
SECURITY'S SAYING WE HAVE TO GO.
WHY?
APPARENTLY A MAN WITH A GUN TRIED TO CRASH OUR OFFICES. POLICE ARE LOCKING DOWN THE WHOLE BUILDING.
ALL RIGHT, I'LL GET MY BRIEFCASE AND WE'LL LEAVE.
ROY, MAYBE YOU SHOULD TAKE SOME TIME OFF, MAYBE--
I KNOW WHAT YOU'RE THINKING, SIR, SO I GUESS THERE'S ONLY ONE THING I CAN DO.
PROVE IT TO YOU... WHATEVER IT TAKES.
WHAT WAS THAT ABOUT, MR. BLACK?
I'M NOT ENTIRELY SURE, TREVOR. IT'S BEEN AN UNUSUAL DAY--

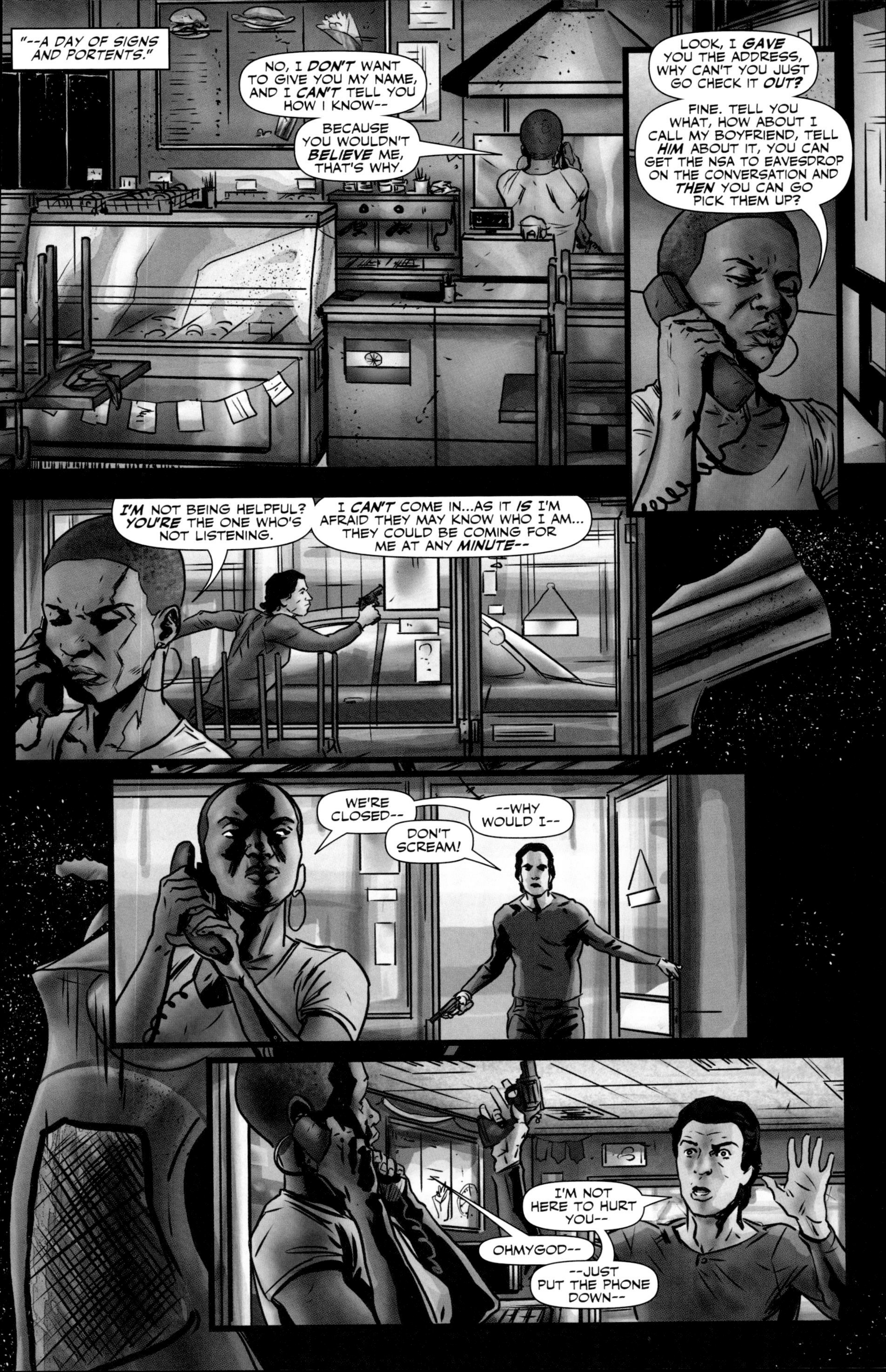
"--A DAY OF SIGNS AND PORTENTS."
NO, I DON'T WANT TO GIVE YOU MY NAME, AND I CAN'T TELL YOU HOW I KNOW--
BECAUSE YOU WOULDN'T BELIEVE ME, THAT'S WHY.
LOOK, I GAVE YOU THE ADDRESS, WHY CAN'T YOU JUST GO CHECK IT OUT?
FINE. TELL YOU WHAT, HOW ABOUT I CALL MY BOYFRIEND, TELL HIM ABOUT IT, YOU CAN GET THE NSA TO EAVESDROP ON THE CONVERSATION AND THEN YOU CAN GO PICK THEM UP?
I'M NOT BEING HELPFUL? YOU'RE THE ONE WHO'S NOT LISTENING.
I CAN'T COME IN...AS IT IS I'M AFRAID THEY MAY KNOW WHO I AM... THEY COULD BE COMING FOR ME AT ANY MINUTE--
WE'RE CLOSED--
--WHY WOULD I--
DON'T SCREAM!
I'M NOT HERE TO HURT YOU--
OHMYGOD--
--JUST PUT THE PHONE DOWN--

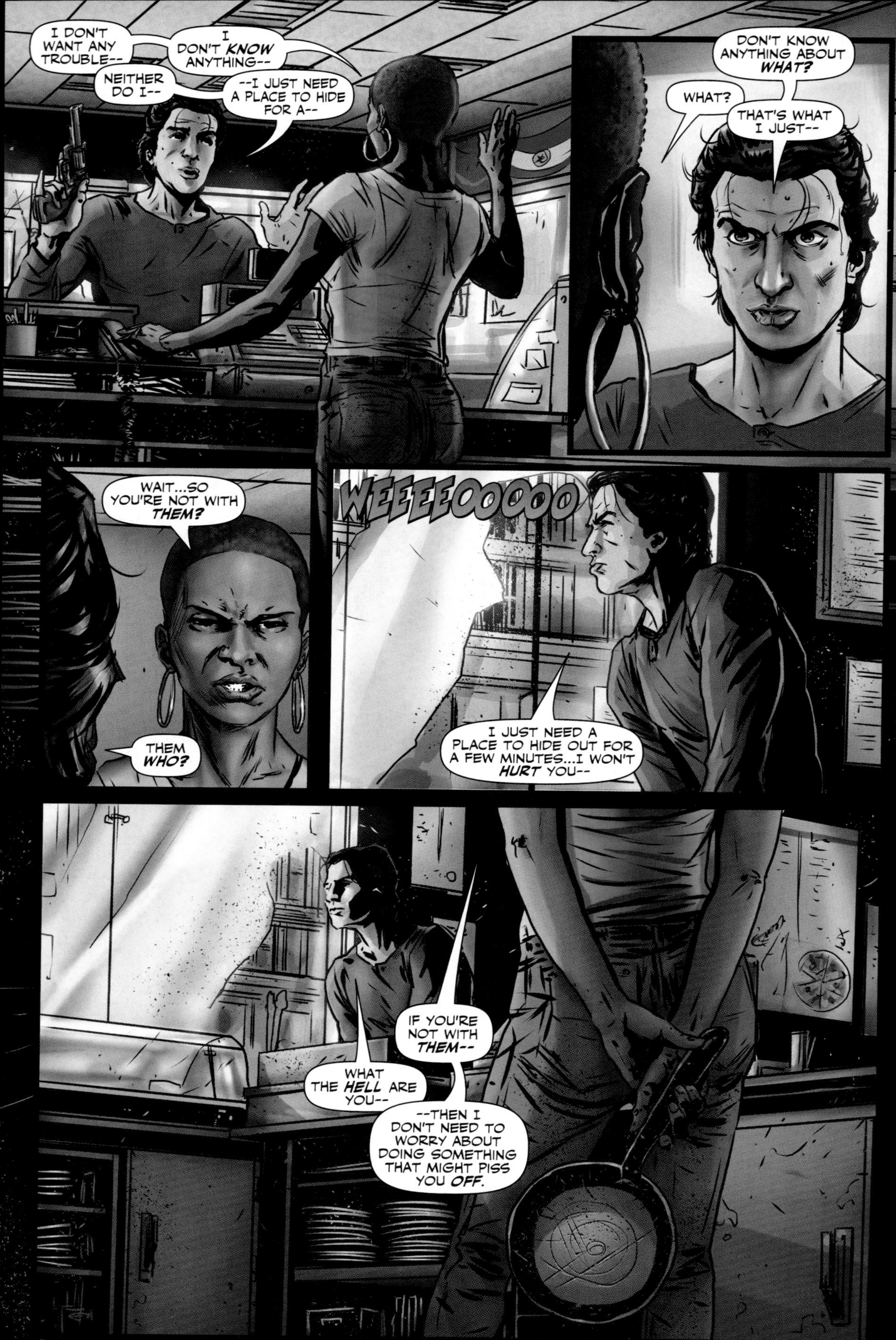
I DON'T WANT ANY TROUBLE--
I DON'T KNOW ANYTHING--
NEITHER DO I--
--I JUST NEED A PLACE TO HIDE FOR A--
DON'T KNOW ANYTHING ABOUT WHAT?
WHAT?
THAT'S WHAT I JUST--
WAIT...SO YOU'RE NOT WITH THEM?
THEM WHO?
WEEEEOOOOO
I JUST NEED A PLACE TO HIDE OUT FOR A FEW MINUTES...I WON'T HURT YOU--
WHAT THE HELL ARE YOU--
IF YOU'RE NOT WITH THEM--
--THEN I DON'T NEED TO WORRY ABOUT DOING SOMETHING THAT MIGHT PISS YOU OFF.

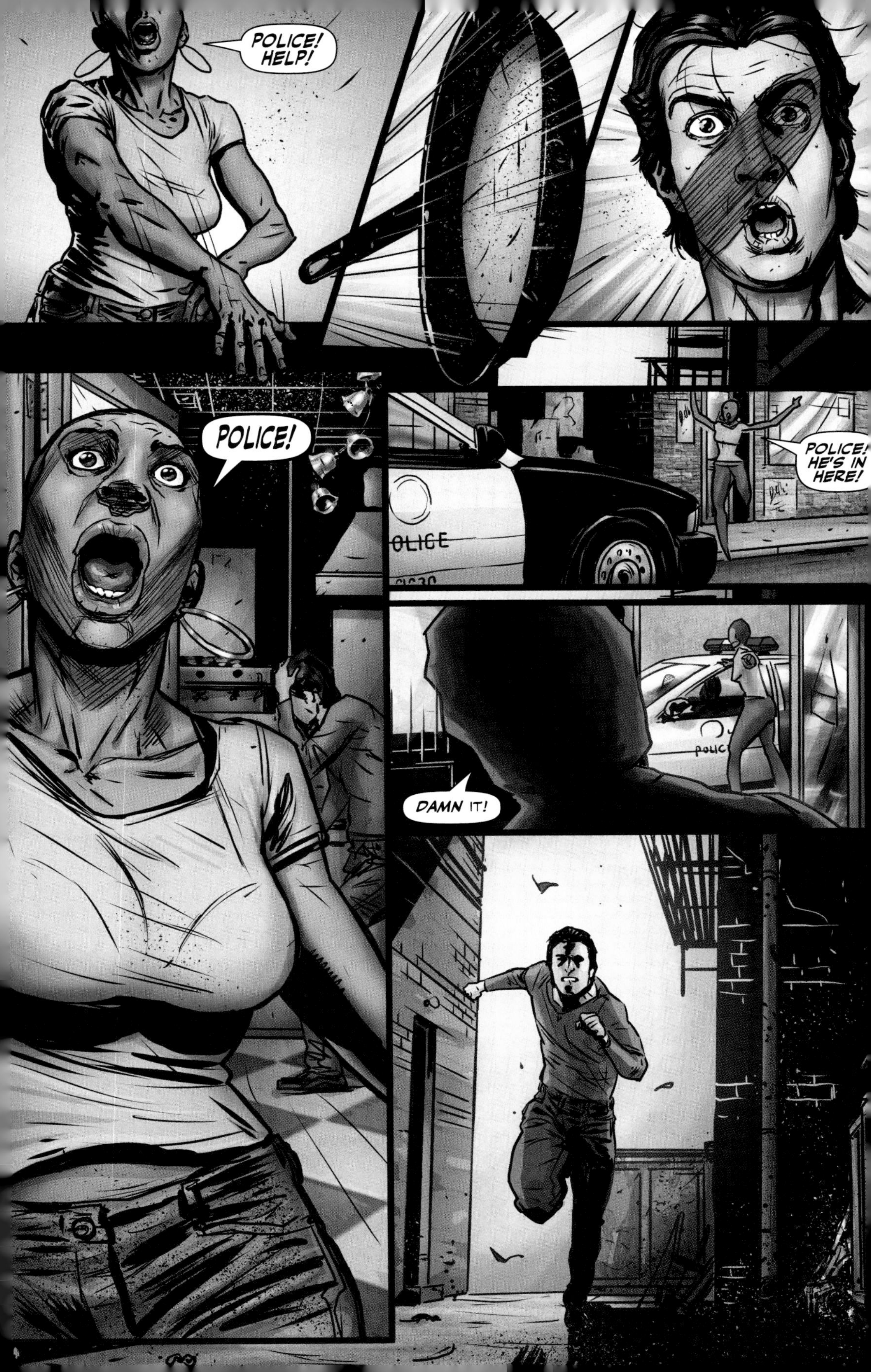
POLICE! HELP!
POLICE!
POLICE! HE'S IN HERE!
DAMN IT!

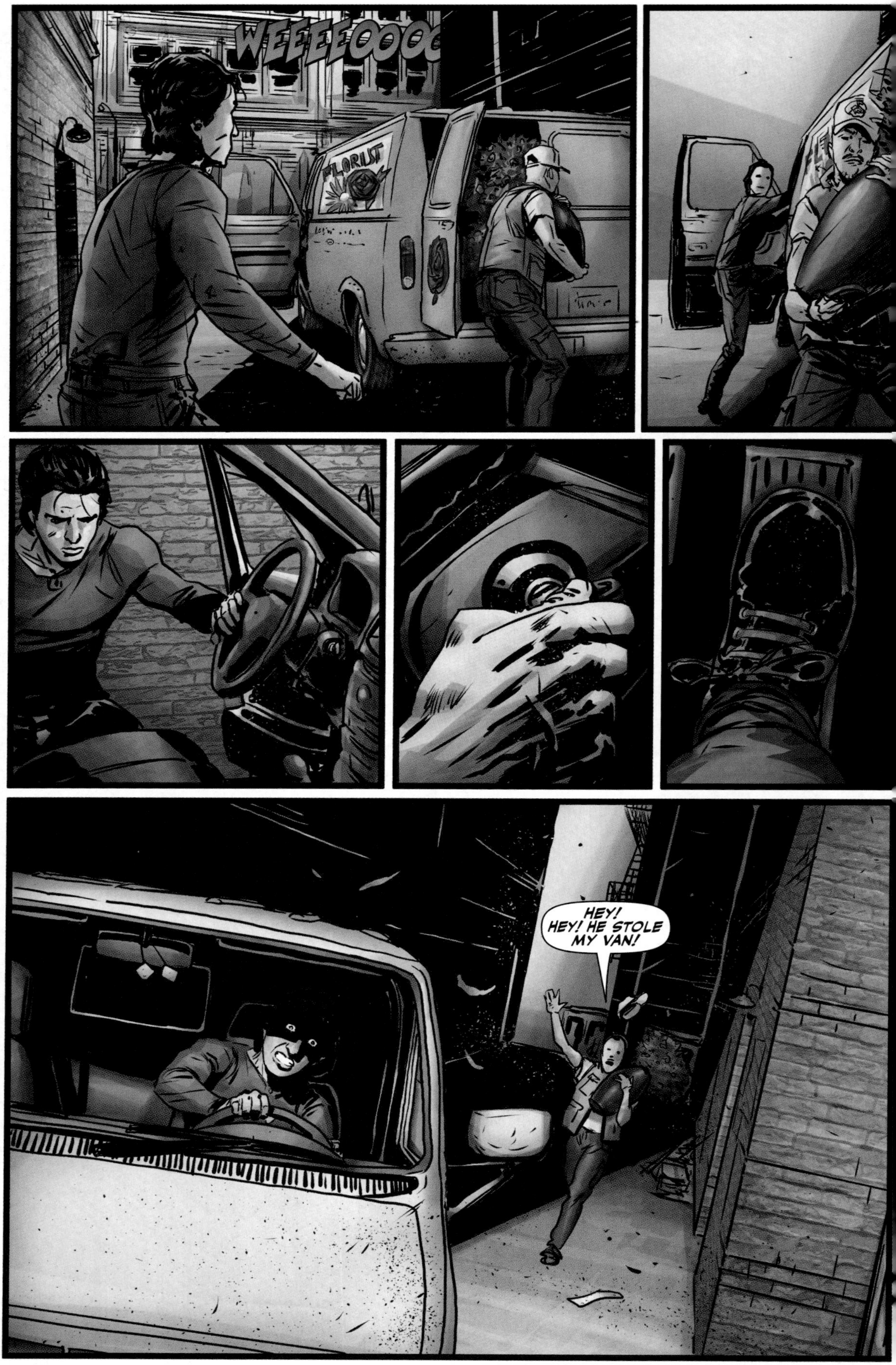
WEEEEOOOO
HEY!
HEY! HE STOLE
MY VAN!

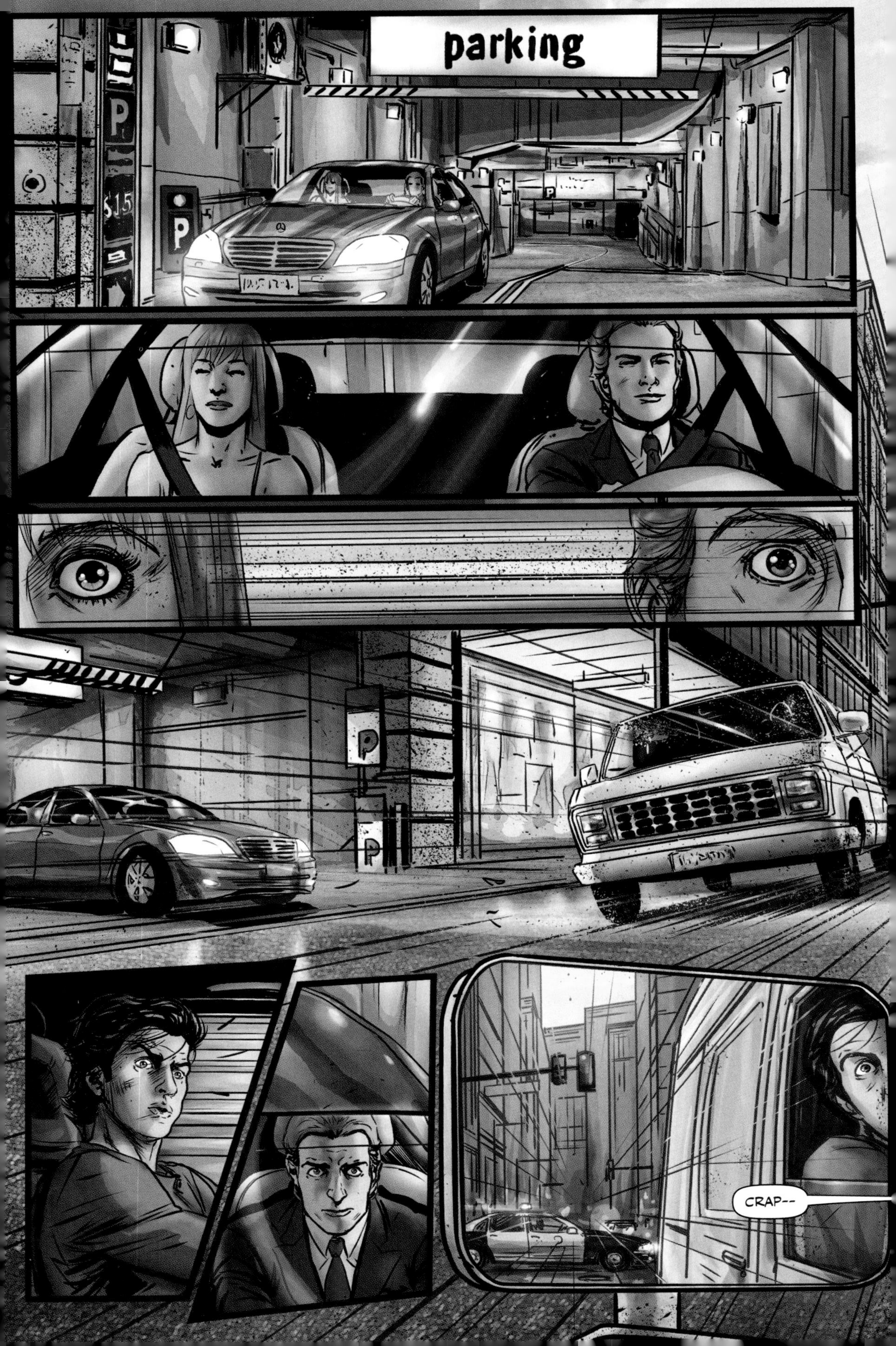
parking
$15
CRAP--

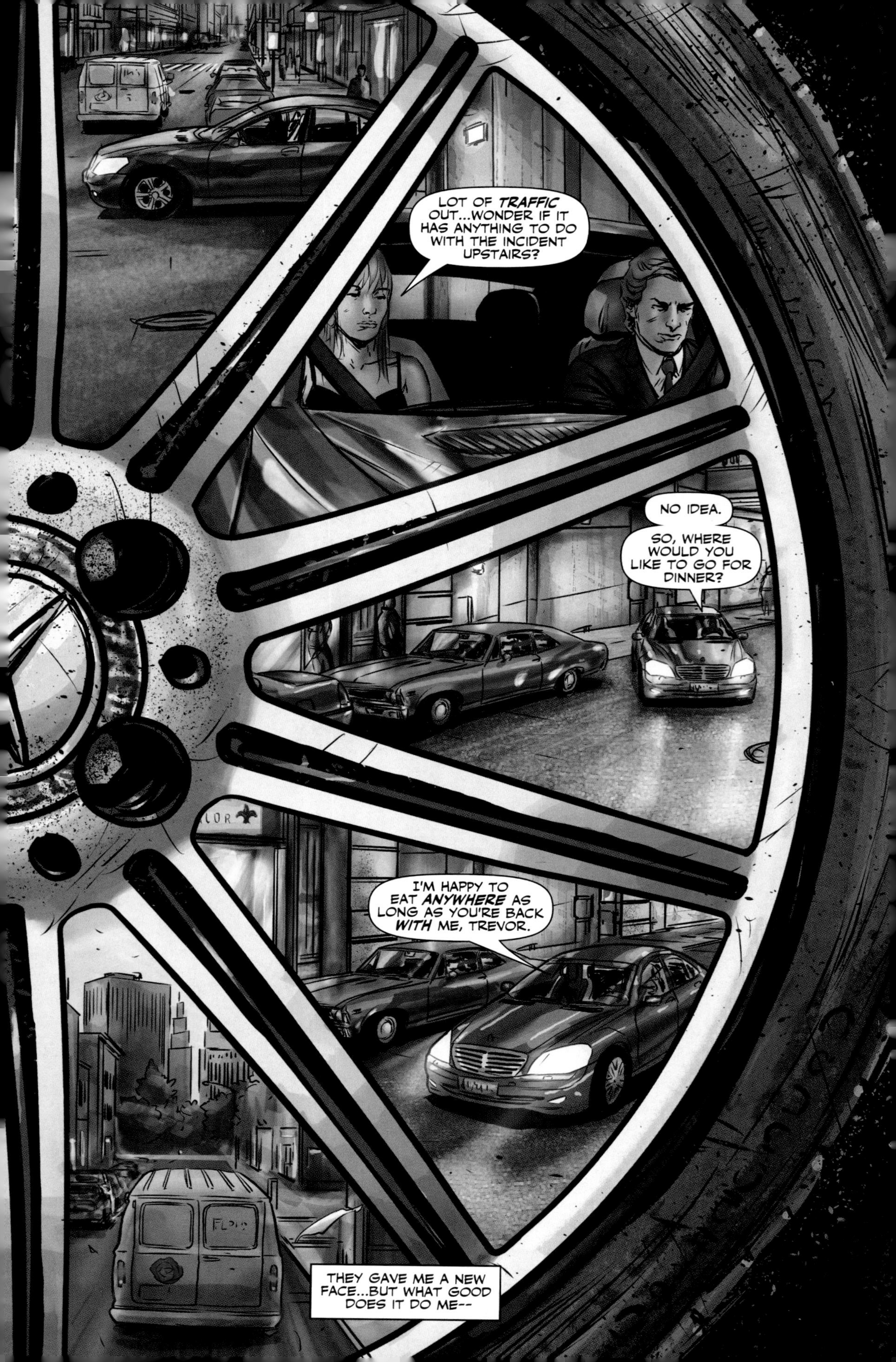
LOT OF *TRAFFIC* OUT...WONDER IF IT HAS ANYTHING TO DO WITH THE INCIDENT UPSTAIRS?
NO IDEA.
SO, WHERE WOULD YOU LIKE TO GO FOR DINNER?
I'M HAPPY TO EAT *ANYWHERE* AS LONG AS YOU'RE BACK *WITH* ME, TREVOR.
THEY GAVE ME A NEW FACE...BUT WHAT GOOD DOES IT DO ME--

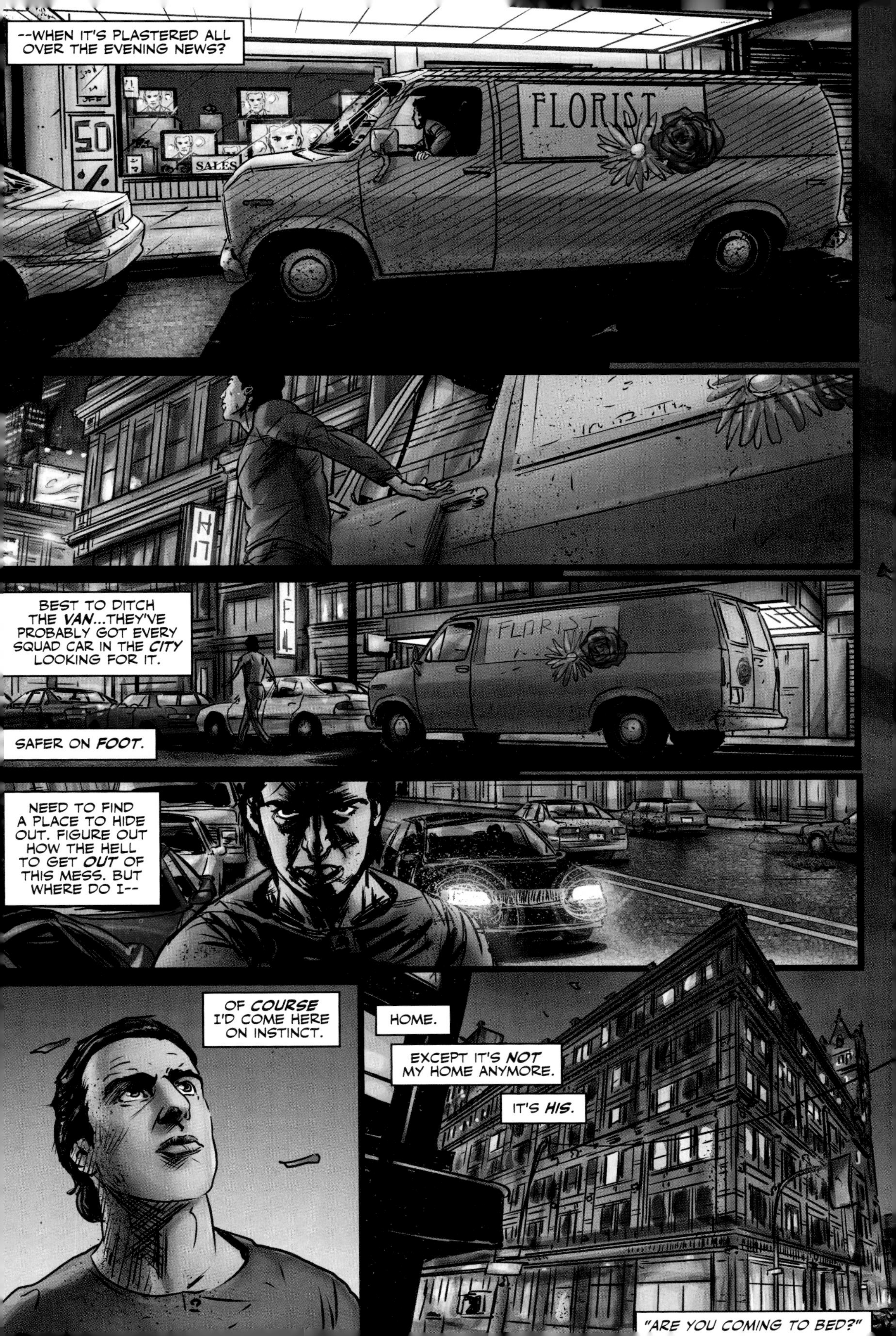
--WHEN IT'S PLASTERED ALL OVER THE EVENING NEWS?
FLORIST
SALES
BEST TO DITCH THE VAN...THEY'VE PROBABLY GOT EVERY SQUAD CAR IN THE CITY LOOKING FOR IT.
SAFER ON FOOT.
NEED TO FIND A PLACE TO HIDE OUT. FIGURE OUT HOW THE HELL TO GET OUT OF THIS MESS. BUT WHERE DO I--
OF COURSE I'D COME HERE ON INSTINCT.
HOME.
EXCEPT IT'S NOT MY HOME ANYMORE.
IT'S HIS.
"ARE YOU COMING TO BED?"

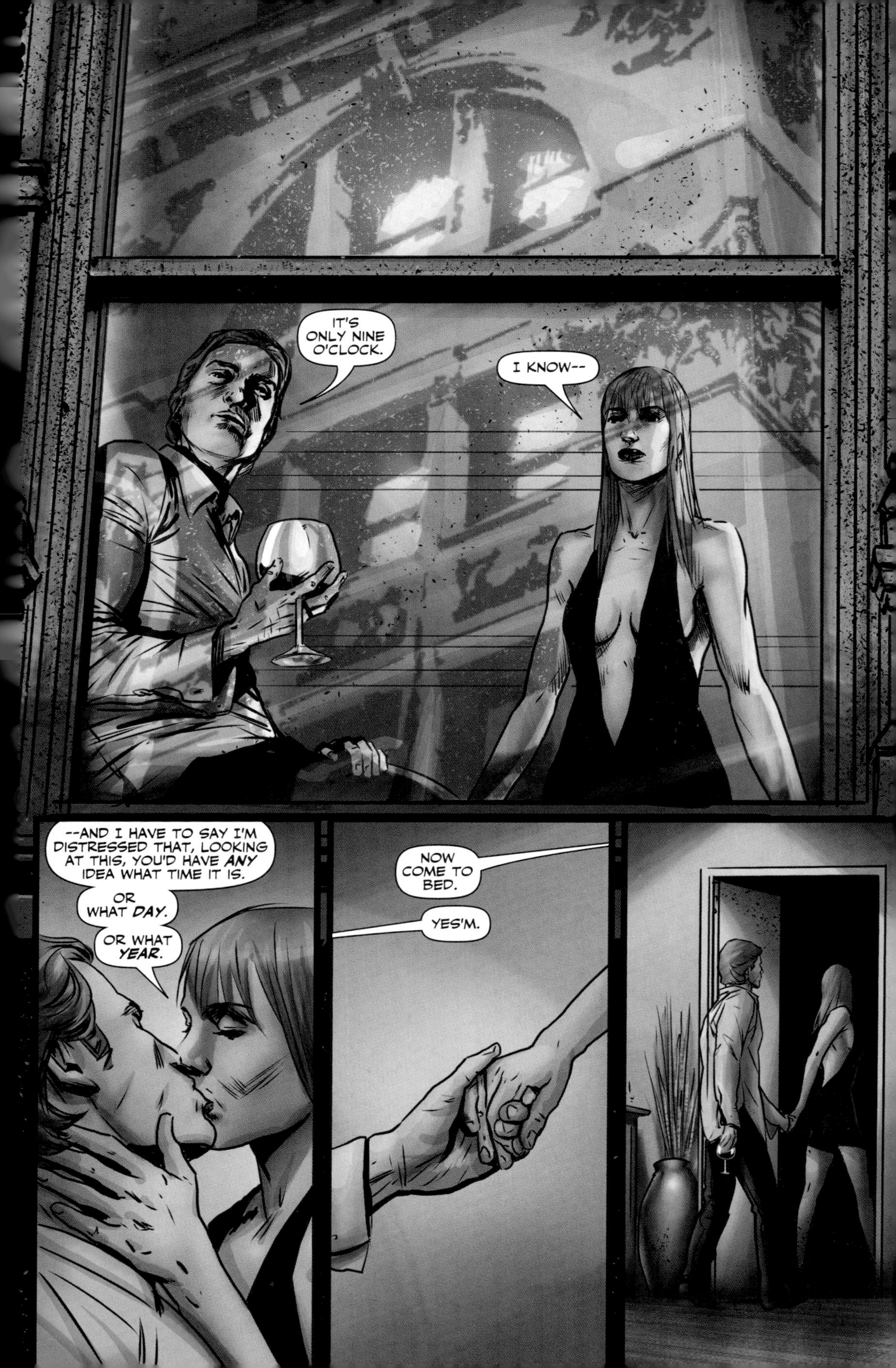
IT'S ONLY NINE O'CLOCK.
I KNOW--
--AND I HAVE TO SAY I'M DISTRESSED THAT, LOOKING AT THIS, YOU'D HAVE *ANY* IDEA WHAT TIME IT IS.
OR WHAT *DAY*.
OR WHAT *YEAR*.
NOW COME TO BED.
YES'M.

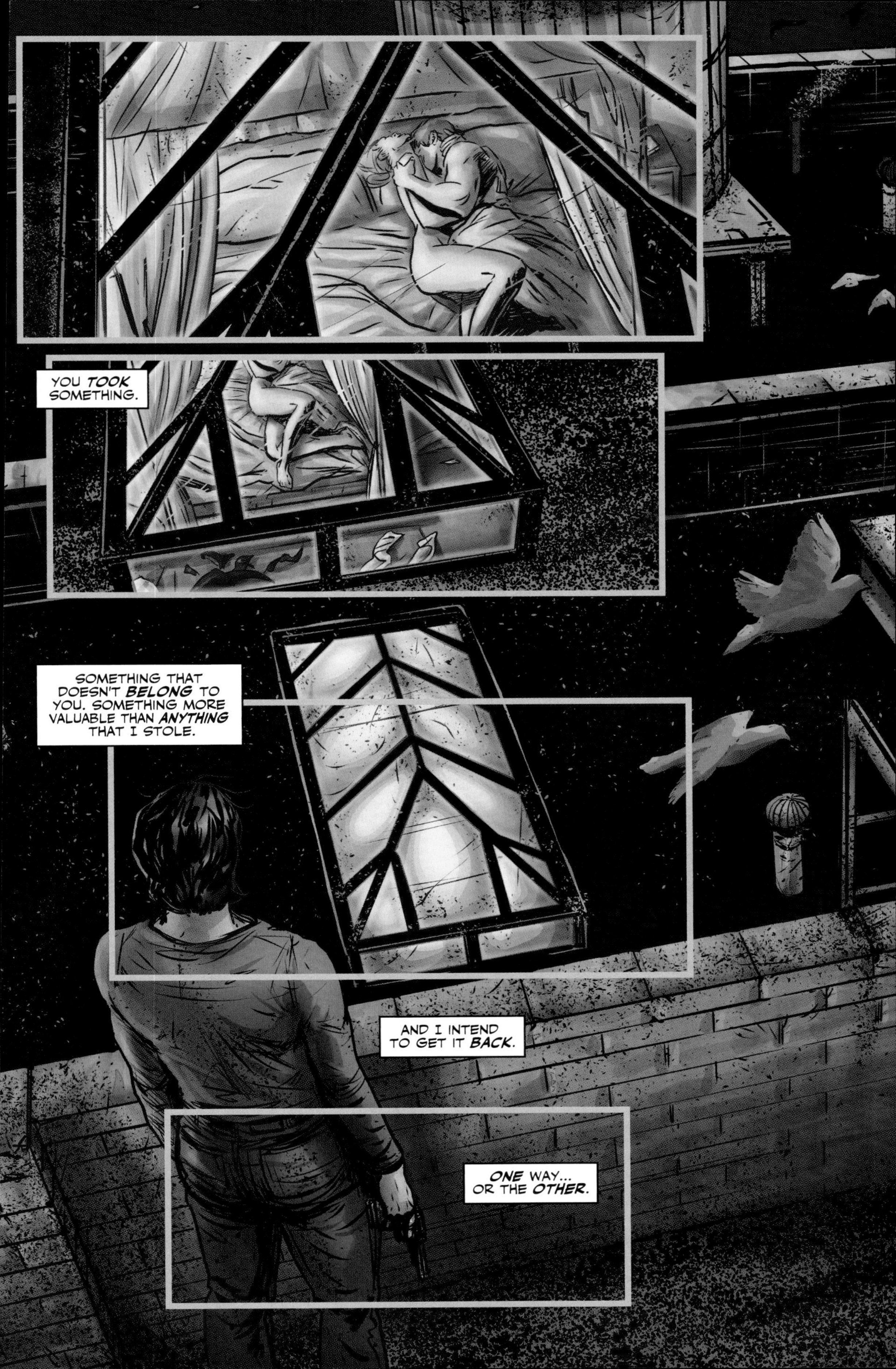

YOU *TOOK* SOMETHING.
SOMETHING THAT DOESN'T *BELONG* TO YOU. SOMETHING MORE VALUABLE THAN *ANYTHING* THAT I STOLE.
AND I INTEND TO GET IT *BACK*.
ONE WAY... OR THE *OTHER*.

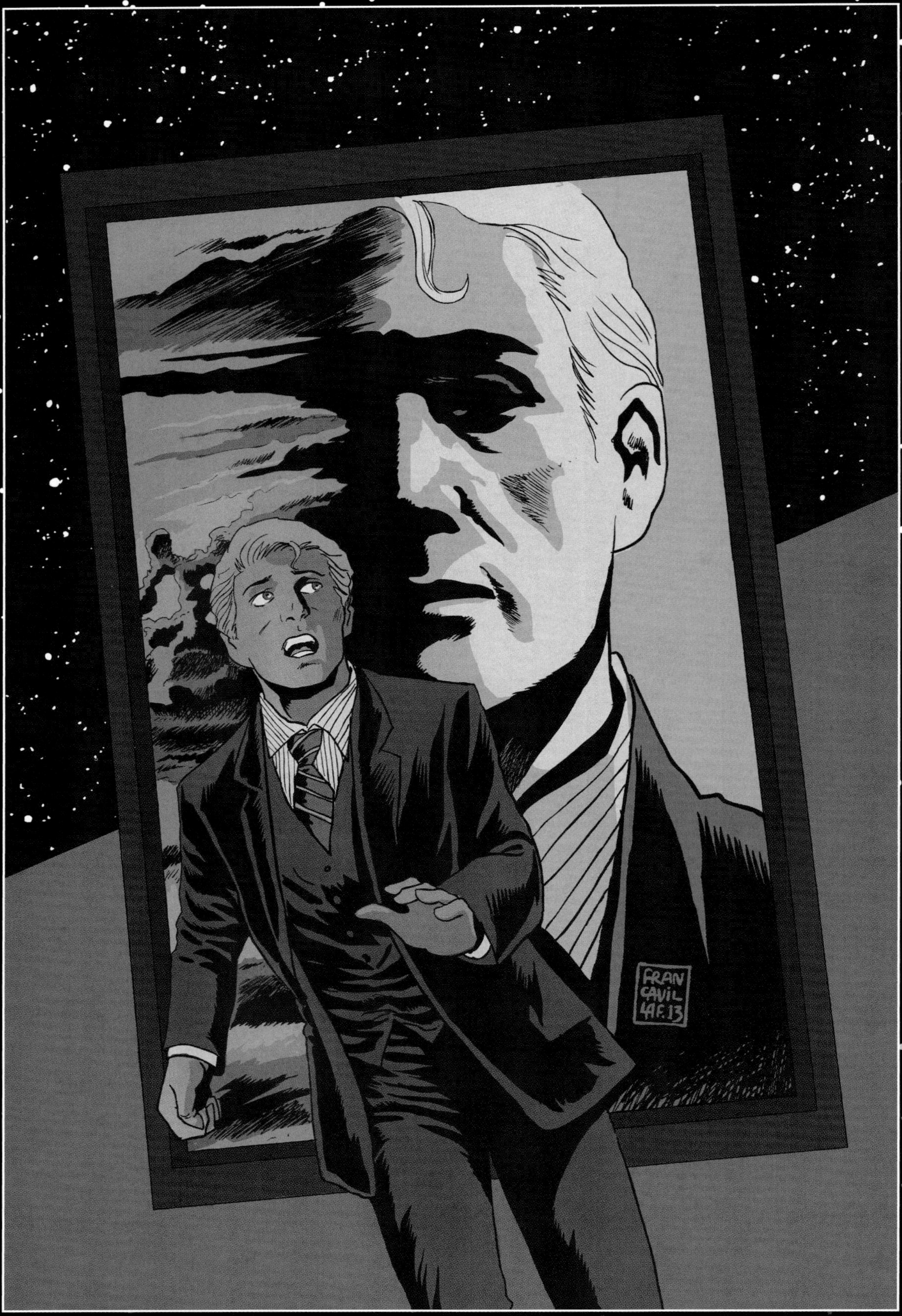
FRAN CAVIL LAF.13

ACT THREE

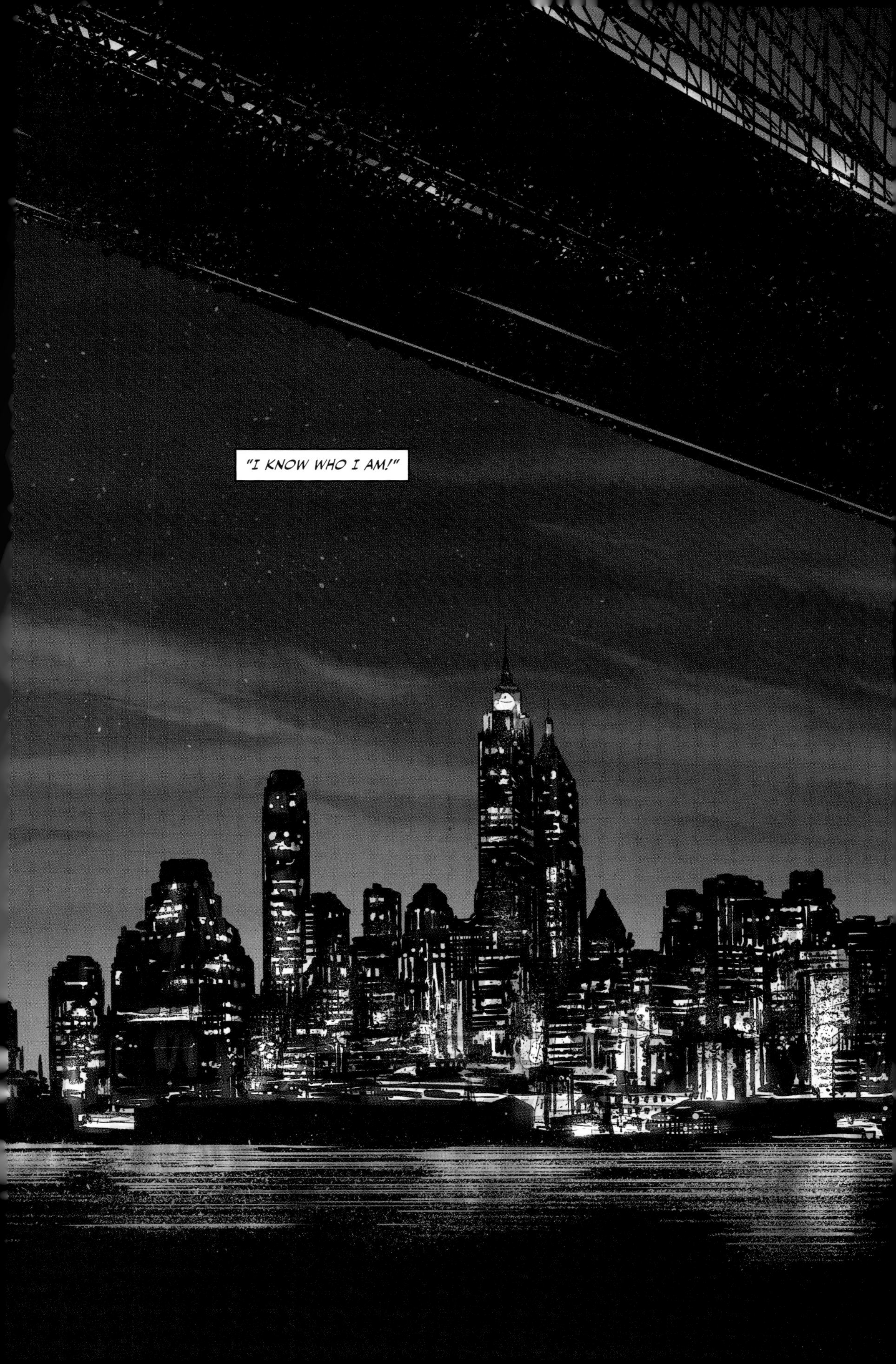
"I KNOW WHO I AM!"

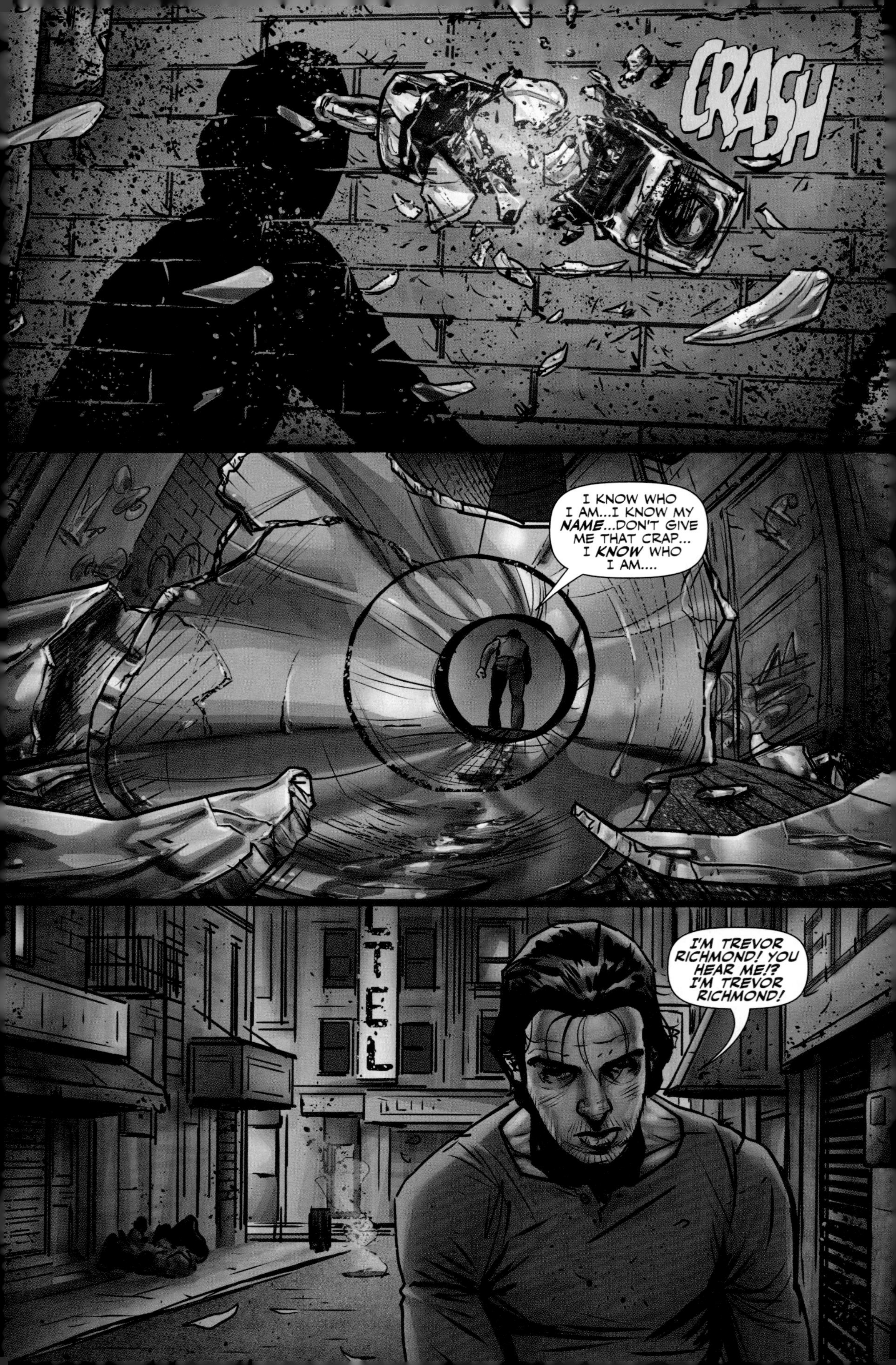
CRASH
I KNOW WHO I AM...I KNOW MY NAME...DON'T GIVE ME THAT CRAP... I KNOW WHO I AM....
I'M TREVOR RICHMOND! YOU HEAR ME!? I'M TREVOR RICHMOND!

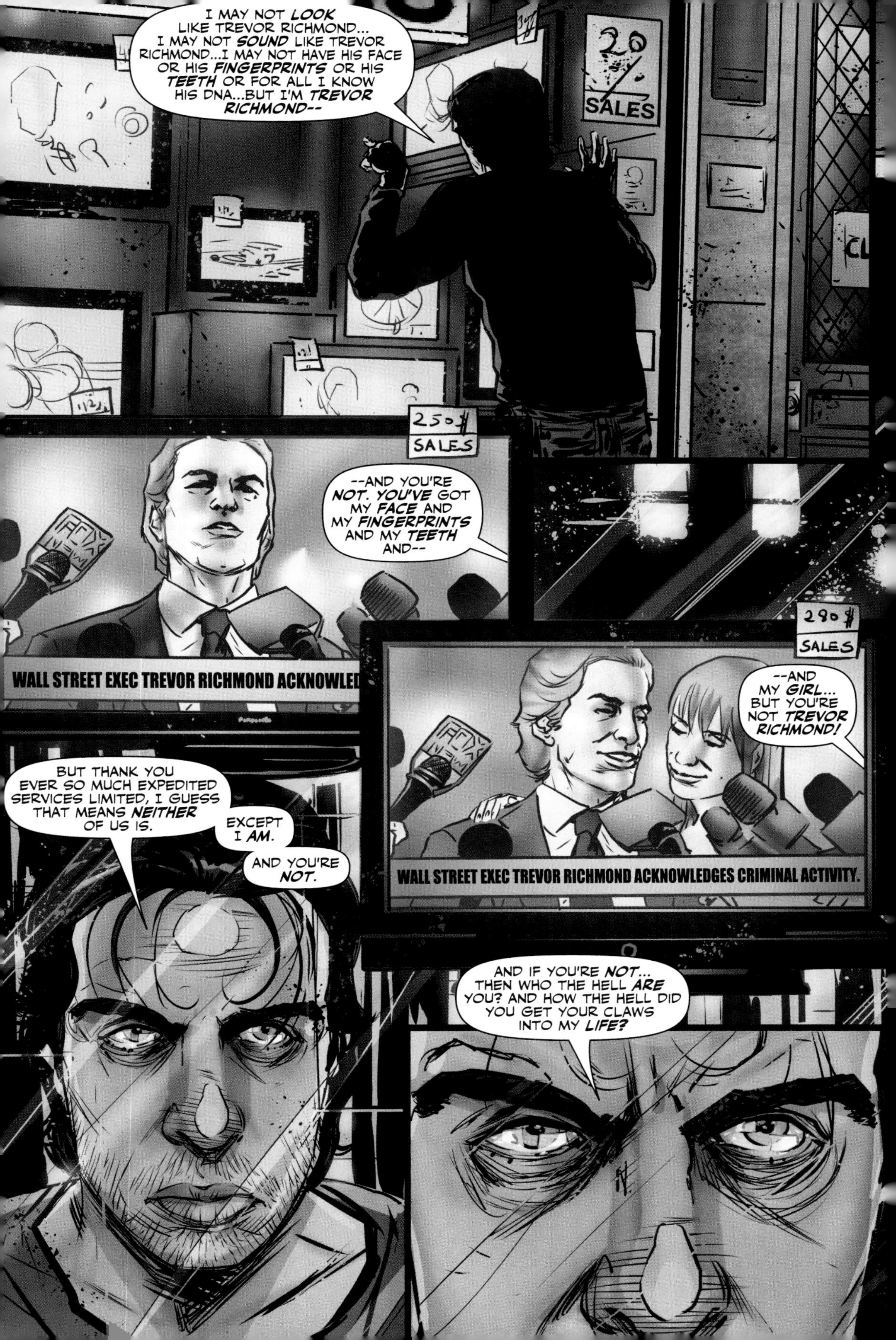
I MAY NOT LOOK LIKE TREVOR RICHMOND... I MAY NOT SOUND LIKE TREVOR RICHMOND...I MAY NOT HAVE HIS FACE OR HIS FINGERPRINTS OR HIS TEETH OR FOR ALL I KNOW HIS DNA...BUT I'M TREVOR RICHMOND--
20 % SALES
250# SALES
--AND YOU'RE NOT. YOU'VE GOT MY FACE AND MY FINGERPRINTS AND MY TEETH AND--
WALL STREET EXEC TREVOR RICHMOND ACKNOWLED
280# SALES
--AND MY GIRL... BUT YOU'RE NOT TREVOR RICHMOND!
WALL STREET EXEC TREVOR RICHMOND ACKNOWLEDGES CRIMINAL ACTIVITY.
BUT THANK YOU EVER SO MUCH EXPEDITED SERVICES LIMITED, I GUESS THAT MEANS NEITHER OF US IS.
EXCEPT I AM.
AND YOU'RE NOT.
AND IF YOU'RE NOT... THEN WHO THE HELL ARE YOU? AND HOW THE HELL DID YOU GET YOUR CLAWS INTO MY LIFE?

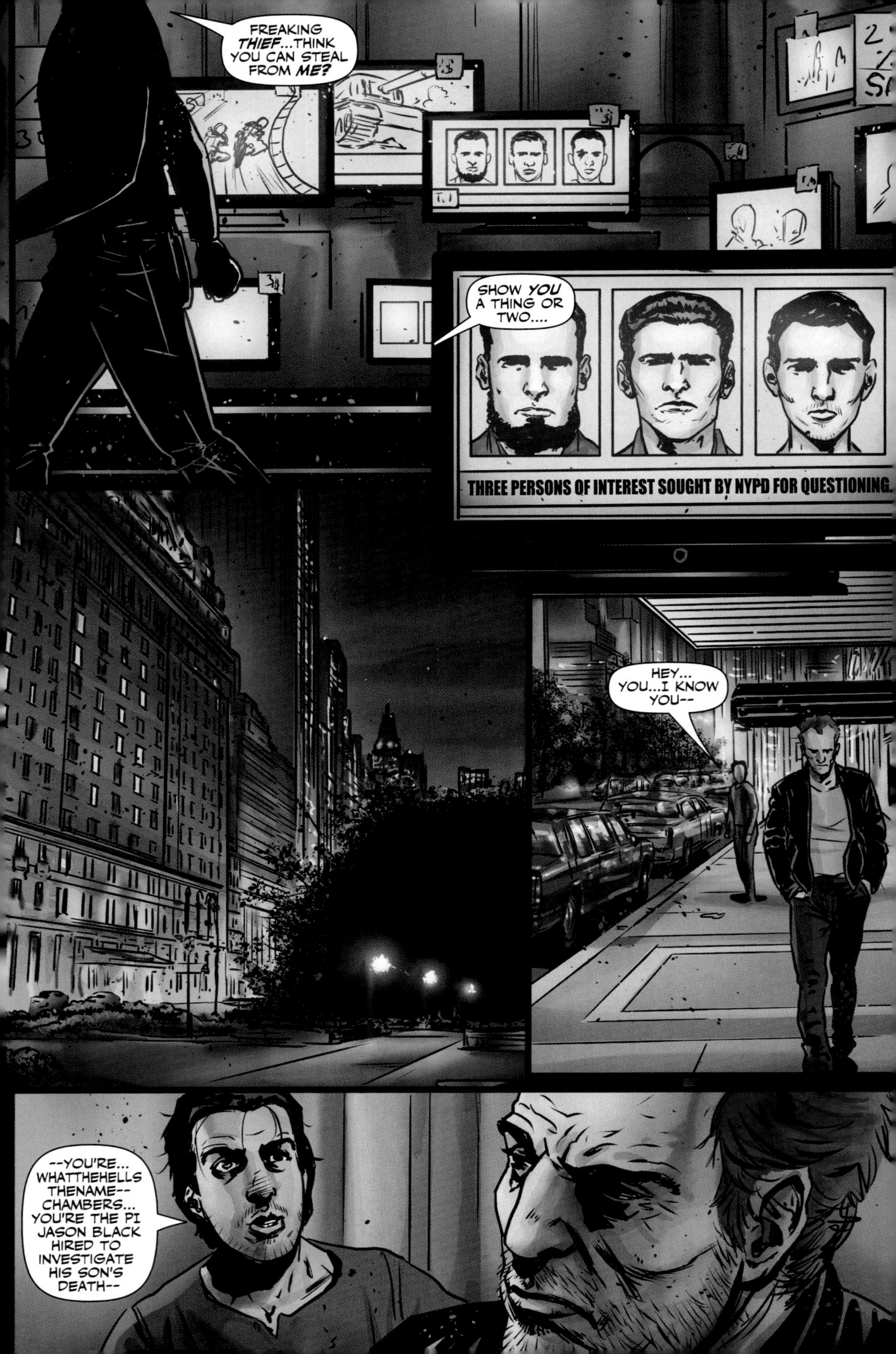
FREAKING THIEF...THINK YOU CAN STEAL FROM ME?
SHOW YOU A THING OR TWO....
THREE PERSONS OF INTEREST SOUGHT BY NYPD FOR QUESTIONING.
HEY... YOU...I KNOW YOU--
--YOU'RE... WHATTHEHELLS THENAME-- CHAMBERS... YOU'RE THE PI JASON BLACK HIRED TO INVESTIGATE HIS SON'S DEATH--

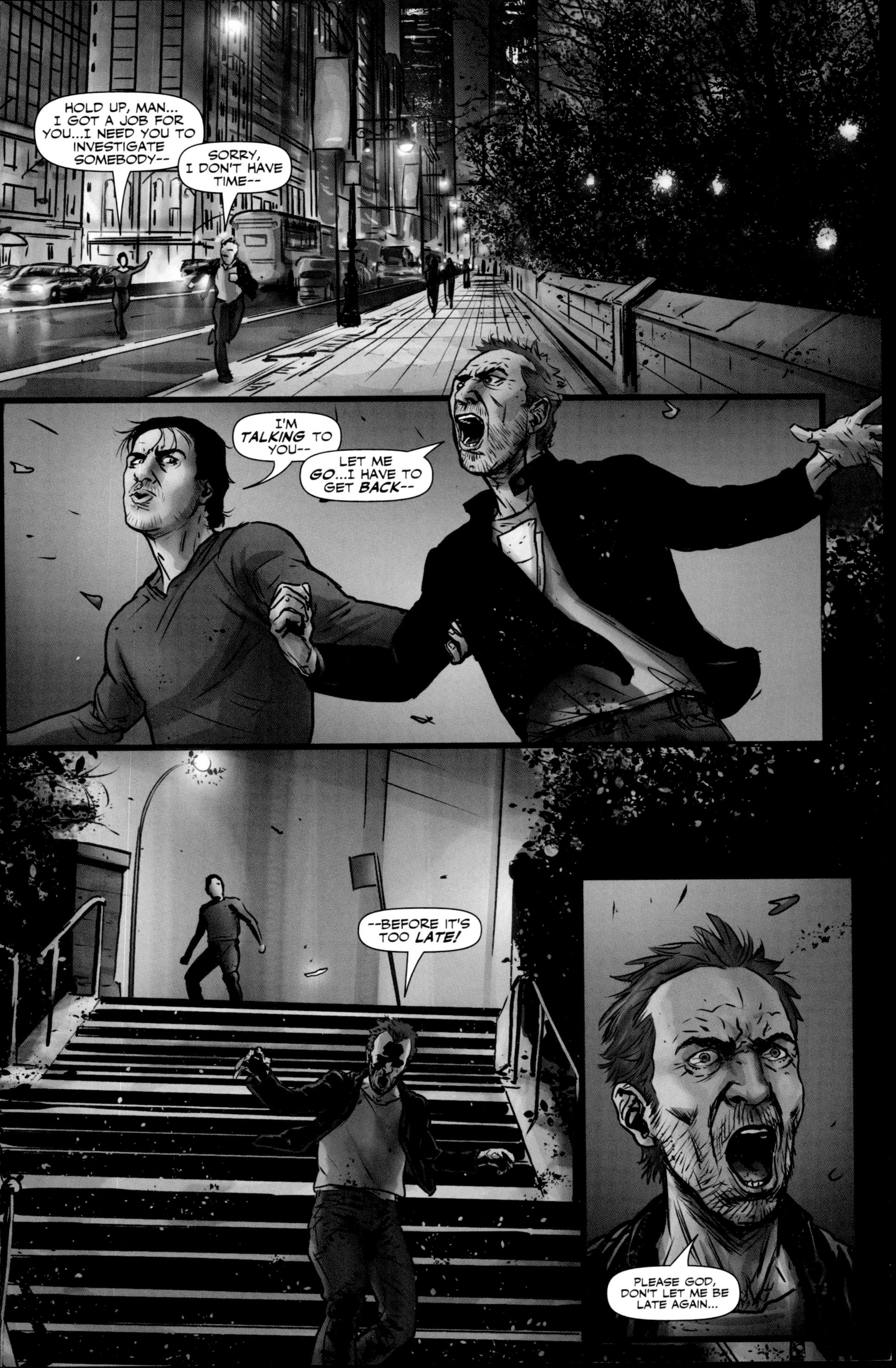
HOLD UP, MAN... I GOT A JOB FOR YOU...I NEED YOU TO INVESTIGATE SOMEBODY--
SORRY, I DON'T HAVE TIME--
I'M *TALKING* TO YOU--
LET ME *GO*...I HAVE TO GET *BACK*--
--BEFORE IT'S TOO *LATE!*
PLEASE GOD, DON'T LET ME BE LATE AGAIN...

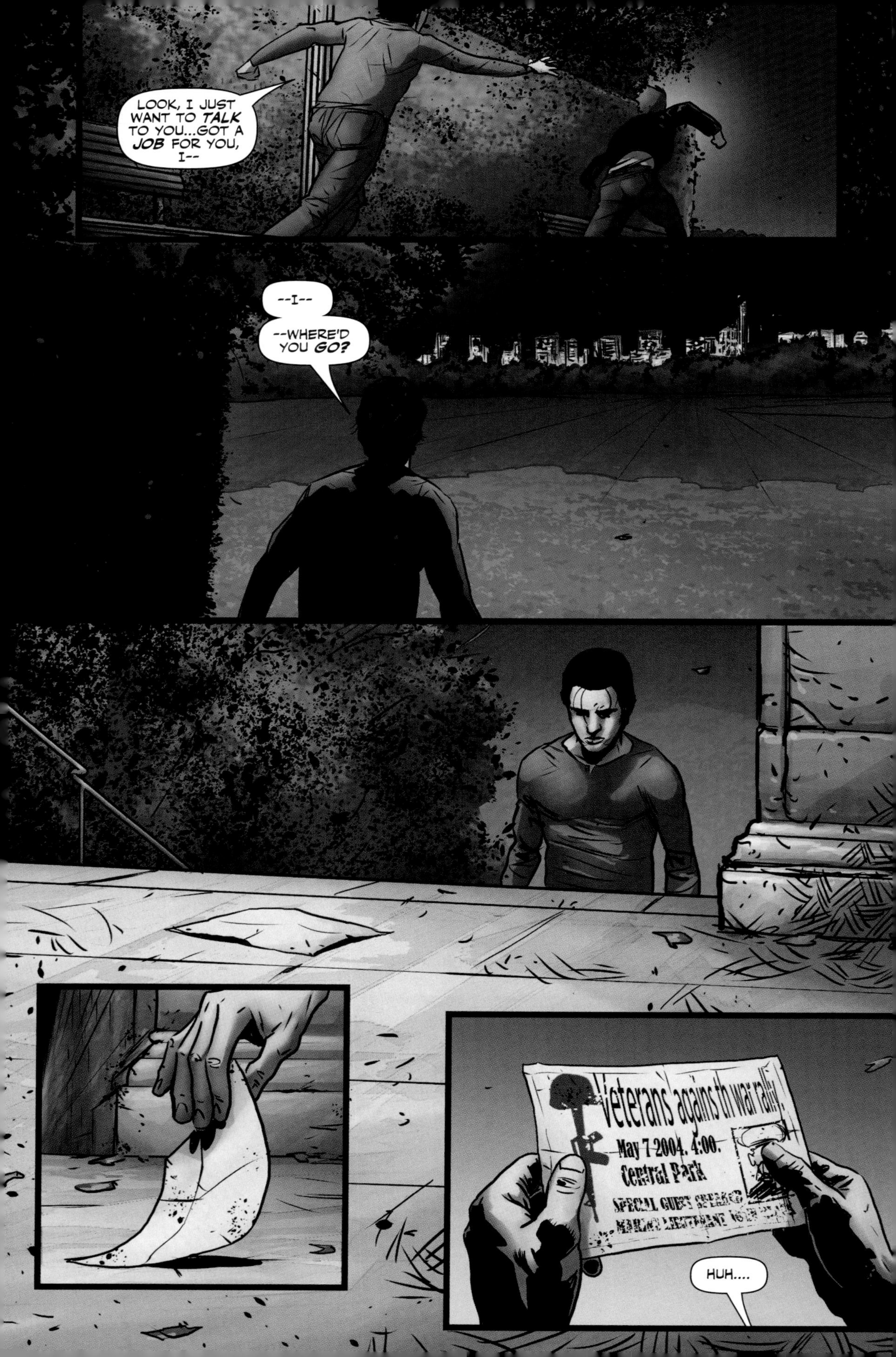
LOOK, I JUST WANT TO TALK TO YOU...GOT A JOB FOR YOU, I--
--I--
--WHERE'D YOU GO?
Veterans agains th war rally
May 7 2004. 4:00.
Central Park
HUH....

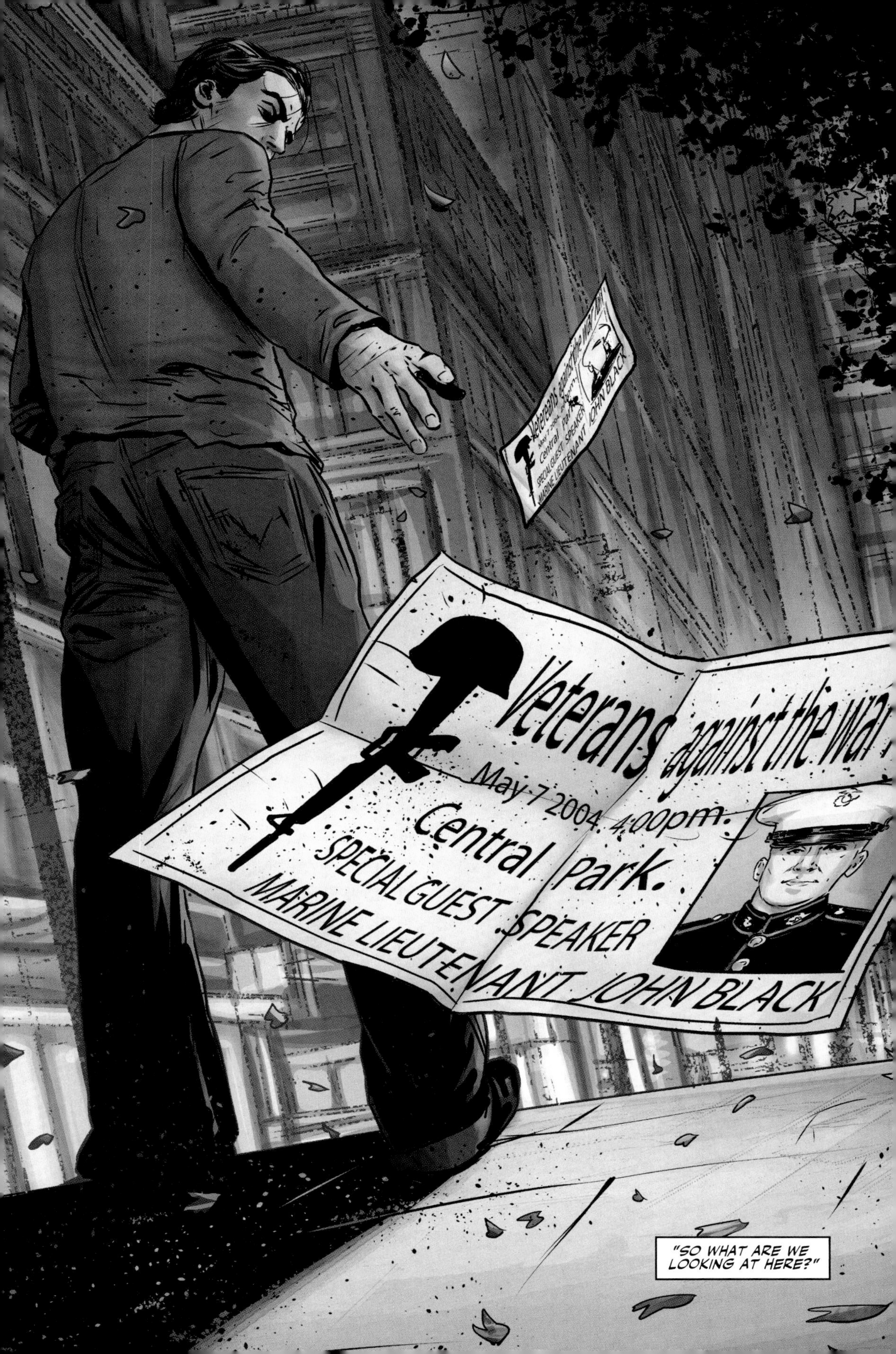
Veterans against the war
May 7 2004 4:00pm.
Central Park.
SPECIAL GUEST SPEAKER
MARINE LIEUTENANT JOHN BLACK
"SO WHAT ARE WE LOOKING AT HERE?"

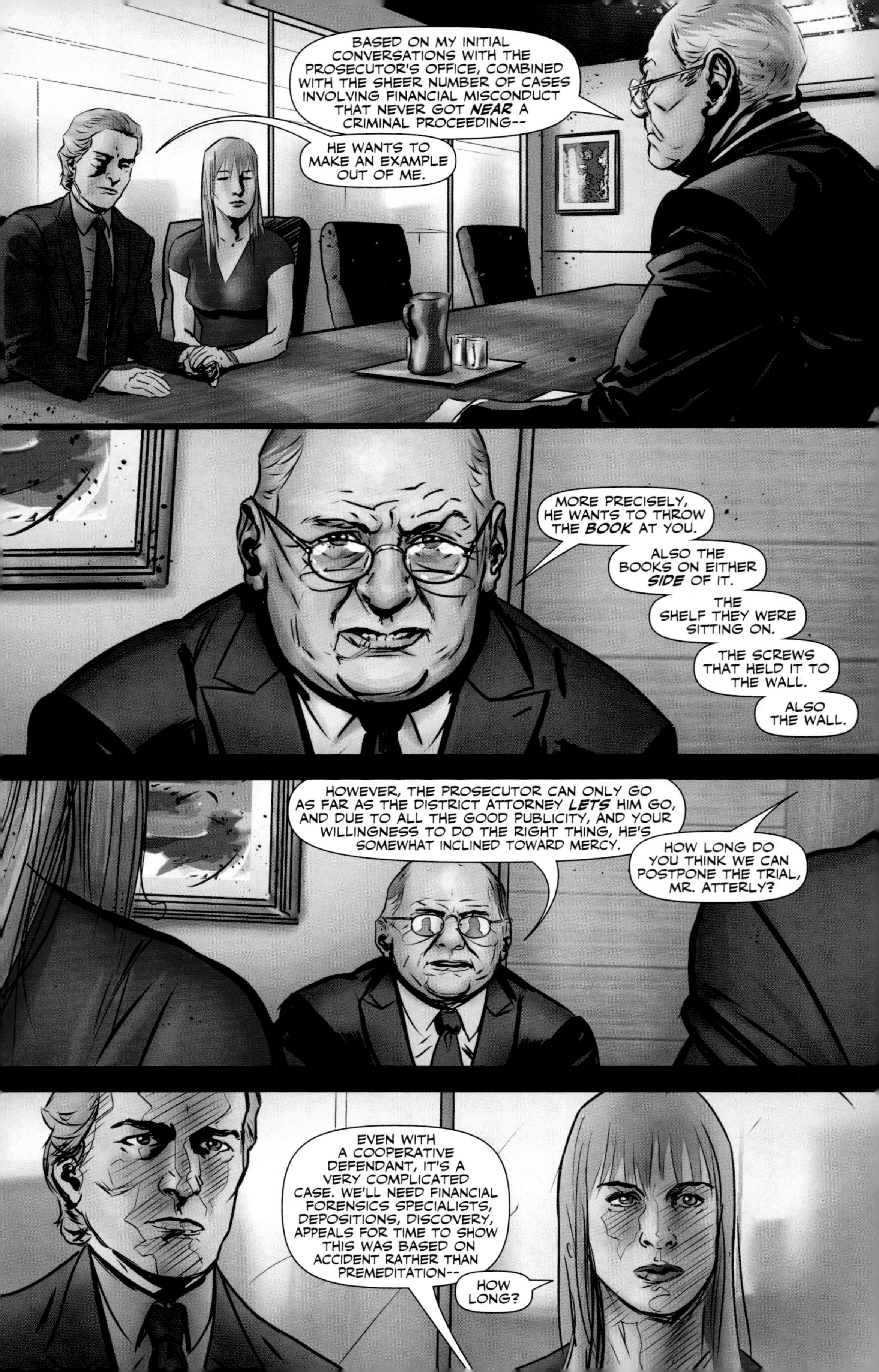
BASED ON MY INITIAL CONVERSATIONS WITH THE PROSECUTOR'S OFFICE, COMBINED WITH THE SHEER NUMBER OF CASES INVOLVING FINANCIAL MISCONDUCT THAT NEVER GOT NEAR A CRIMINAL PROCEEDING--
HE WANTS TO MAKE AN EXAMPLE OUT OF ME.
MORE PRECISELY, HE WANTS TO THROW THE BOOK AT YOU.
ALSO THE BOOKS ON EITHER SIDE OF IT.
THE SHELF THEY WERE SITTING ON.
THE SCREWS THAT HELD IT TO THE WALL.
ALSO THE WALL.
HOWEVER, THE PROSECUTOR CAN ONLY GO AS FAR AS THE DISTRICT ATTORNEY LETS HIM GO, AND DUE TO ALL THE GOOD PUBLICITY, AND YOUR WILLINGNESS TO DO THE RIGHT THING, HE'S SOMEWHAT INCLINED TOWARD MERCY.
HOW LONG DO YOU THINK WE CAN POSTPONE THE TRIAL, MR. ATTERLY?
EVEN WITH A COOPERATIVE DEFENDANT, IT'S A VERY COMPLICATED CASE. WE'LL NEED FINANCIAL FORENSICS SPECIALISTS, DEPOSITIONS, DISCOVERY, APPEALS FOR TIME TO SHOW THIS WAS BASED ON ACCIDENT RATHER THAN PREMEDITATION--
HOW LONG?

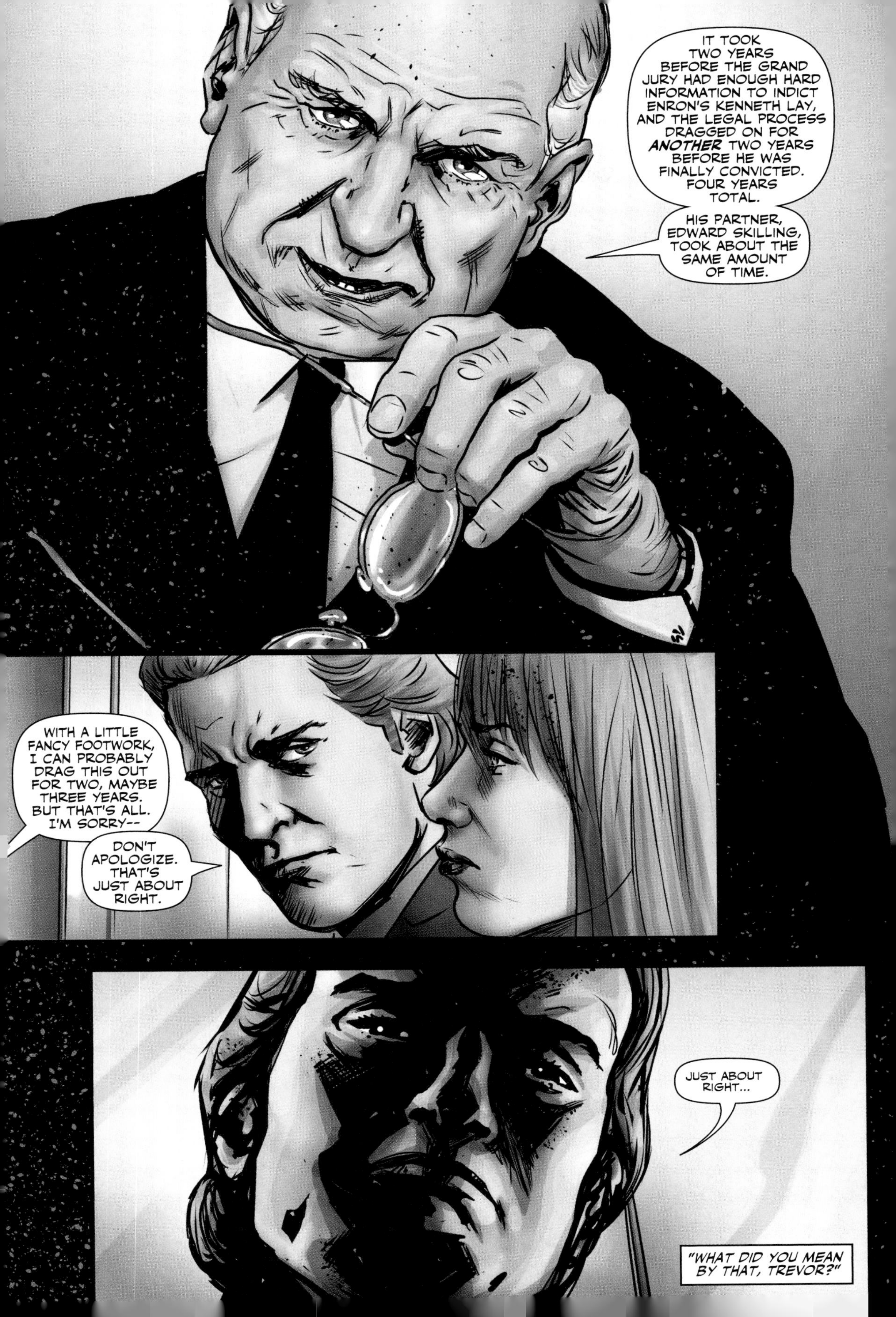
IT TOOK TWO YEARS BEFORE THE GRAND JURY HAD ENOUGH HARD INFORMATION TO INDICT ENRON'S KENNETH LAY, AND THE LEGAL PROCESS DRAGGED ON FOR ANOTHER TWO YEARS BEFORE HE WAS FINALLY CONVICTED. FOUR YEARS TOTAL.
HIS PARTNER, EDWARD SKILLING, TOOK ABOUT THE SAME AMOUNT OF TIME.
WITH A LITTLE FANCY FOOTWORK, I CAN PROBABLY DRAG THIS OUT FOR TWO, MAYBE THREE YEARS. BUT THAT'S ALL. I'M SORRY--
DON'T APOLOGIZE. THAT'S JUST ABOUT RIGHT.
JUST ABOUT RIGHT...
"WHAT DID YOU MEAN BY THAT, TREVOR?"

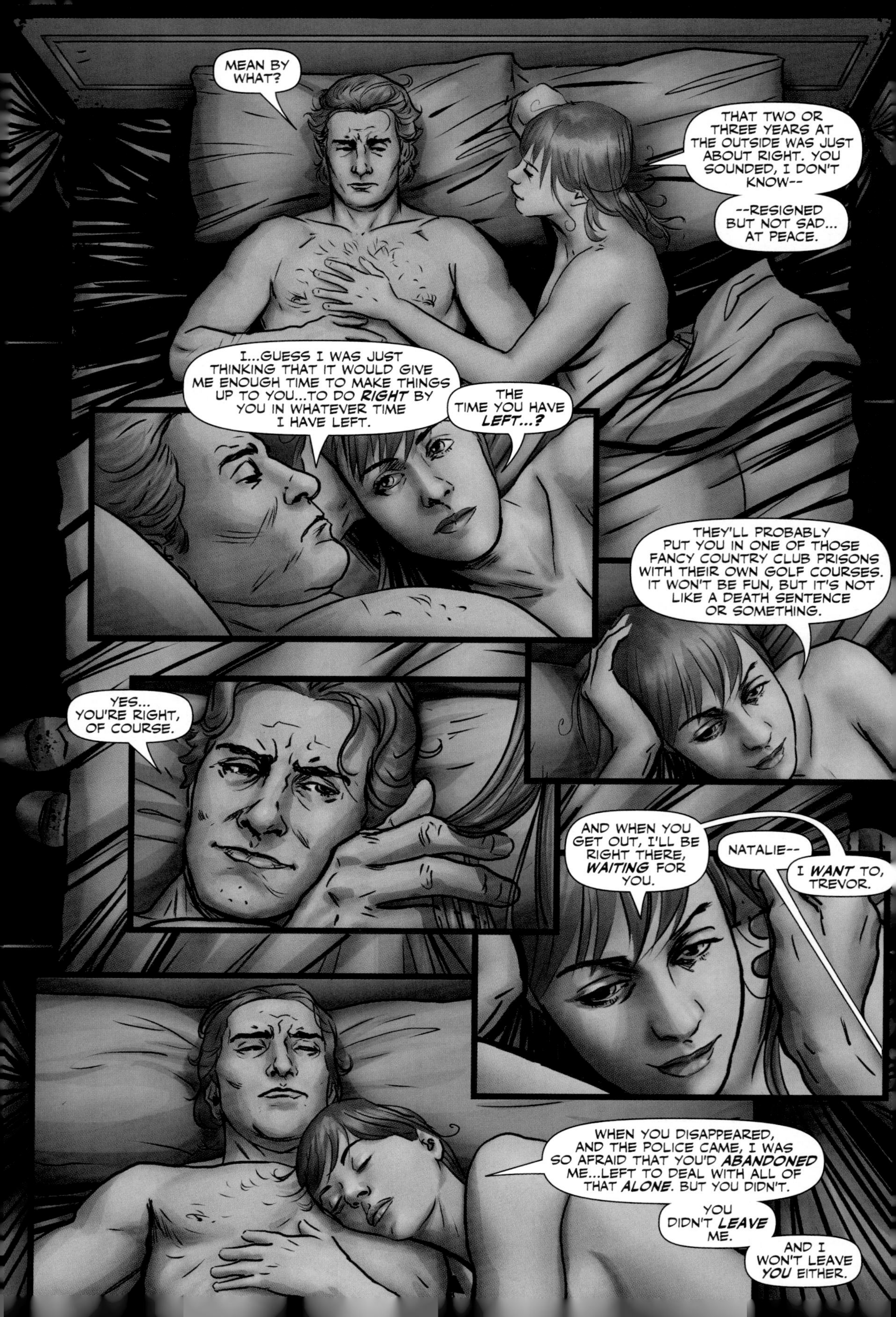
MEAN BY WHAT?
THAT TWO OR THREE YEARS AT THE OUTSIDE WAS JUST ABOUT RIGHT. YOU SOUNDED, I DON'T KNOW--
--RESIGNED BUT NOT SAD... AT PEACE.
I...GUESS I WAS JUST THINKING THAT IT WOULD GIVE ME ENOUGH TIME TO MAKE THINGS UP TO YOU...TO DO RIGHT BY YOU IN WHATEVER TIME I HAVE LEFT.
THE TIME YOU HAVE LEFT...?
THEY'LL PROBABLY PUT YOU IN ONE OF THOSE FANCY COUNTRY CLUB PRISONS WITH THEIR OWN GOLF COURSES. IT WON'T BE FUN, BUT IT'S NOT LIKE A DEATH SENTENCE OR SOMETHING.
YES... YOU'RE RIGHT, OF COURSE.
AND WHEN YOU GET OUT, I'LL BE RIGHT THERE, WAITING FOR YOU.
NATALIE--
I WANT TO, TREVOR.
WHEN YOU DISAPPEARED, AND THE POLICE CAME, I WAS SO AFRAID THAT YOU'D ABANDONED ME...LEFT TO DEAL WITH ALL OF THAT ALONE. BUT YOU DIDN'T.
YOU DIDN'T LEAVE ME.
AND I WON'T LEAVE YOU EITHER.

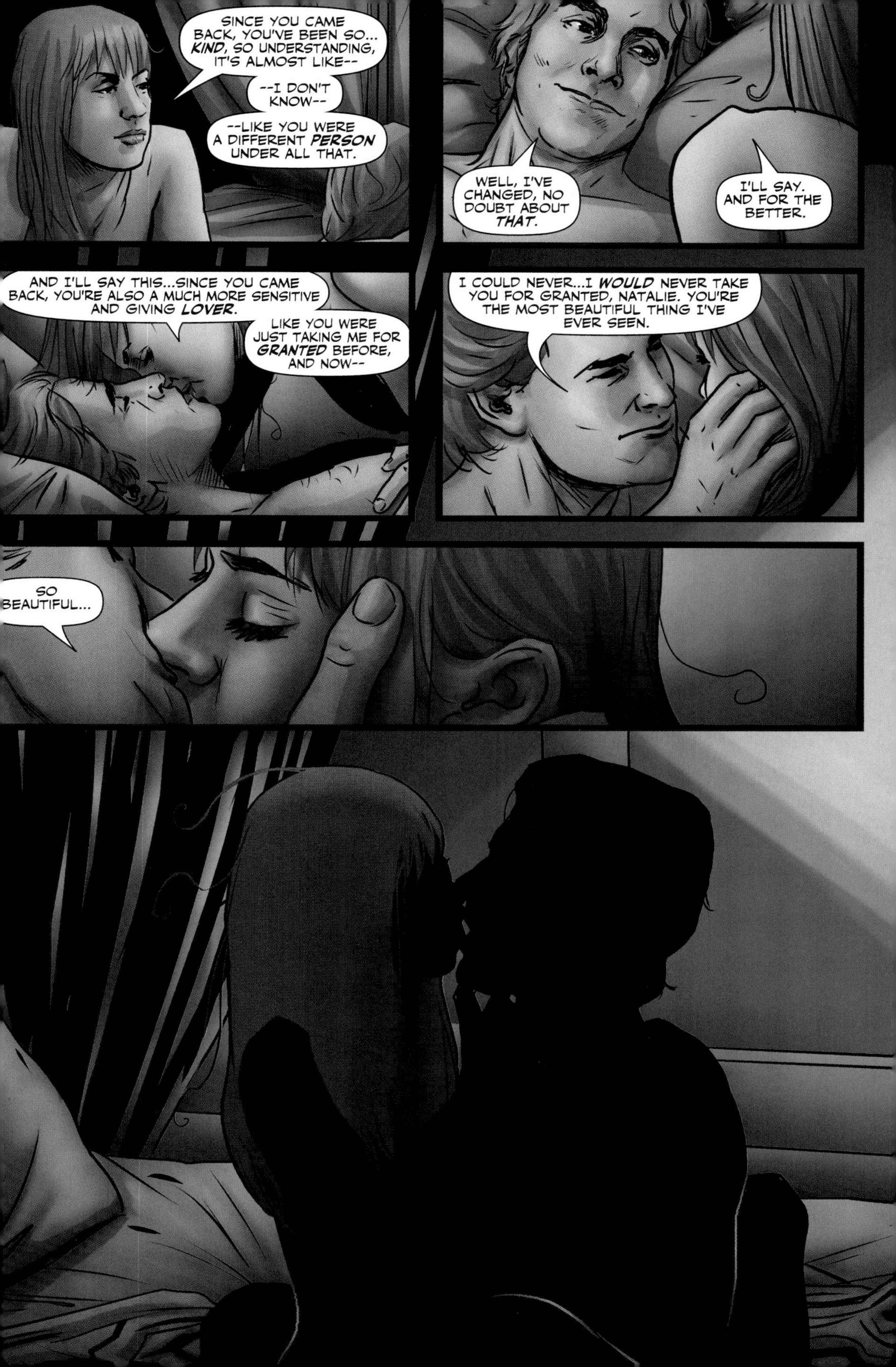
SINCE YOU CAME BACK, YOU'VE BEEN SO... *KIND*, SO UNDERSTANDING, IT'S ALMOST LIKE--
--I DON'T KNOW--
--LIKE YOU WERE A DIFFERENT *PERSON* UNDER ALL THAT.
WELL, I'VE CHANGED, NO DOUBT ABOUT *THAT*.
I'LL SAY. AND FOR THE BETTER.
AND I'LL SAY THIS...SINCE YOU CAME BACK, YOU'RE ALSO A MUCH MORE SENSITIVE AND GIVING *LOVER*.
LIKE YOU WERE JUST TAKING ME FOR *GRANTED* BEFORE, AND NOW--
I COULD NEVER...I *WOULD* NEVER TAKE YOU FOR GRANTED, NATALIE. YOU'RE THE MOST BEAUTIFUL THING I'VE EVER SEEN.
SO BEAUTIFUL...

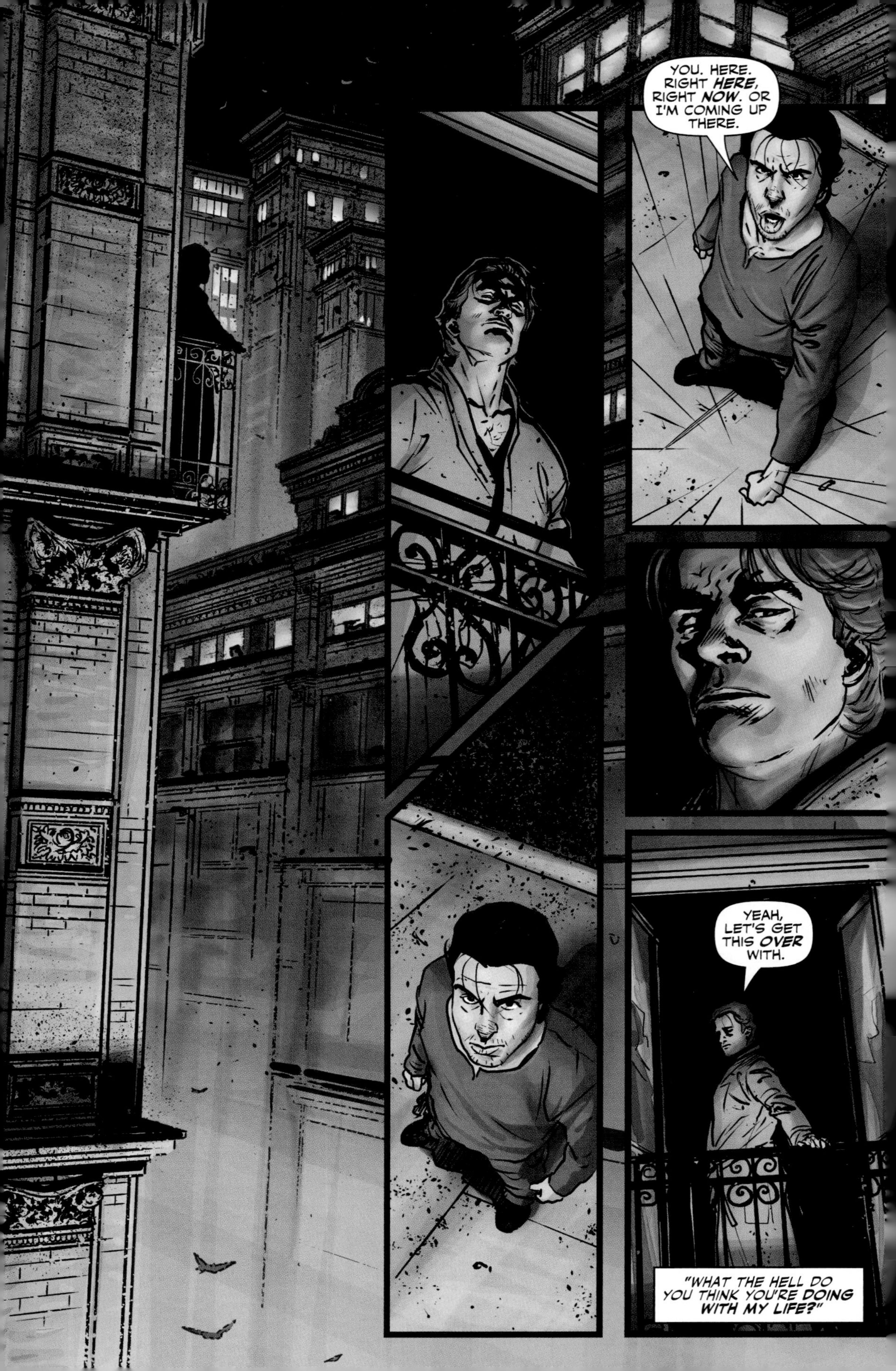
YOU. HERE. RIGHT HERE, RIGHT NOW. OR I'M COMING UP THERE.
YEAH, LET'S GET THIS OVER WITH.
"WHAT THE HELL DO YOU THINK YOU'RE DOING WITH MY LIFE?"

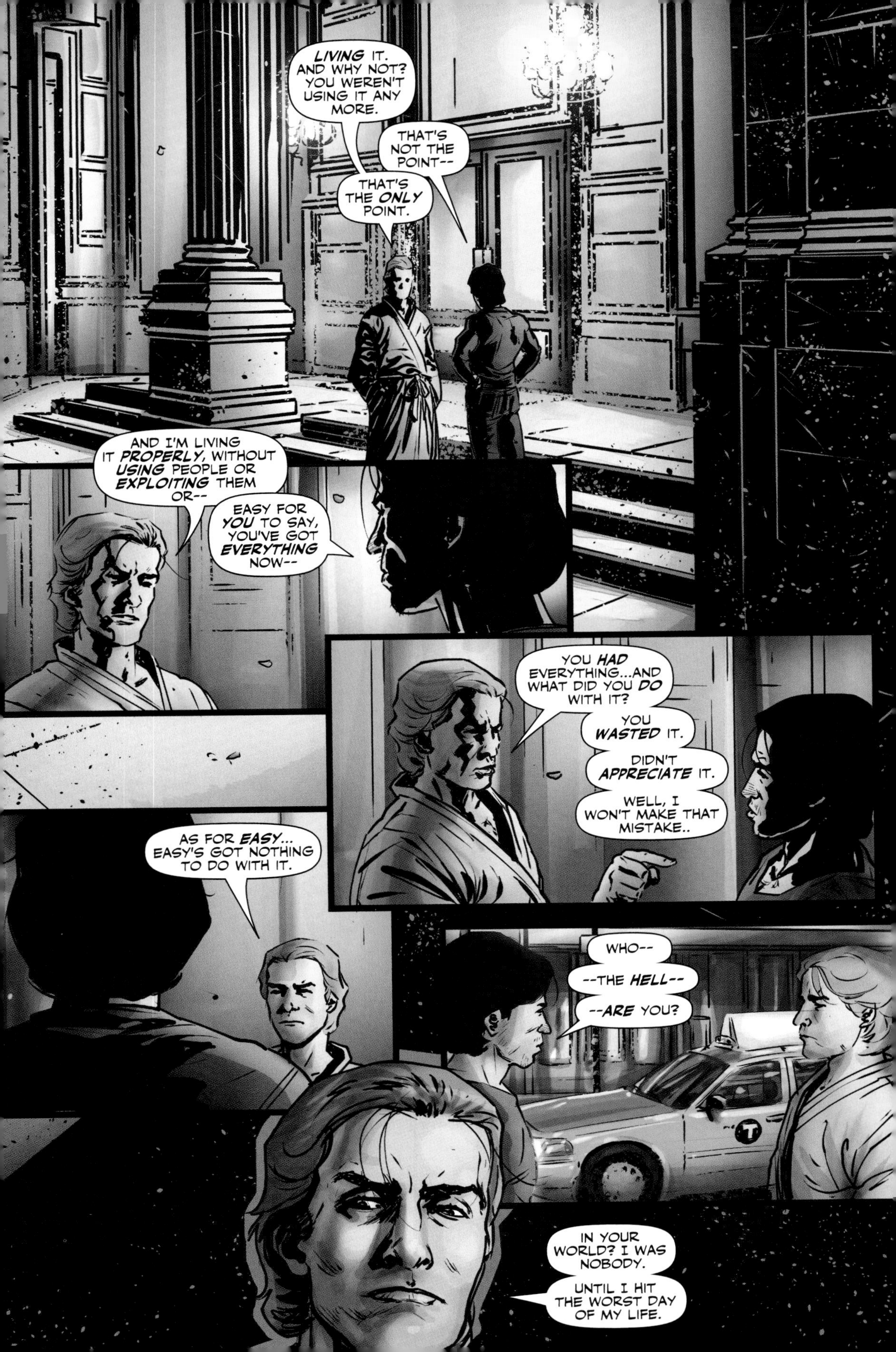
LIVING IT. AND WHY NOT? YOU WEREN'T USING IT ANY MORE.
THAT'S NOT THE POINT--
THAT'S THE ONLY POINT.
AND I'M LIVING IT PROPERLY, WITHOUT USING PEOPLE OR EXPLOITING THEM OR--
EASY FOR YOU TO SAY, YOU'VE GOT EVERYTHING NOW--
YOU HAD EVERYTHING...AND WHAT DID YOU DO WITH IT?
YOU WASTED IT.
DIDN'T APPRECIATE IT.
WELL, I WON'T MAKE THAT MISTAKE..
AS FOR EASY... EASY'S GOT NOTHING TO DO WITH IT.
WHO--
--THE HELL--
--ARE YOU?
IN YOUR WORLD? I WAS NOBODY.
UNTIL I HIT THE WORST DAY OF MY LIFE.

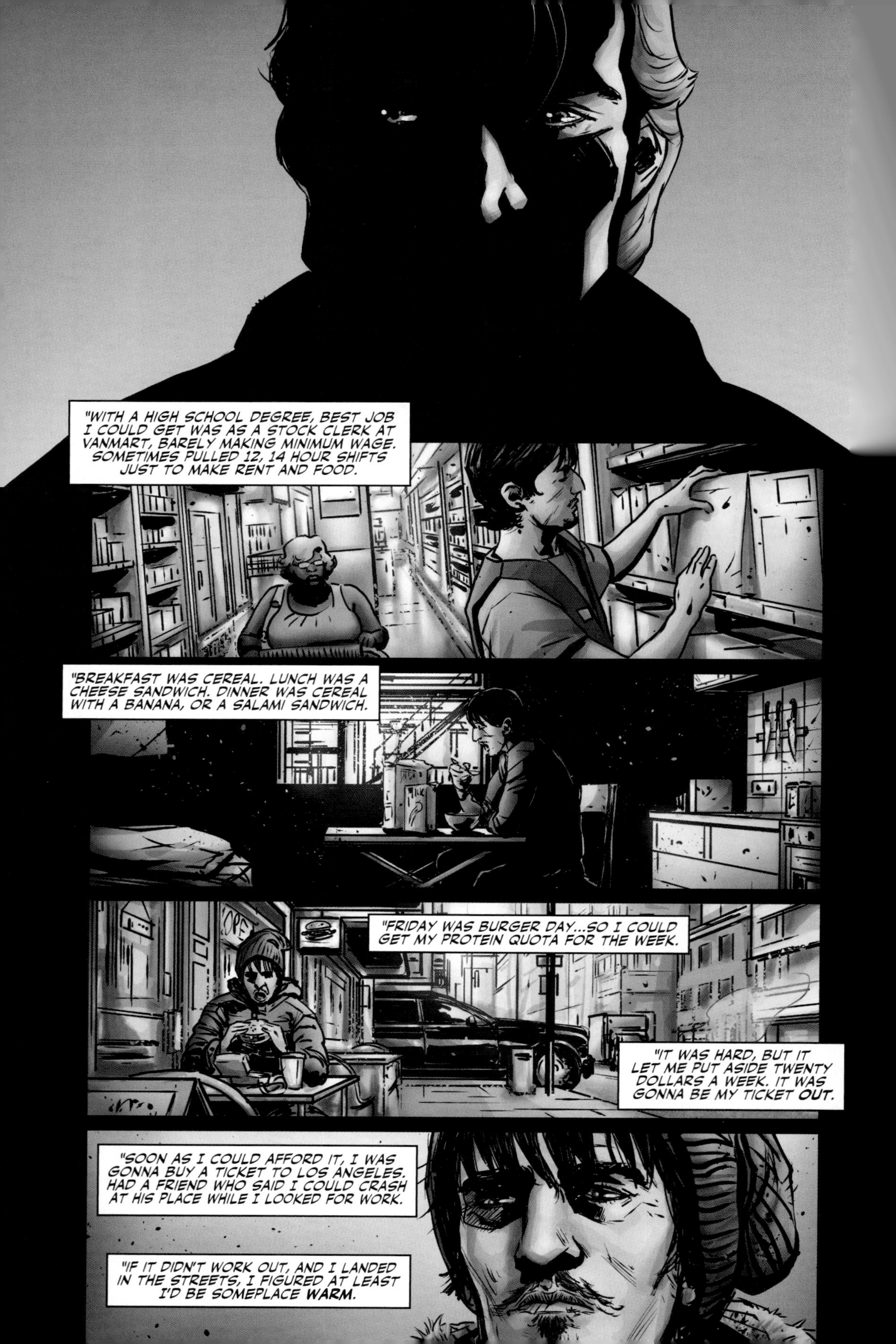
"WITH A HIGH SCHOOL DEGREE, BEST JOB I COULD GET WAS AS A STOCK CLERK AT VANMART, BARELY MAKING MINIMUM WAGE. SOMETIMES PULLED 12, 14 HOUR SHIFTS JUST TO MAKE RENT AND FOOD.
"BREAKFAST WAS CEREAL. LUNCH WAS A CHEESE SANDWICH. DINNER WAS CEREAL WITH A BANANA, OR A SALAMI SANDWICH.
"FRIDAY WAS BURGER DAY...SO I COULD GET MY PROTEIN QUOTA FOR THE WEEK.
"IT WAS HARD, BUT IT LET ME PUT ASIDE TWENTY DOLLARS A WEEK. IT WAS GONNA BE MY TICKET **OUT**.
"SOON AS I COULD AFFORD IT, I WAS GONNA BUY A TICKET TO LOS ANGELES. HAD A FRIEND WHO SAID I COULD CRASH AT HIS PLACE WHILE I LOOKED FOR WORK.
"IF IT DIDN'T WORK OUT, AND I LANDED IN THE STREETS, I FIGURED AT LEAST I'D BE SOMEPLACE **WARM**.

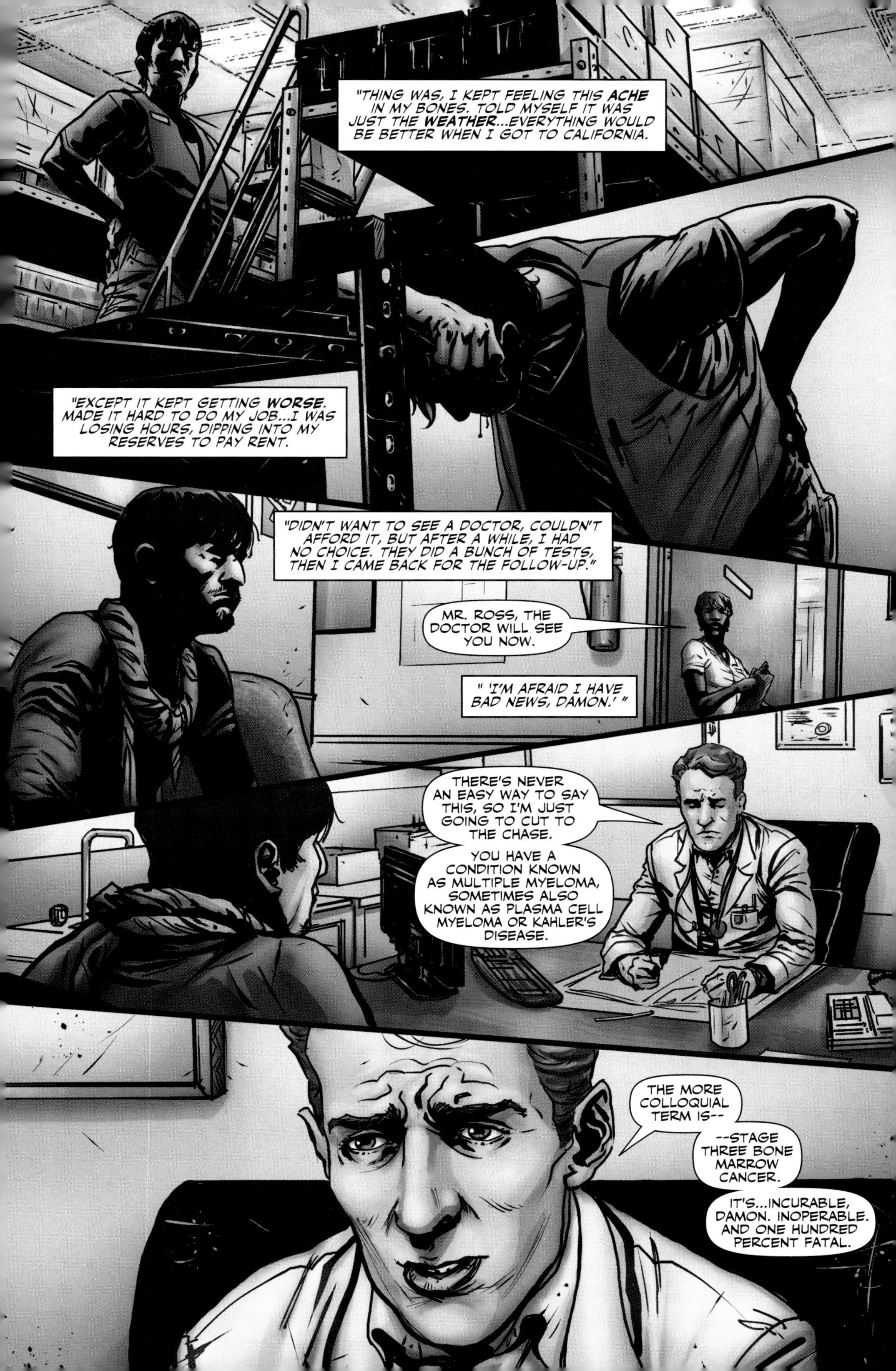
"THING WAS, I KEPT FEELING THIS **ACHE** IN MY BONES. TOLD MYSELF IT WAS JUST THE **WEATHER**...EVERYTHING WOULD BE BETTER WHEN I GOT TO CALIFORNIA.
"EXCEPT IT KEPT GETTING **WORSE**. MADE IT HARD TO DO MY JOB...I WAS LOSING HOURS, DIPPING INTO MY RESERVES TO PAY RENT.
"DIDN'T WANT TO SEE A DOCTOR, COULDN'T AFFORD IT, BUT AFTER A WHILE, I HAD NO CHOICE. THEY DID A BUNCH OF TESTS, THEN I CAME BACK FOR THE FOLLOW-UP."
MR. ROSS, THE DOCTOR WILL SEE YOU NOW.
" 'I'M AFRAID I HAVE BAD NEWS, DAMON.' "
THERE'S NEVER AN EASY WAY TO SAY THIS, SO I'M JUST GOING TO CUT TO THE CHASE.
YOU HAVE A CONDITION KNOWN AS MULTIPLE MYELOMA, SOMETIMES ALSO KNOWN AS PLASMA CELL MYELOMA OR KAHLER'S DISEASE.
THE MORE COLLOQUIAL TERM IS--
--STAGE THREE BONE MARROW CANCER.
IT'S...INCURABLE, DAMON. INOPERABLE. AND ONE HUNDRED PERCENT FATAL.

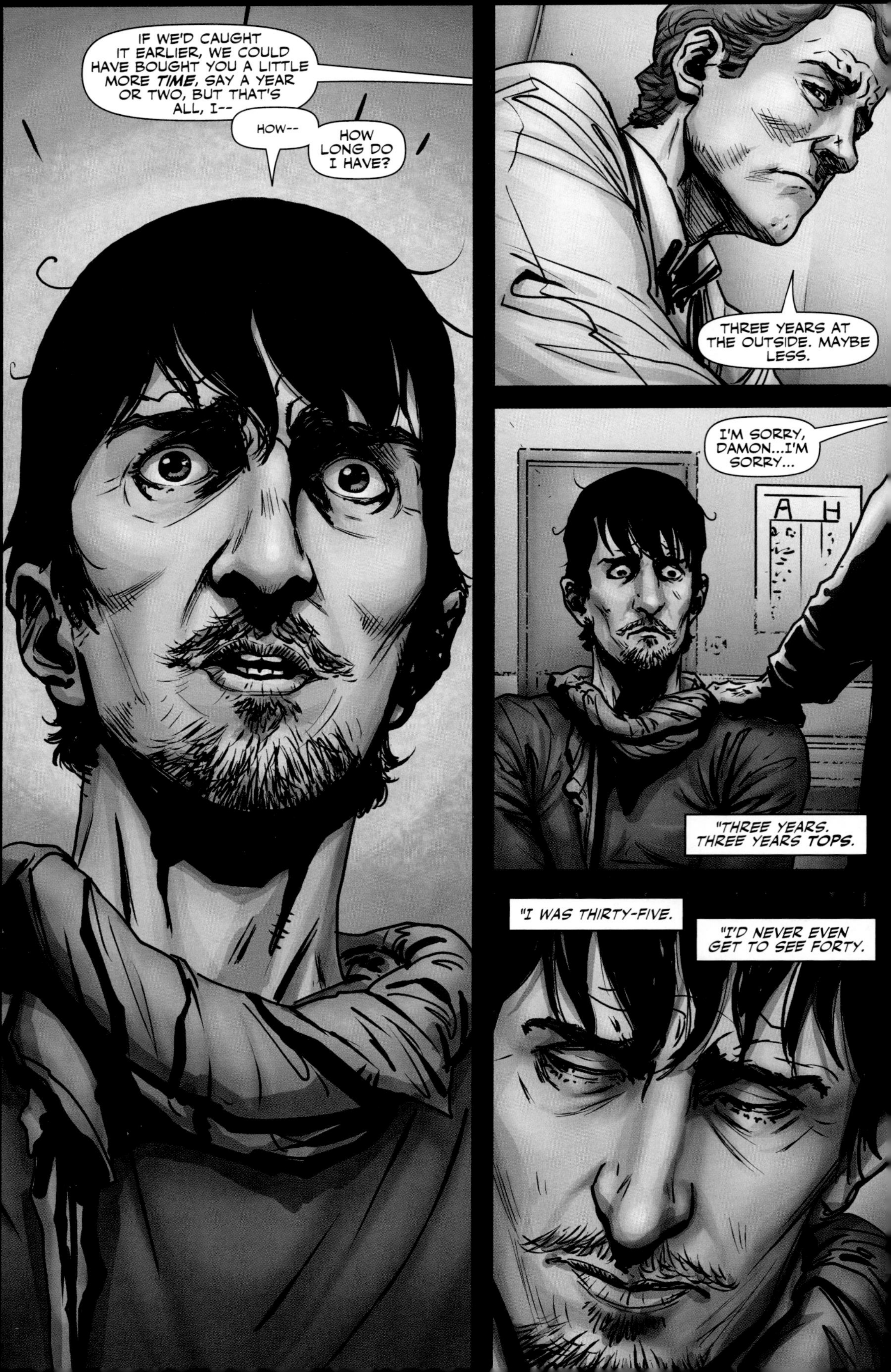
IF WE'D CAUGHT IT EARLIER, WE COULD HAVE BOUGHT YOU A LITTLE MORE *TIME*, SAY A YEAR OR TWO, BUT THAT'S ALL, I--
HOW--
HOW LONG DO I HAVE?
THREE YEARS AT THE OUTSIDE. MAYBE LESS.
I'M SORRY, DAMON...I'M SORRY...
"THREE YEARS. THREE YEARS *TOPS*.
"I WAS THIRTY-FIVE.
"I'D NEVER EVEN GET TO SEE FORTY.

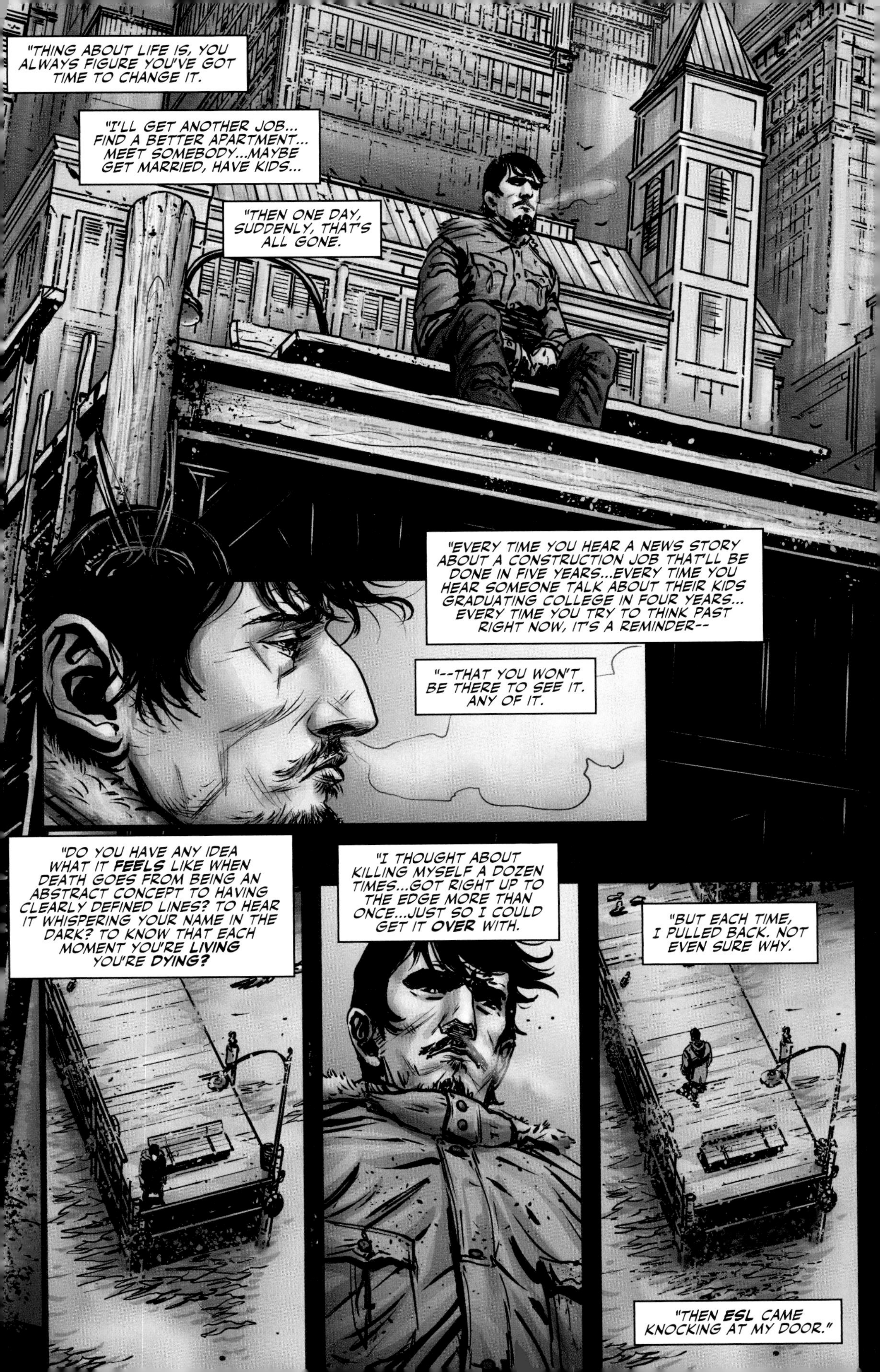
"THING ABOUT LIFE IS, YOU ALWAYS FIGURE YOU'VE GOT TIME TO CHANGE IT.
"I'LL GET ANOTHER JOB... FIND A BETTER APARTMENT... MEET SOMEBODY...MAYBE GET MARRIED, HAVE KIDS...
"THEN ONE DAY, SUDDENLY, THAT'S ALL GONE.
"EVERY TIME YOU HEAR A NEWS STORY ABOUT A CONSTRUCTION JOB THAT'LL BE DONE IN FIVE YEARS...EVERY TIME YOU HEAR SOMEONE TALK ABOUT THEIR KIDS GRADUATING COLLEGE IN FOUR YEARS... EVERY TIME YOU TRY TO THINK PAST RIGHT NOW, IT'S A REMINDER--
"--THAT YOU WON'T BE THERE TO SEE IT. ANY OF IT.
"DO YOU HAVE ANY IDEA WHAT IT **FEELS** LIKE WHEN DEATH GOES FROM BEING AN ABSTRACT CONCEPT TO HAVING CLEARLY DEFINED LINES? TO HEAR IT WHISPERING YOUR NAME IN THE DARK? TO KNOW THAT EACH MOMENT YOU'RE **LIVING** YOU'RE **DYING?**
"I THOUGHT ABOUT KILLING MYSELF A DOZEN TIMES...GOT RIGHT UP TO THE EDGE MORE THAN ONCE...JUST SO I COULD GET IT **OVER** WITH.
"BUT EACH TIME, I PULLED BACK. NOT EVEN SURE WHY.
"THEN **ESL** CAME KNOCKING AT MY DOOR."

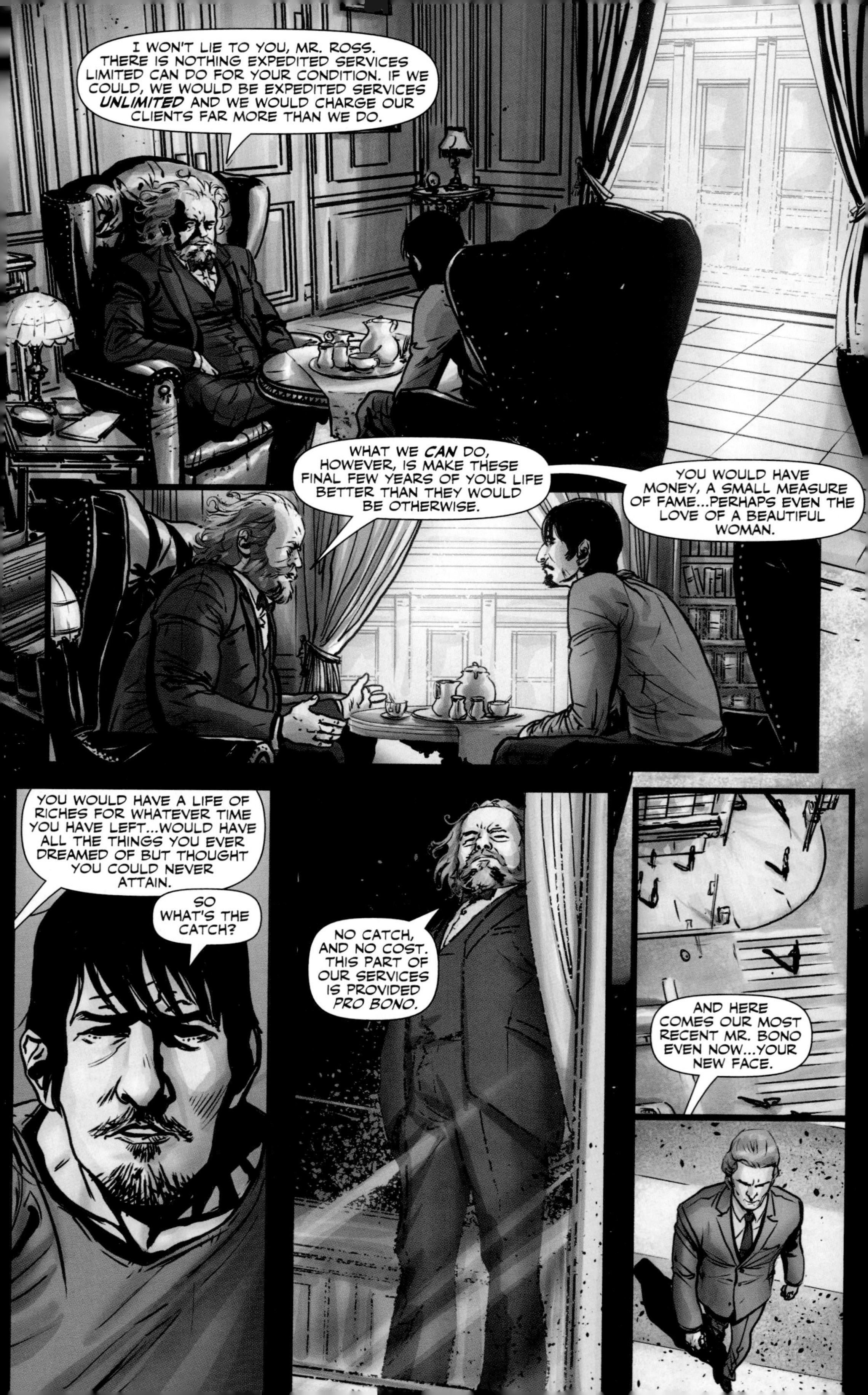
I WON'T LIE TO YOU, MR. ROSS. THERE IS NOTHING EXPEDITED SERVICES LIMITED CAN DO FOR YOUR CONDITION. IF WE COULD, WE WOULD BE EXPEDITED SERVICES *UNLIMITED* AND WE WOULD CHARGE OUR CLIENTS FAR MORE THAN WE DO.
WHAT WE *CAN* DO, HOWEVER, IS MAKE THESE FINAL FEW YEARS OF YOUR LIFE BETTER THAN THEY WOULD BE OTHERWISE.
YOU WOULD HAVE MONEY, A SMALL MEASURE OF FAME...PERHAPS EVEN THE LOVE OF A BEAUTIFUL WOMAN.
YOU WOULD HAVE A LIFE OF RICHES FOR WHATEVER TIME YOU HAVE LEFT...WOULD HAVE ALL THE THINGS YOU EVER DREAMED OF BUT THOUGHT YOU COULD NEVER ATTAIN.
SO WHAT'S THE CATCH?
NO CATCH, AND NO COST. THIS PART OF OUR SERVICES IS PROVIDED *PRO BONO*.
AND HERE COMES OUR MOST RECENT MR. BONO EVEN NOW...YOUR NEW FACE.

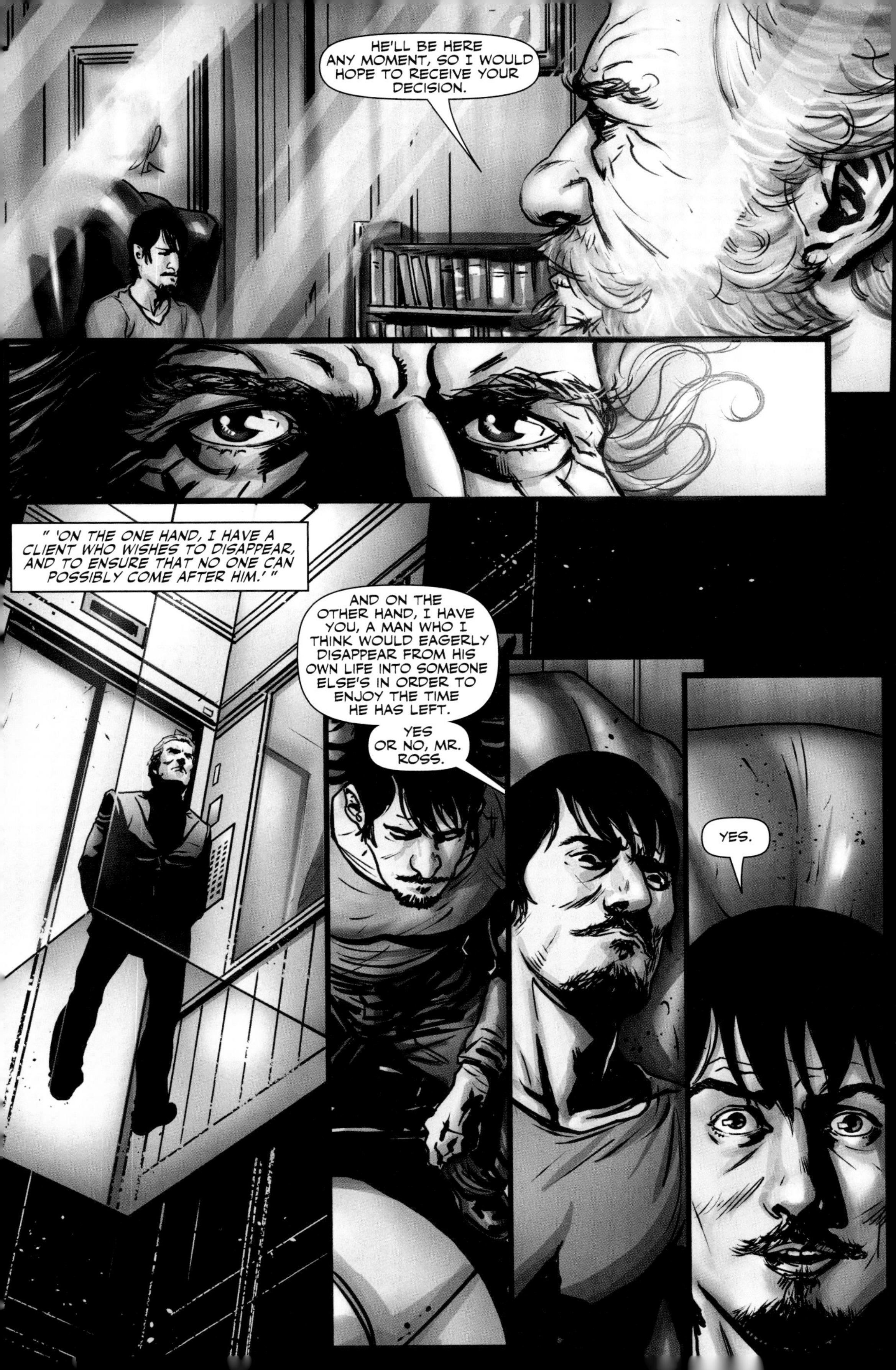
HE'LL BE HERE ANY MOMENT, SO I WOULD HOPE TO RECEIVE YOUR DECISION.
" 'ON THE ONE HAND, I HAVE A CLIENT WHO WISHES TO DISAPPEAR, AND TO ENSURE THAT NO ONE CAN POSSIBLY COME AFTER HIM.' "
AND ON THE OTHER HAND, I HAVE YOU, A MAN WHO I THINK WOULD EAGERLY DISAPPEAR FROM HIS OWN LIFE INTO SOMEONE ELSE'S IN ORDER TO ENJOY THE TIME HE HAS LEFT.
YES OR NO, MR. ROSS.
YES.

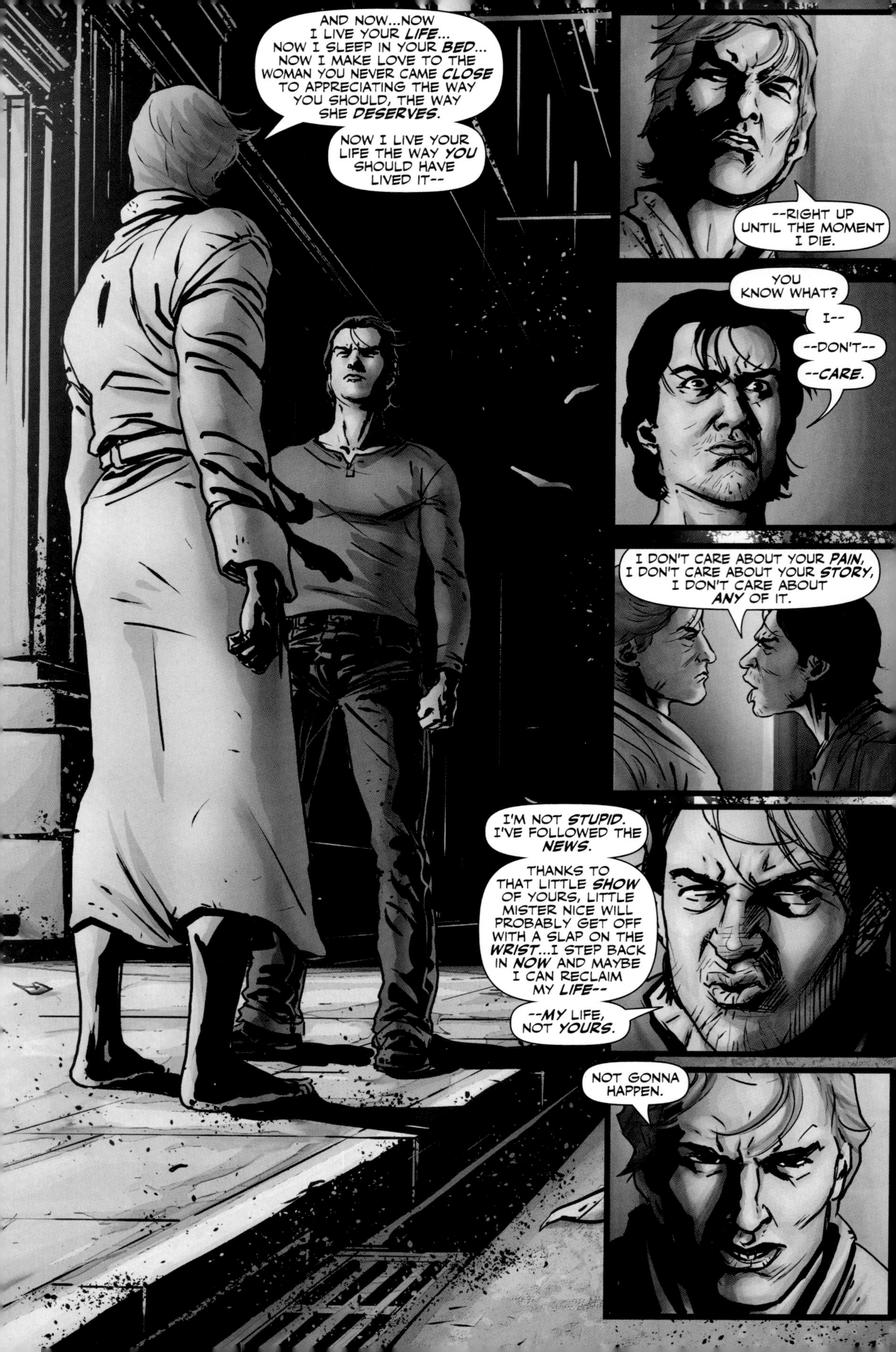
AND NOW...NOW I LIVE YOUR LIFE... NOW I SLEEP IN YOUR BED... NOW I MAKE LOVE TO THE WOMAN YOU NEVER CAME CLOSE TO APPRECIATING THE WAY YOU SHOULD, THE WAY SHE DESERVES.
NOW I LIVE YOUR LIFE THE WAY YOU SHOULD HAVE LIVED IT--
--RIGHT UP UNTIL THE MOMENT I DIE.
YOU KNOW WHAT?
I--
--DON'T--
--CARE.
I DON'T CARE ABOUT YOUR PAIN, I DON'T CARE ABOUT YOUR STORY, I DON'T CARE ABOUT ANY OF IT.
I'M NOT STUPID. I'VE FOLLOWED THE NEWS.
THANKS TO THAT LITTLE SHOW OF YOURS, LITTLE MISTER NICE WILL PROBABLY GET OFF WITH A SLAP ON THE WRIST...I STEP BACK IN NOW AND MAYBE I CAN RECLAIM MY LIFE--
--MY LIFE, NOT YOURS.
NOT GONNA HAPPEN.

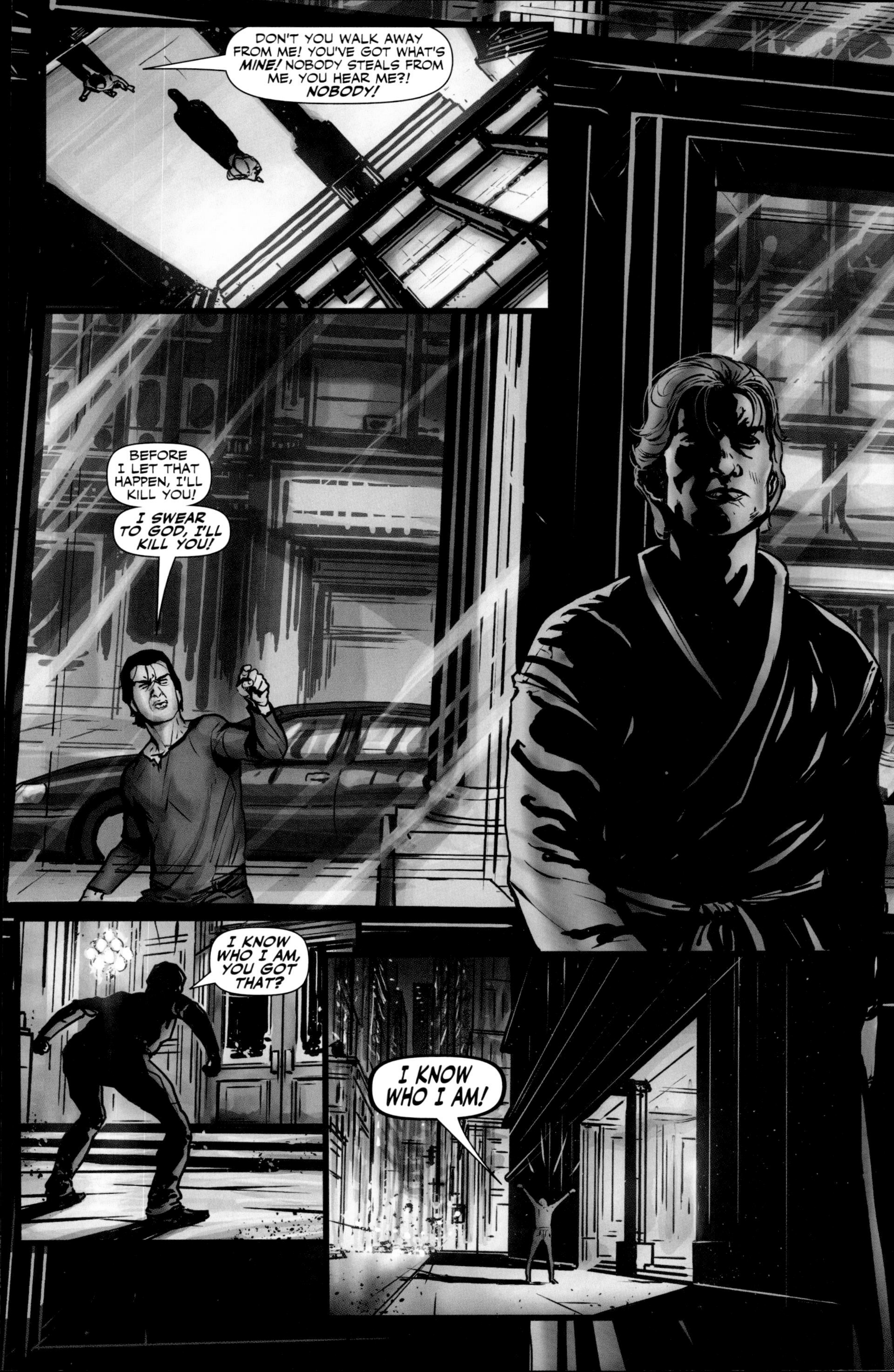
DON'T YOU WALK AWAY FROM ME! YOU'VE GOT WHAT'S *MINE!* NOBODY STEALS FROM ME, YOU HEAR ME?! *NOBODY!*
BEFORE I LET THAT HAPPEN, I'LL KILL YOU!
I SWEAR TO GOD, I'LL KILL YOU!
I KNOW WHO I AM, YOU GOT THAT?
I KNOW WHO I AM!

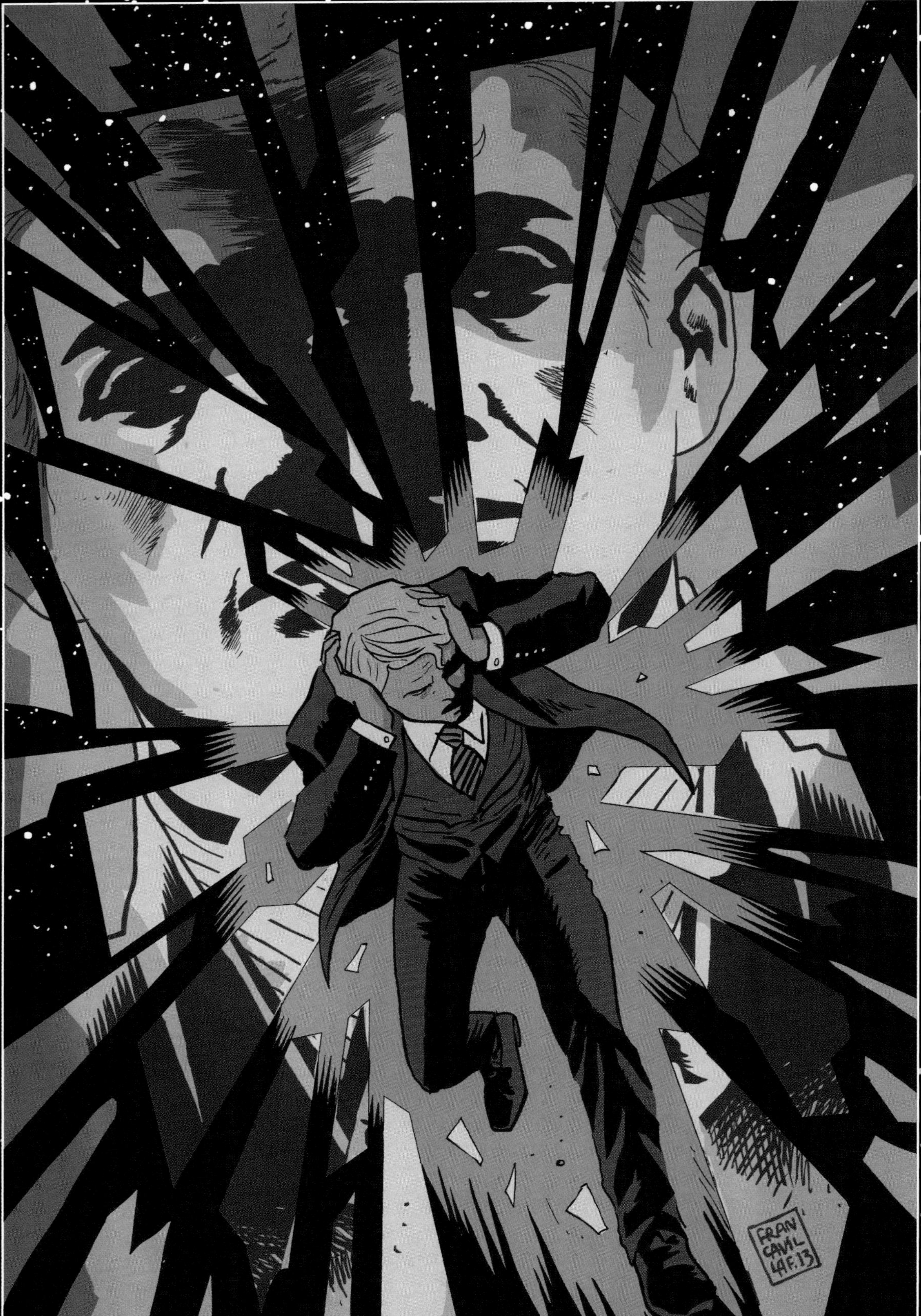
FRAN
CAVIL
LA F. 13

ACT FOUR

cover art by FRANCESCO FRANCAVILLA

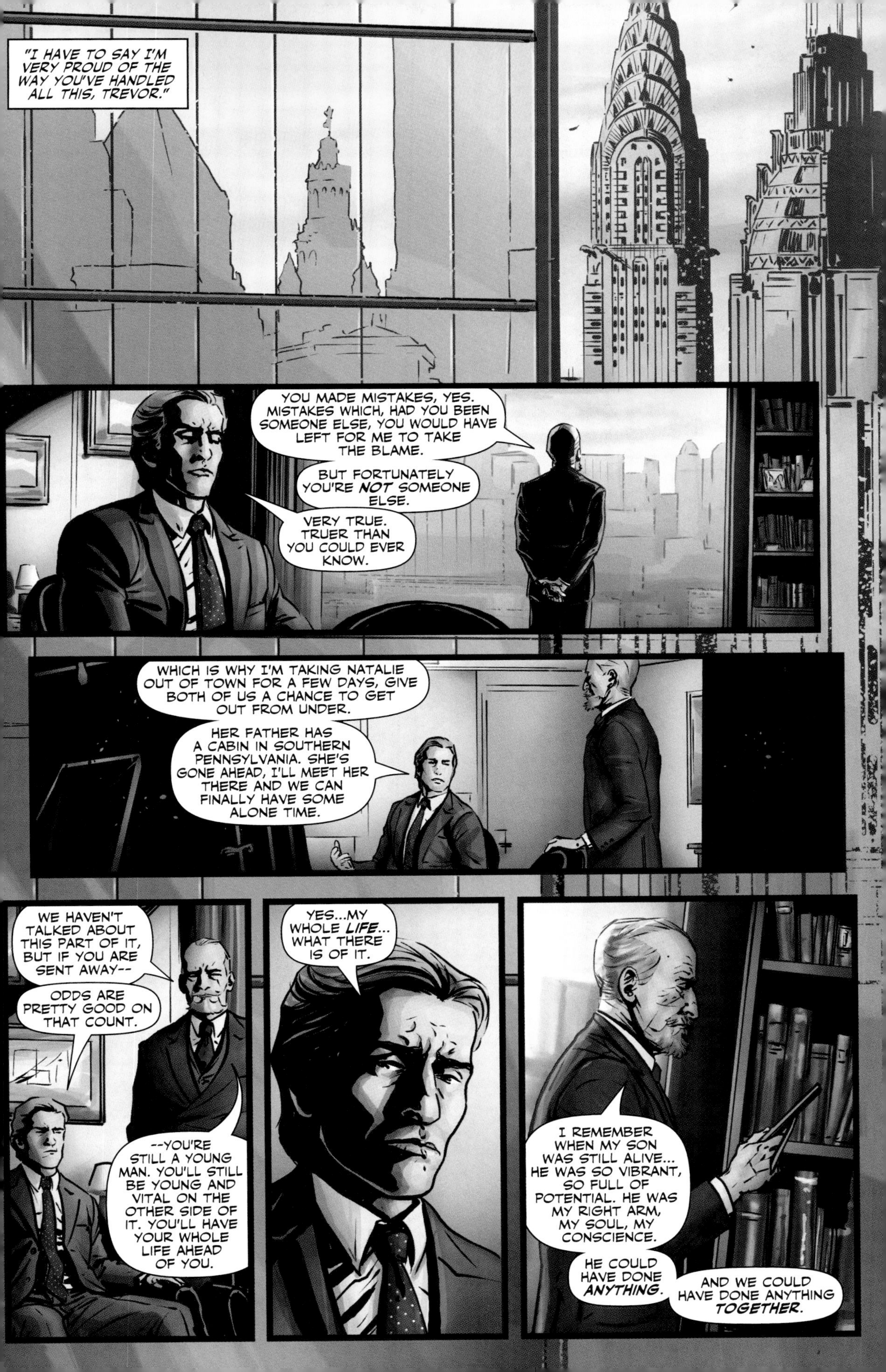
"I HAVE TO SAY I'M VERY PROUD OF THE WAY YOU'VE HANDLED ALL THIS, TREVOR."
YOU MADE MISTAKES, YES. MISTAKES WHICH, HAD YOU BEEN SOMEONE ELSE, YOU WOULD HAVE LEFT FOR ME TO TAKE THE BLAME.
BUT FORTUNATELY YOU'RE NOT SOMEONE ELSE.
VERY TRUE. TRUER THAN YOU COULD EVER KNOW.
WHICH IS WHY I'M TAKING NATALIE OUT OF TOWN FOR A FEW DAYS, GIVE BOTH OF US A CHANCE TO GET OUT FROM UNDER.
HER FATHER HAS A CABIN IN SOUTHERN PENNSYLVANIA. SHE'S GONE AHEAD, I'LL MEET HER THERE AND WE CAN FINALLY HAVE SOME ALONE TIME.
WE HAVEN'T TALKED ABOUT THIS PART OF IT, BUT IF YOU ARE SENT AWAY--
ODDS ARE PRETTY GOOD ON THAT COUNT.
--YOU'RE STILL A YOUNG MAN. YOU'LL STILL BE YOUNG AND VITAL ON THE OTHER SIDE OF IT. YOU'LL HAVE YOUR WHOLE LIFE AHEAD OF YOU.
YES...MY WHOLE LIFE... WHAT THERE IS OF IT.
I REMEMBER WHEN MY SON WAS STILL ALIVE... HE WAS SO VIBRANT, SO FULL OF POTENTIAL. HE WAS MY RIGHT ARM, MY SOUL, MY CONSCIENCE.
HE COULD HAVE DONE ANYTHING.
AND WE COULD HAVE DONE ANYTHING TOGETHER.

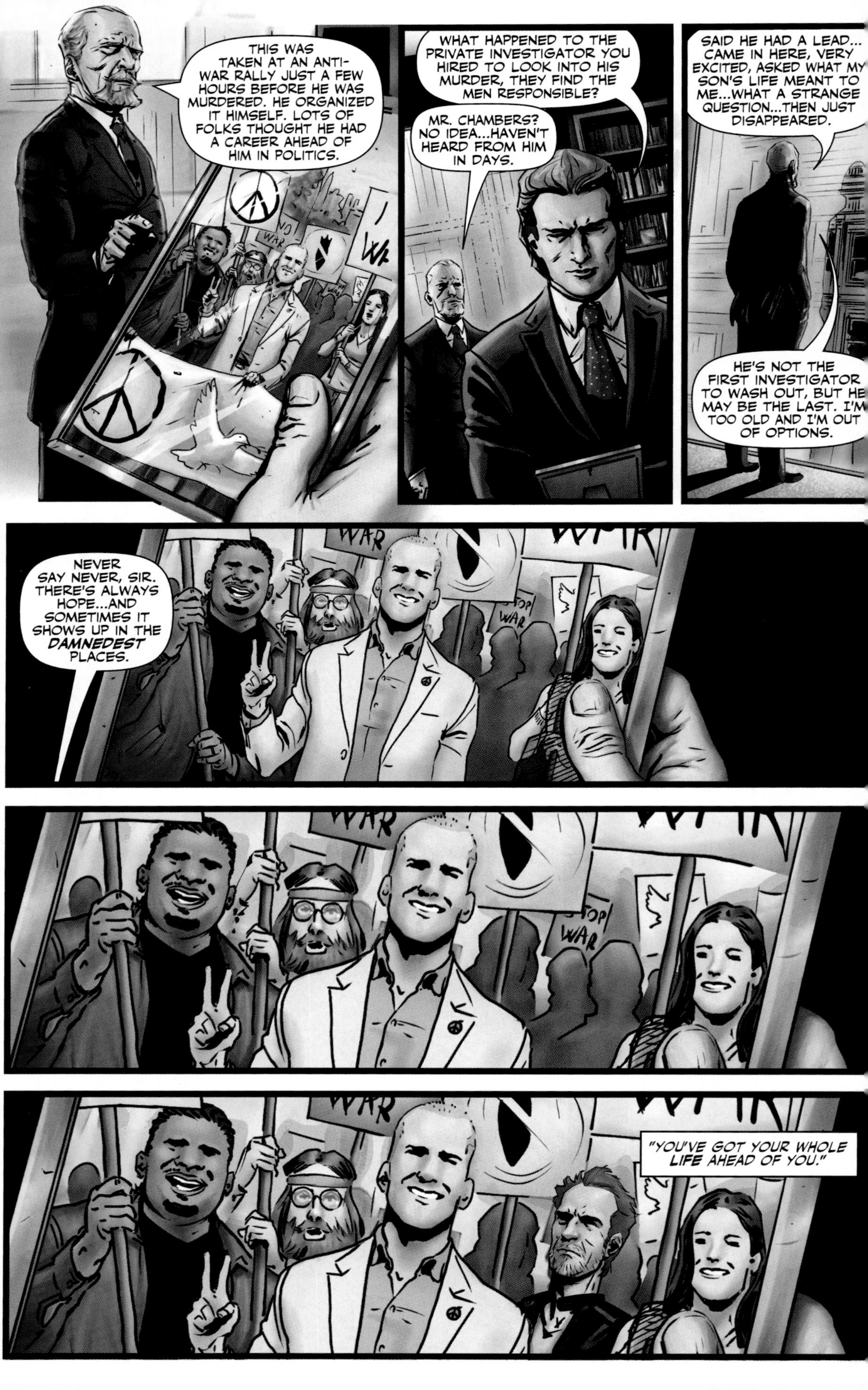
THIS WAS TAKEN AT AN ANTI-WAR RALLY JUST A FEW HOURS BEFORE HE WAS MURDERED. HE ORGANIZED IT HIMSELF. LOTS OF FOLKS THOUGHT HE HAD A CAREER AHEAD OF HIM IN POLITICS.
WHAT HAPPENED TO THE PRIVATE INVESTIGATOR YOU HIRED TO LOOK INTO HIS MURDER, THEY FIND THE MEN RESPONSIBLE?
MR. CHAMBERS? NO IDEA...HAVEN'T HEARD FROM HIM IN DAYS.
SAID HE HAD A LEAD... CAME IN HERE, VERY EXCITED, ASKED WHAT MY SON'S LIFE MEANT TO ME...WHAT A STRANGE QUESTION...THEN JUST DISAPPEARED.
HE'S NOT THE FIRST INVESTIGATOR TO WASH OUT, BUT HE MAY BE THE LAST. I'M TOO OLD AND I'M OUT OF OPTIONS.
NEVER SAY NEVER, SIR. THERE'S ALWAYS HOPE...AND SOMETIMES IT SHOWS UP IN THE DAMNEDEST PLACES.
"YOU'VE GOT YOUR WHOLE LIFE AHEAD OF YOU."

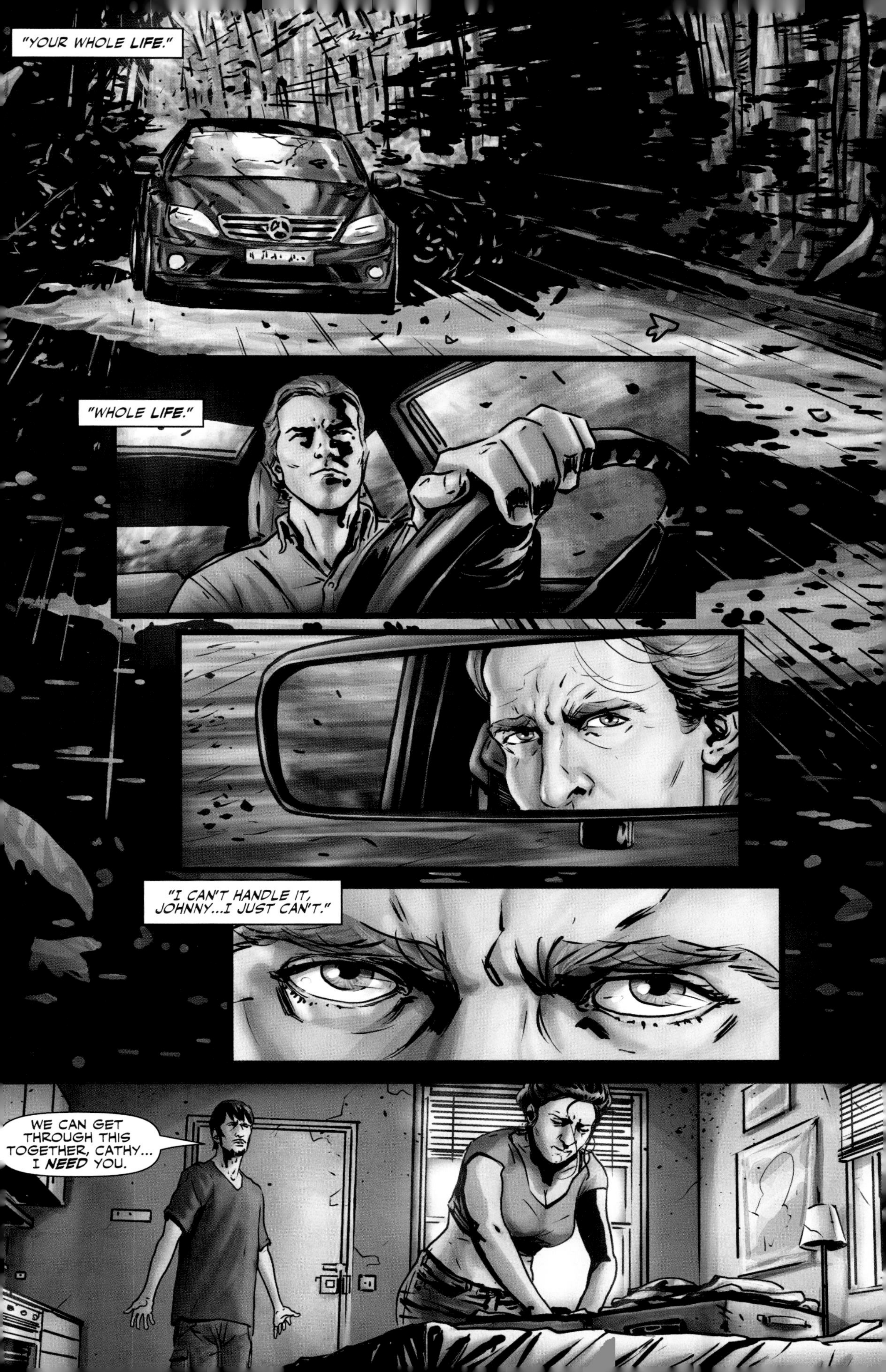
"YOUR WHOLE LIFE."
"WHOLE LIFE."
"I CAN'T HANDLE IT, JOHNNY...I JUST CAN'T."
WE CAN GET THROUGH THIS TOGETHER, CATHY... I NEED YOU.

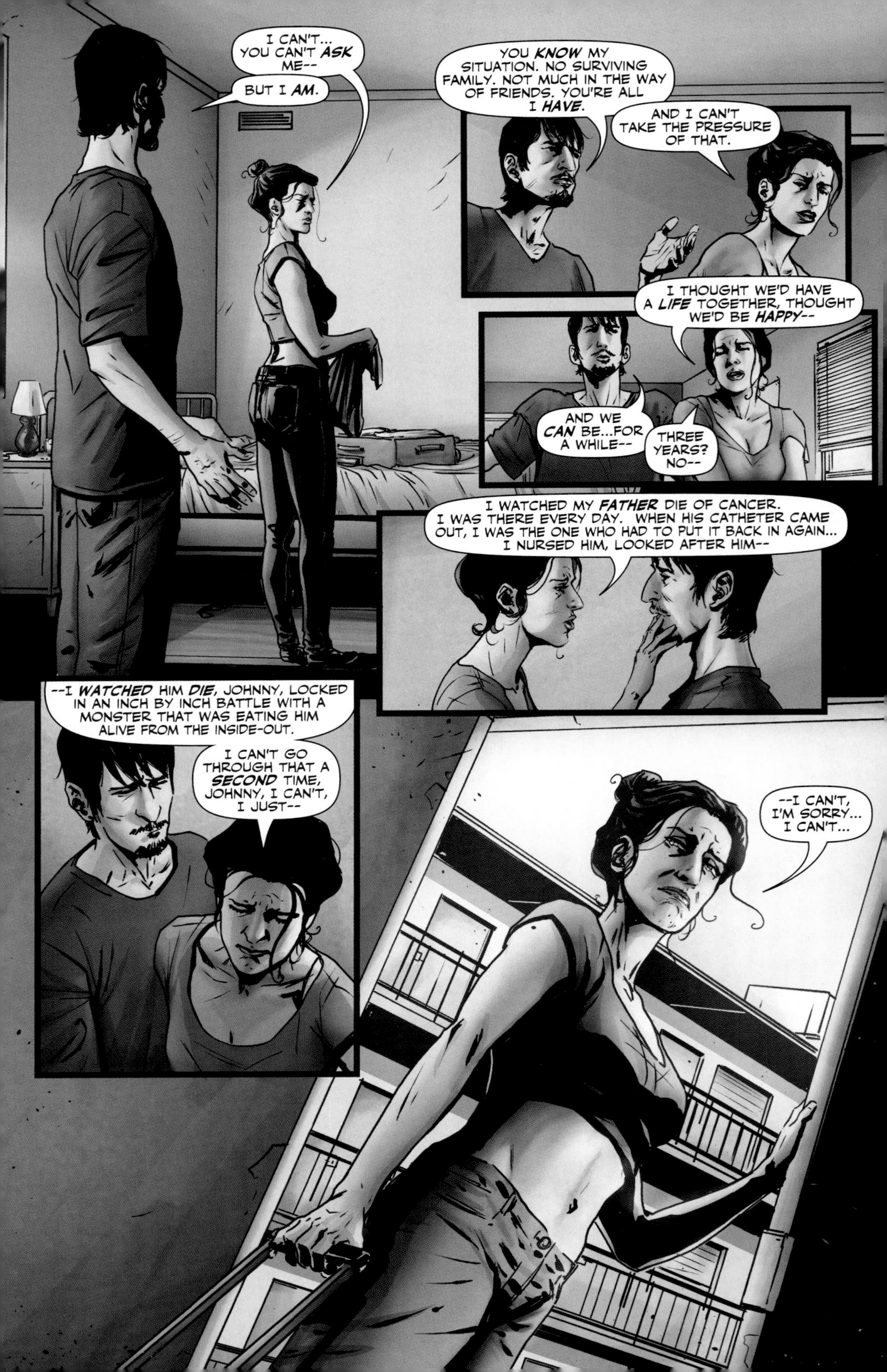
I CAN'T... YOU CAN'T ASK ME--
BUT I AM.
YOU KNOW MY SITUATION. NO SURVIVING FAMILY. NOT MUCH IN THE WAY OF FRIENDS. YOU'RE ALL I HAVE.
AND I CAN'T TAKE THE PRESSURE OF THAT.
I THOUGHT WE'D HAVE A LIFE TOGETHER, THOUGHT WE'D BE HAPPY--
AND WE CAN BE...FOR A WHILE--
THREE YEARS? NO--
I WATCHED MY FATHER DIE OF CANCER. I WAS THERE EVERY DAY. WHEN HIS CATHETER CAME OUT, I WAS THE ONE WHO HAD TO PUT IT BACK IN AGAIN... I NURSED HIM, LOOKED AFTER HIM--
--I WATCHED HIM DIE, JOHNNY, LOCKED IN AN INCH BY INCH BATTLE WITH A MONSTER THAT WAS EATING HIM ALIVE FROM THE INSIDE-OUT.
I CAN'T GO THROUGH THAT A SECOND TIME, JOHNNY, I CAN'T, I JUST--
--I CAN'T, I'M SORRY... I CAN'T...

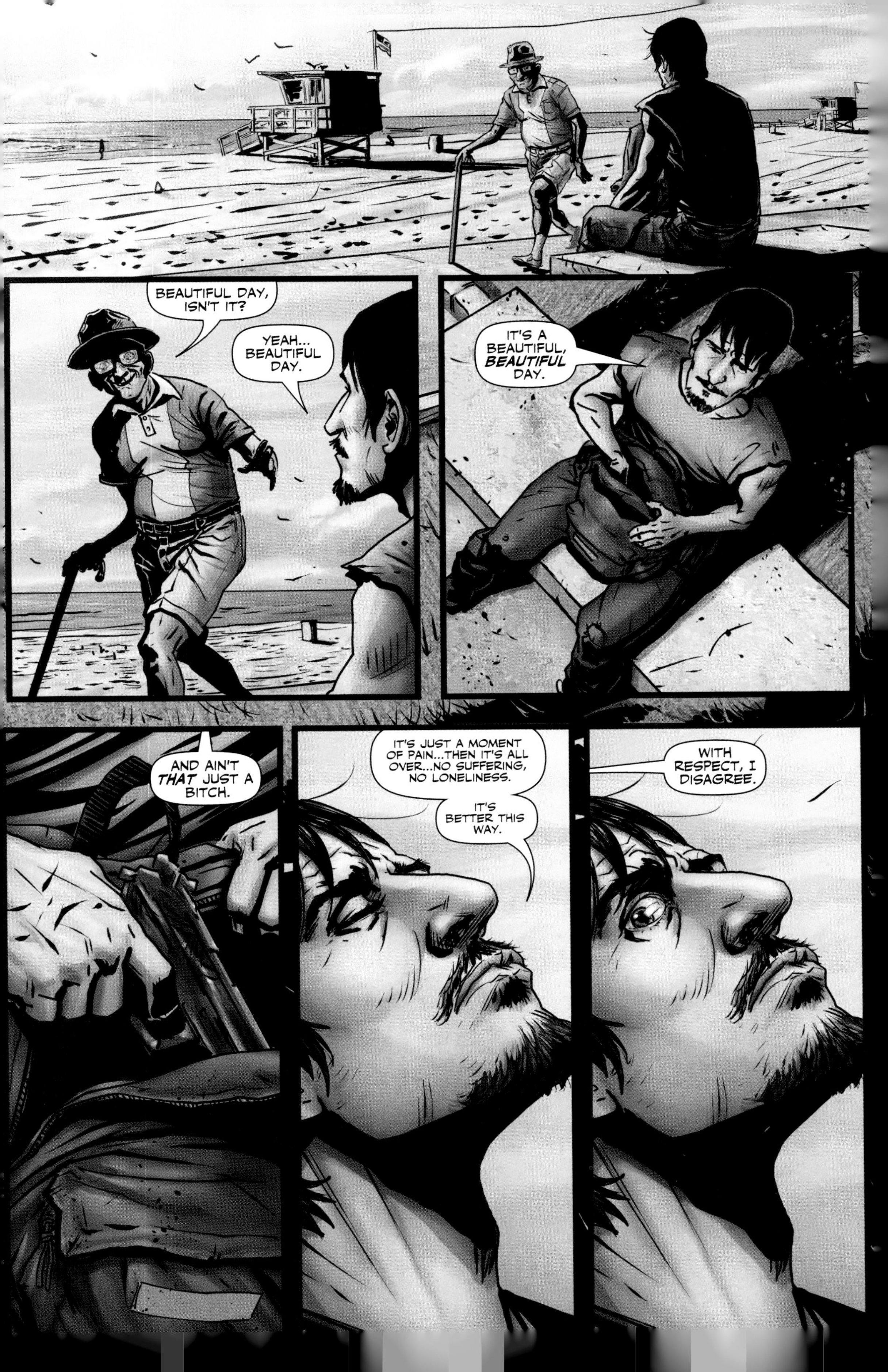
BEAUTIFUL DAY, ISN'T IT?
YEAH... BEAUTIFUL DAY.
IT'S A BEAUTIFUL, *BEAUTIFUL* DAY.
AND AIN'T *THAT* JUST A BITCH.
IT'S JUST A MOMENT OF PAIN...THEN IT'S ALL OVER...NO SUFFERING, NO LONELINESS.
IT'S BETTER THIS WAY.
WITH RESPECT, I DISAGREE.

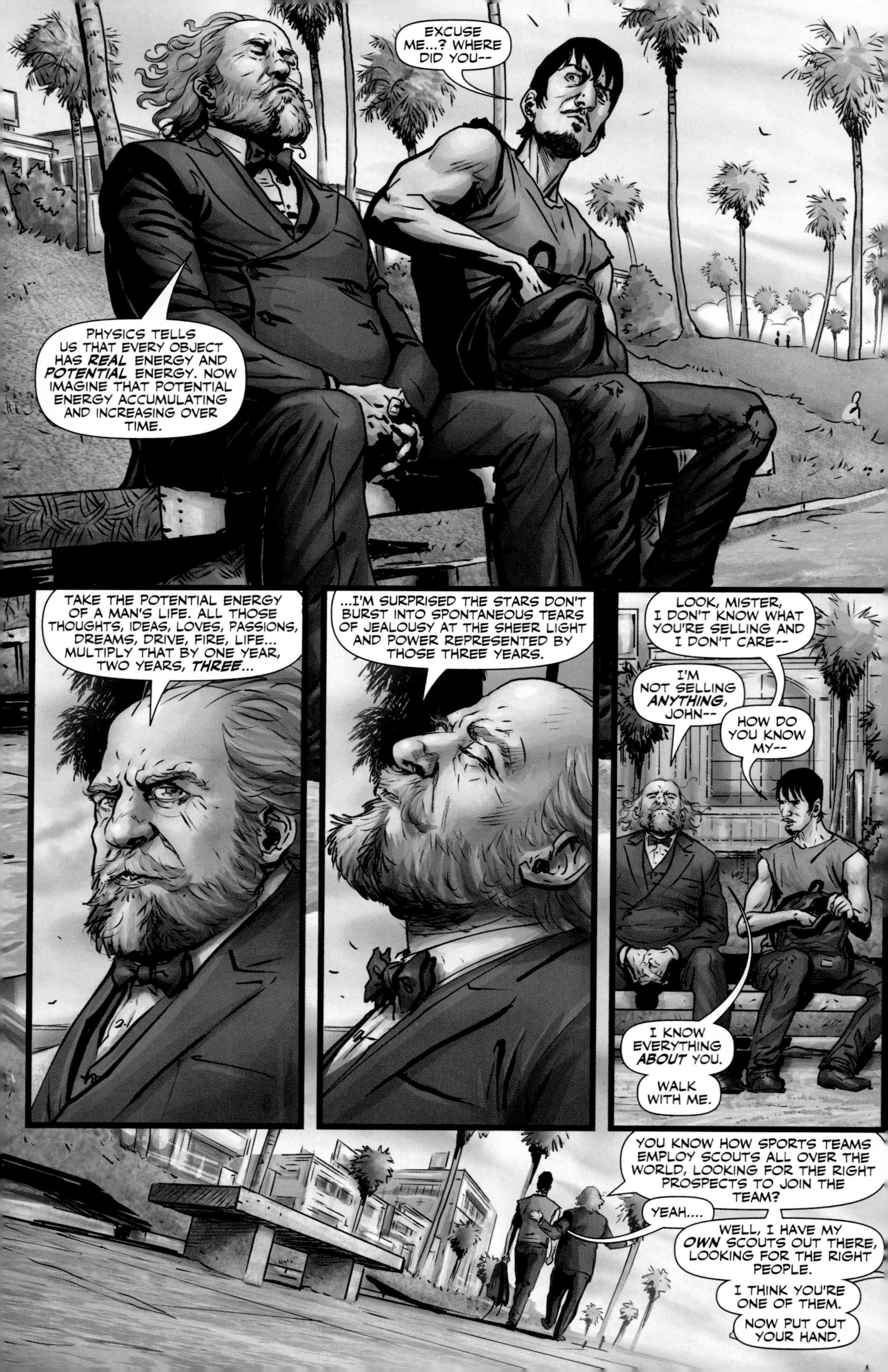
EXCUSE ME...? WHERE DID YOU--
PHYSICS TELLS US THAT EVERY OBJECT HAS **REAL** ENERGY AND **POTENTIAL** ENERGY. NOW IMAGINE THAT POTENTIAL ENERGY ACCUMULATING AND INCREASING OVER TIME.
TAKE THE POTENTIAL ENERGY OF A MAN'S LIFE. ALL THOSE THOUGHTS, IDEAS, LOVES, PASSIONS, DREAMS, DRIVE, FIRE, LIFE... MULTIPLY THAT BY ONE YEAR, TWO YEARS, **THREE**...
...I'M SURPRISED THE STARS DON'T BURST INTO SPONTANEOUS TEARS OF JEALOUSY AT THE SHEER LIGHT AND POWER REPRESENTED BY THOSE THREE YEARS.
LOOK, MISTER, I DON'T KNOW WHAT YOU'RE SELLING AND I DON'T CARE--
I'M NOT SELLING **ANYTHING**, JOHN--
HOW DO YOU KNOW MY--
I KNOW EVERYTHING **ABOUT** YOU.
WALK WITH ME.
YOU KNOW HOW SPORTS TEAMS EMPLOY SCOUTS ALL OVER THE WORLD, LOOKING FOR THE RIGHT PROSPECTS TO JOIN THE TEAM?
YEAH....
WELL, I HAVE MY **OWN** SCOUTS OUT THERE, LOOKING FOR THE RIGHT PEOPLE.
I THINK YOU'RE ONE OF THEM.
NOW PUT OUT YOUR HAND.

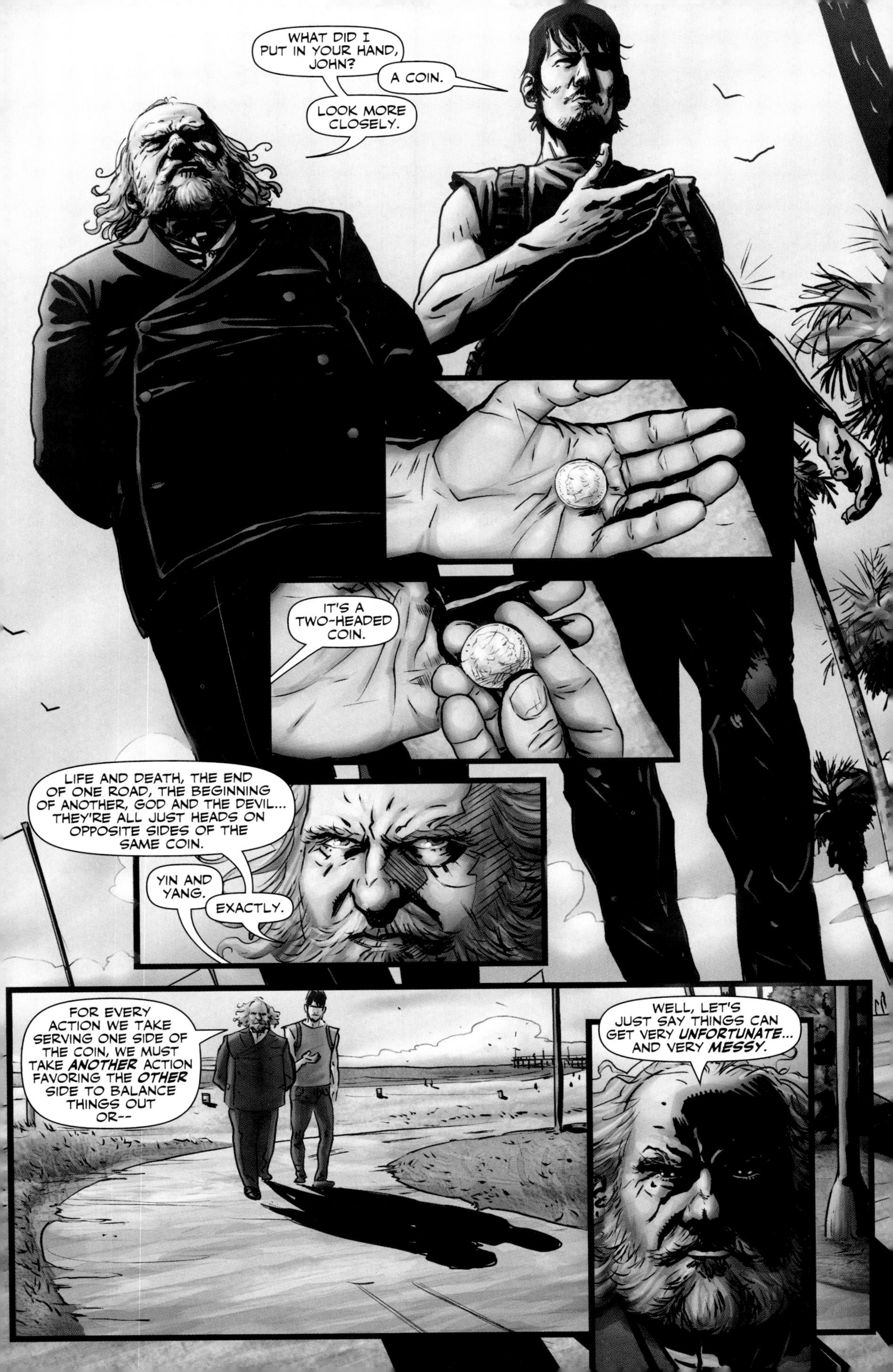
WHAT DID I PUT IN YOUR HAND, JOHN?
A COIN.
LOOK MORE CLOSELY.
IT'S A TWO-HEADED COIN.
LIFE AND DEATH, THE END OF ONE ROAD, THE BEGINNING OF ANOTHER, GOD AND THE DEVIL... THEY'RE ALL JUST HEADS ON OPPOSITE SIDES OF THE SAME COIN.
YIN AND YANG.
EXACTLY.
FOR EVERY ACTION WE TAKE SERVING ONE SIDE OF THE COIN, WE MUST TAKE *ANOTHER* ACTION FAVORING THE *OTHER* SIDE TO BALANCE THINGS OUT OR--
WELL, LET'S JUST SAY THINGS CAN GET VERY *UNFORTUNATE*... AND VERY *MESSY*.

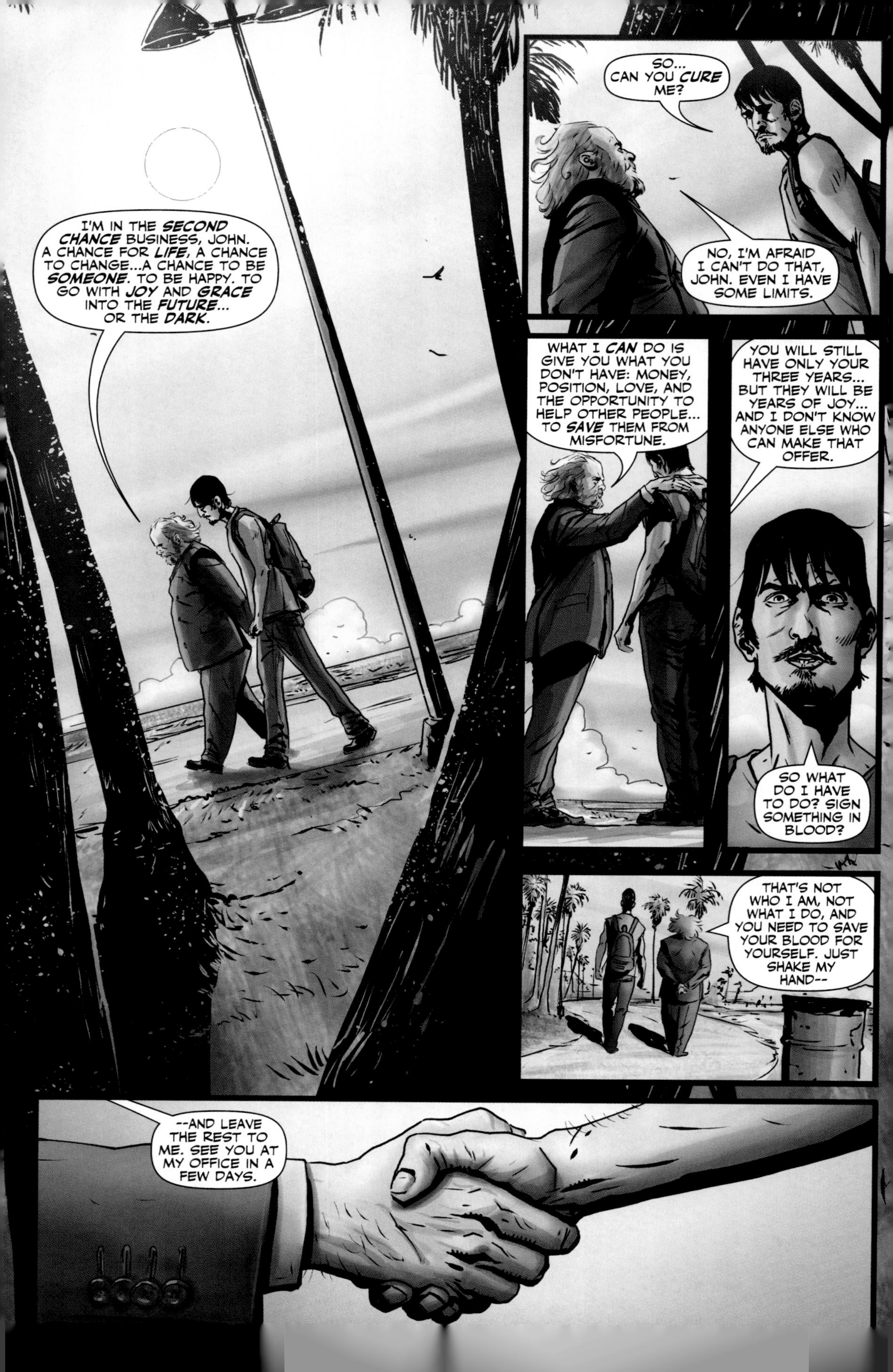
I'M IN THE SECOND CHANCE BUSINESS, JOHN. A CHANCE FOR LIFE, A CHANCE TO CHANGE...A CHANCE TO BE SOMEONE. TO BE HAPPY. TO GO WITH JOY AND GRACE INTO THE FUTURE... OR THE DARK.
SO... CAN YOU CURE ME?
NO, I'M AFRAID I CAN'T DO THAT, JOHN. EVEN I HAVE SOME LIMITS.
WHAT I CAN DO IS GIVE YOU WHAT YOU DON'T HAVE: MONEY, POSITION, LOVE, AND THE OPPORTUNITY TO HELP OTHER PEOPLE... TO SAVE THEM FROM MISFORTUNE.
YOU WILL STILL HAVE ONLY YOUR THREE YEARS... BUT THEY WILL BE YEARS OF JOY... AND I DON'T KNOW ANYONE ELSE WHO CAN MAKE THAT OFFER.
SO WHAT DO I HAVE TO DO? SIGN SOMETHING IN BLOOD?
THAT'S NOT WHO I AM, NOT WHAT I DO, AND YOU NEED TO SAVE YOUR BLOOD FOR YOURSELF. JUST SHAKE MY HAND--
--AND LEAVE THE REST TO ME. SEE YOU AT MY OFFICE IN A FEW DAYS.

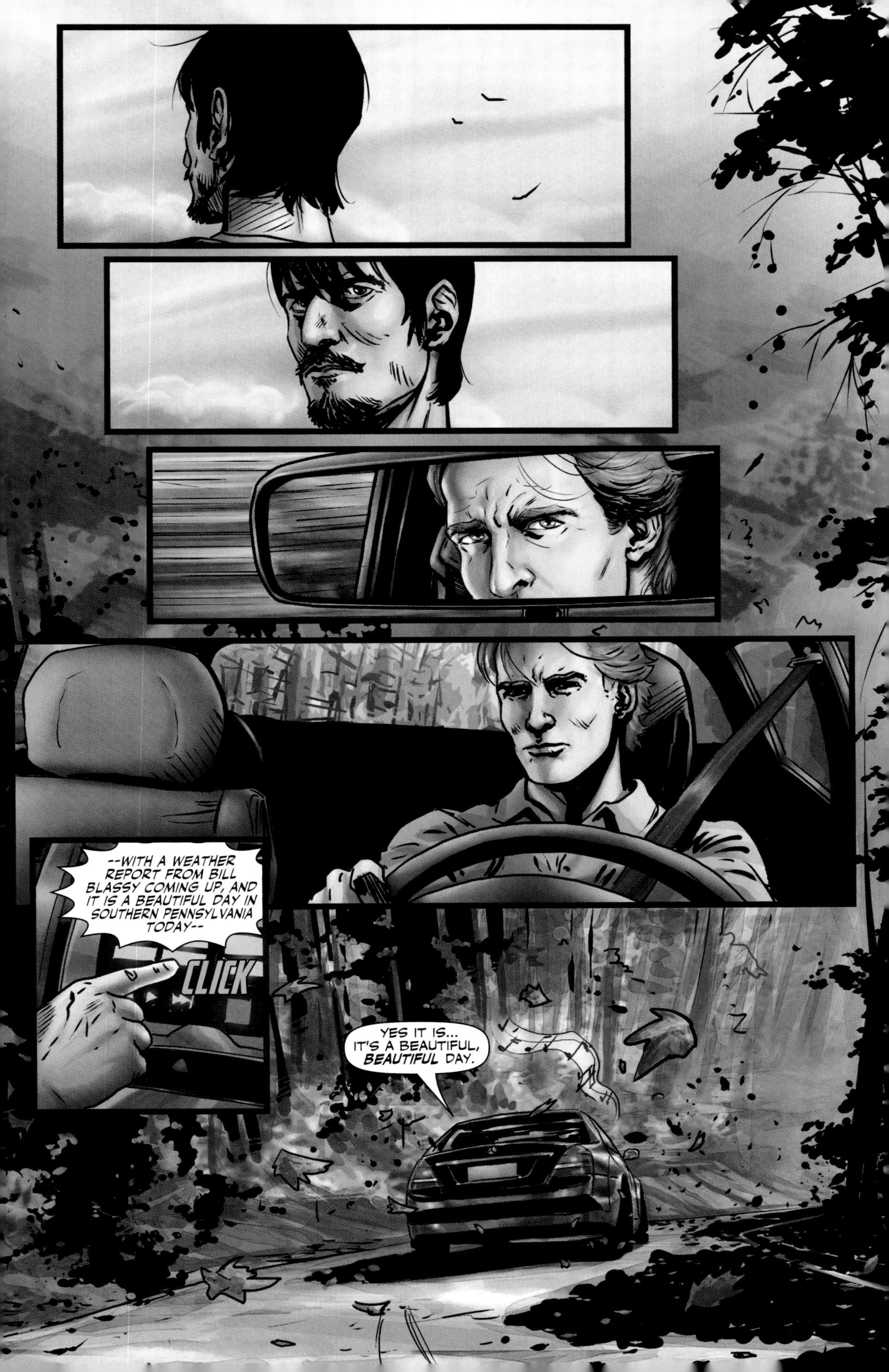
--WITH A WEATHER REPORT FROM BILL BLASSY COMING UP, AND IT IS A BEAUTIFUL DAY IN SOUTHERN PENNSYLVANIA TODAY--
CLICK
YES IT IS... IT'S A BEAUTIFUL, BEAUTIFUL DAY.

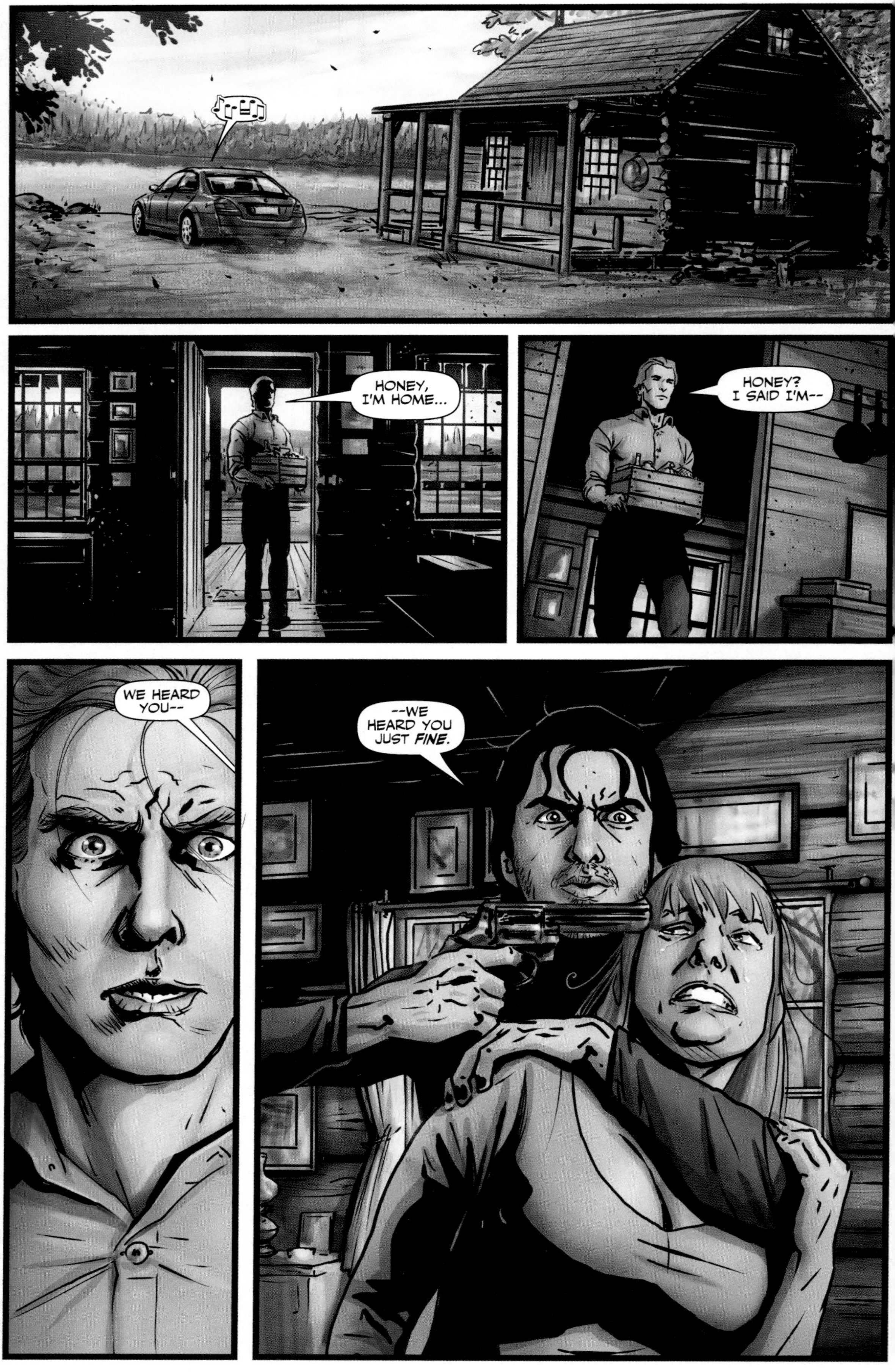
HONEY, I'M HOME...
HONEY? I SAID I'M--
WE HEARD YOU--
--WE HEARD YOU JUST *FINE*.

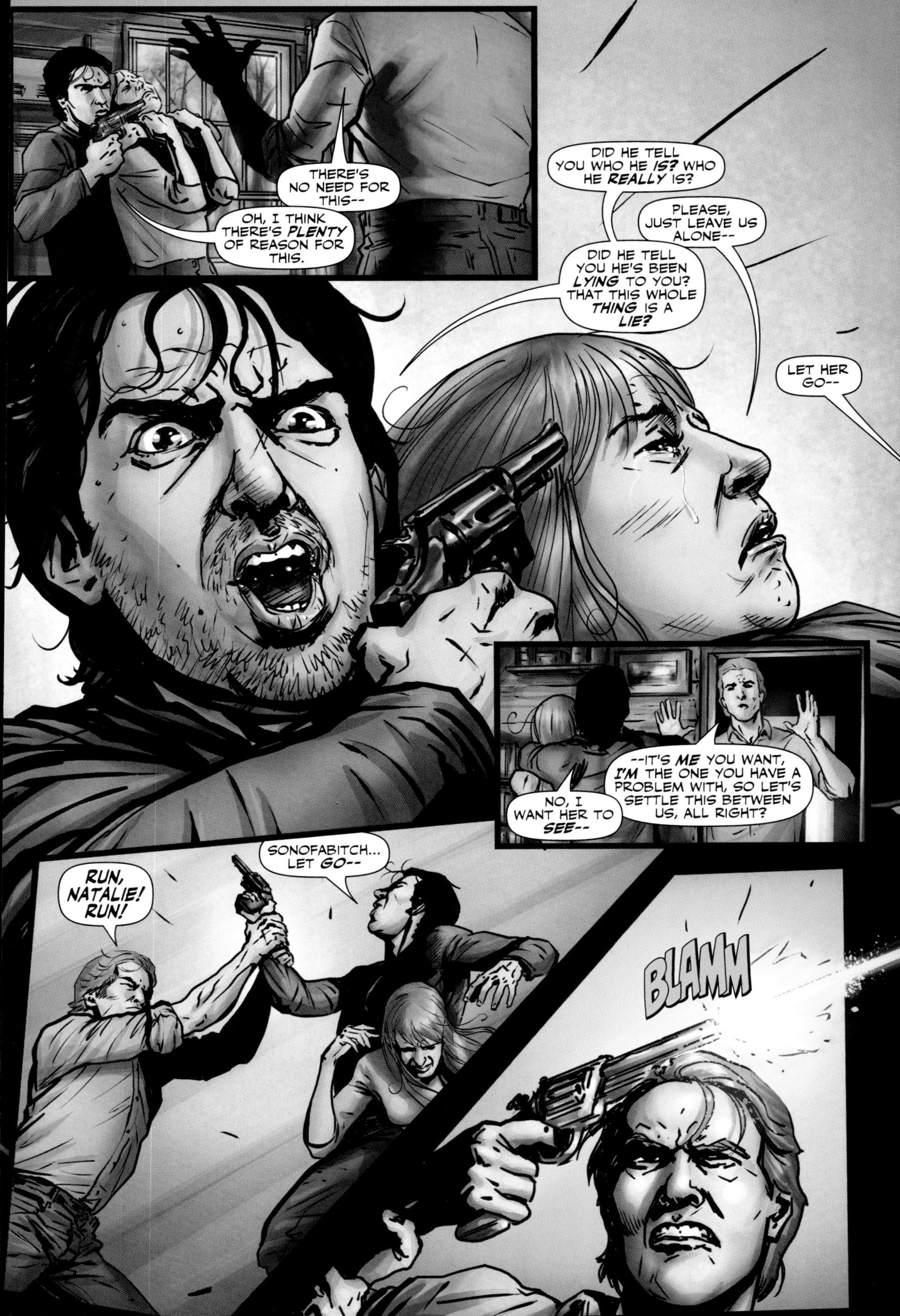
THERE'S NO NEED FOR THIS--
OH, I THINK THERE'S PLENTY OF REASON FOR THIS.
DID HE TELL YOU WHO HE IS? WHO HE REALLY IS?
PLEASE, JUST LEAVE US ALONE--
DID HE TELL YOU HE'S BEEN LYING TO YOU? THAT THIS WHOLE THING IS A LIE?
LET HER GO--
--IT'S ME YOU WANT, I'M THE ONE YOU HAVE A PROBLEM WITH, SO LET'S SETTLE THIS BETWEEN US, ALL RIGHT?
NO, I WANT HER TO SEE--
RUN, NATALIE! RUN!
SONOFABITCH... LET GO--
BLAMM

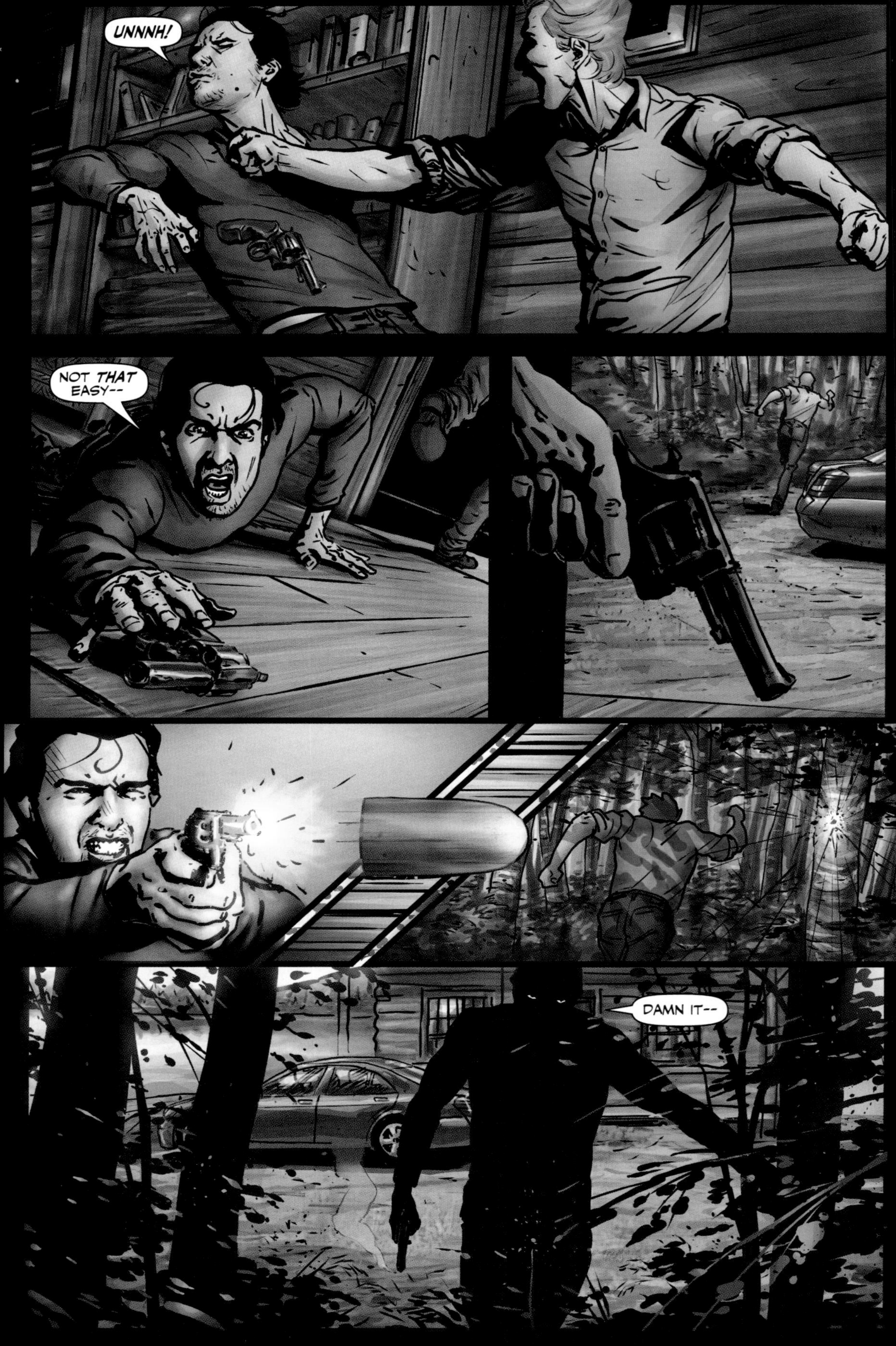
UNNNH!
NOT *THAT* EASY--
DAMN IT--

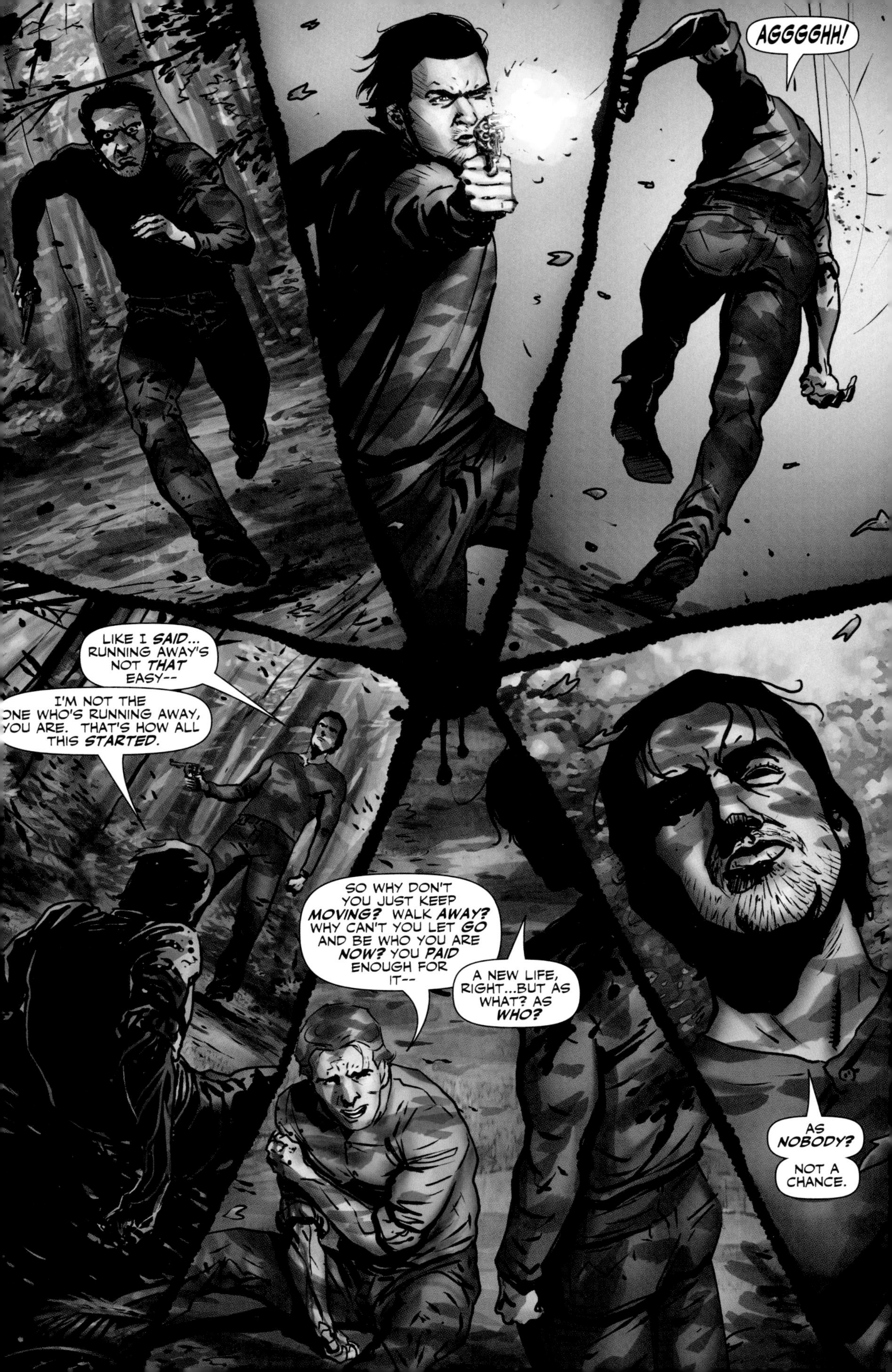

AGGGGHH!
LIKE I *SAID*... RUNNING AWAY'S NOT *THAT* EASY--
I'M NOT THE ONE WHO'S RUNNING AWAY, YOU ARE. THAT'S HOW ALL THIS *STARTED*.
SO WHY DON'T YOU JUST KEEP *MOVING?* WALK *AWAY?* WHY CAN'T YOU LET *GO* AND BE WHO YOU ARE *NOW?* YOU *PAID* ENOUGH FOR IT--
A NEW LIFE, RIGHT...BUT AS WHAT? AS *WHO?*
AS *NOBODY?*
NOT A CHANCE.

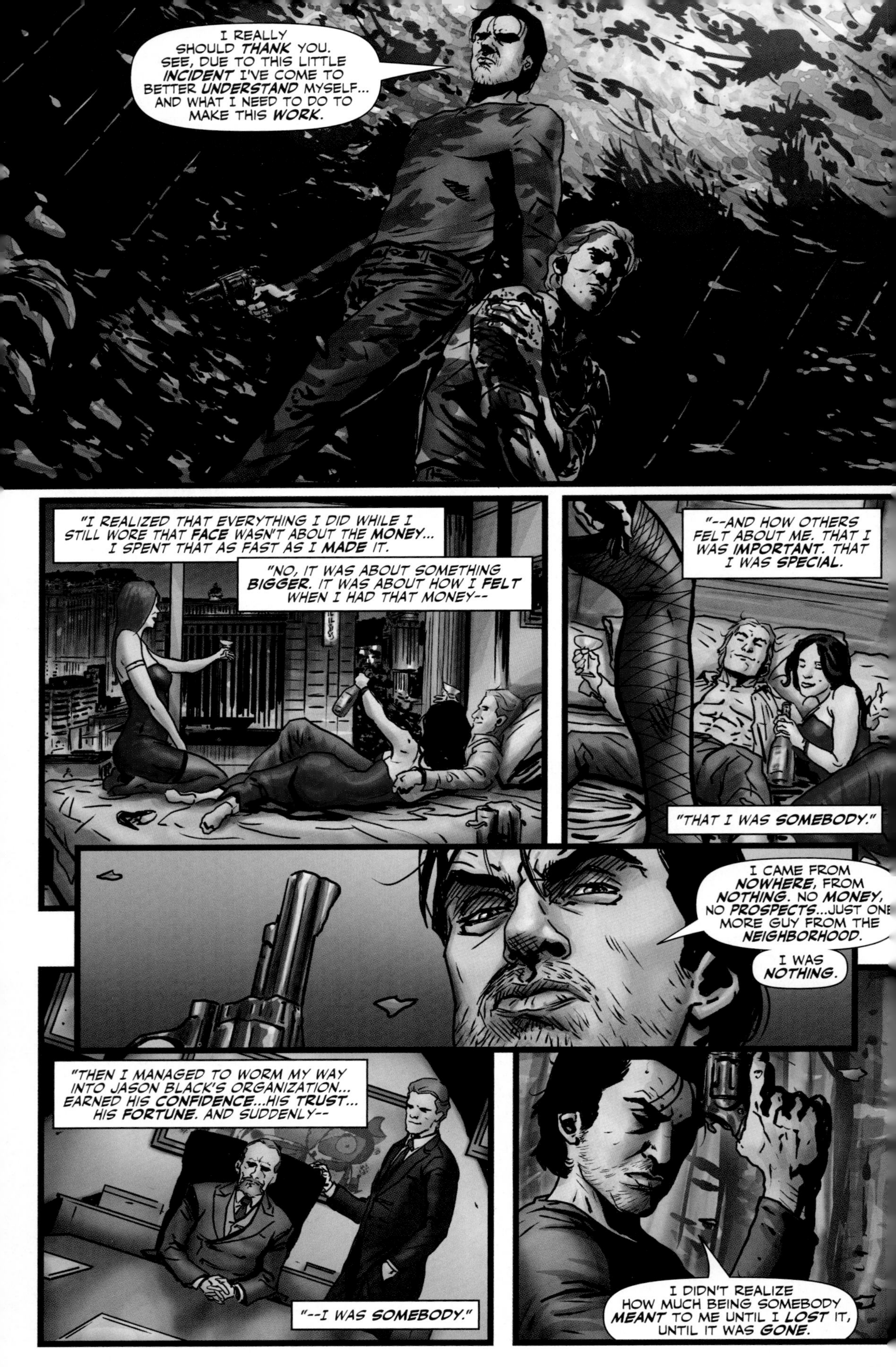
I REALLY SHOULD THANK YOU. SEE, DUE TO THIS LITTLE INCIDENT I'VE COME TO BETTER UNDERSTAND MYSELF... AND WHAT I NEED TO DO TO MAKE THIS WORK.
"I REALIZED THAT EVERYTHING I DID WHILE I STILL WORE THAT FACE WASN'T ABOUT THE MONEY... I SPENT THAT AS FAST AS I MADE IT.
"NO, IT WAS ABOUT SOMETHING BIGGER. IT WAS ABOUT HOW I FELT WHEN I HAD THAT MONEY--
"--AND HOW OTHERS FELT ABOUT ME. THAT I WAS IMPORTANT. THAT I WAS SPECIAL.
"THAT I WAS SOMEBODY."
I CAME FROM NOWHERE, FROM NOTHING. NO MONEY, NO PROSPECTS...JUST ONE MORE GUY FROM THE NEIGHBORHOOD.
I WAS NOTHING.
"THEN I MANAGED TO WORM MY WAY INTO JASON BLACK'S ORGANIZATION... EARNED HIS CONFIDENCE...HIS TRUST... HIS FORTUNE. AND SUDDENLY--
"--I WAS SOMEBODY."
I DIDN'T REALIZE HOW MUCH BEING SOMEBODY MEANT TO ME UNTIL I LOST IT, UNTIL IT WAS GONE.

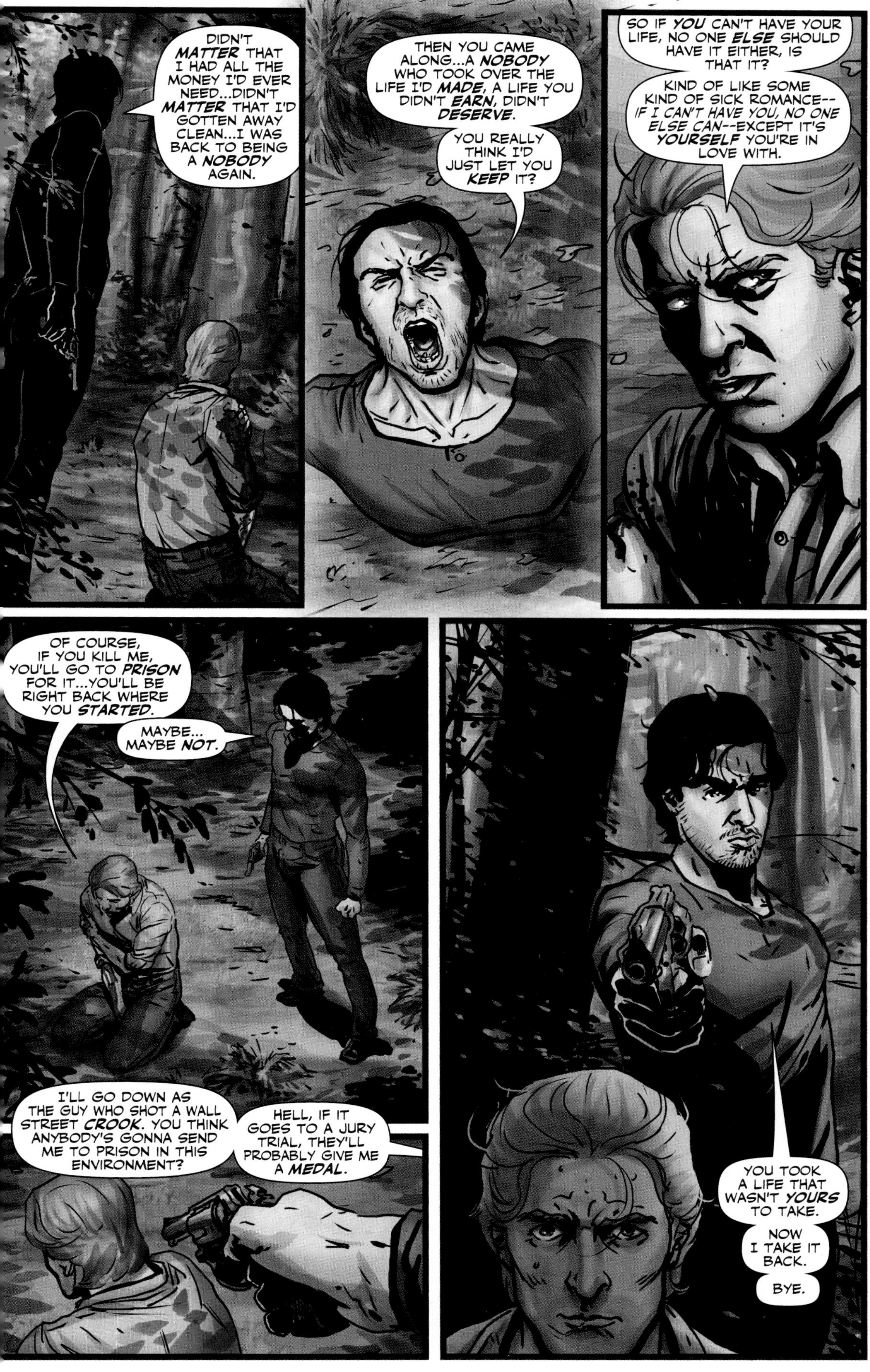
DIDN'T MATTER THAT I HAD ALL THE MONEY I'D EVER NEED...DIDN'T MATTER THAT I'D GOTTEN AWAY CLEAN...I WAS BACK TO BEING A NOBODY AGAIN.
THEN YOU CAME ALONG...A NOBODY WHO TOOK OVER THE LIFE I'D MADE, A LIFE YOU DIDN'T EARN, DIDN'T DESERVE.
YOU REALLY THINK I'D JUST LET YOU KEEP IT?
SO IF YOU CAN'T HAVE YOUR LIFE, NO ONE ELSE SHOULD HAVE IT EITHER, IS THAT IT?
KIND OF LIKE SOME KIND OF SICK ROMANCE--IF I CAN'T HAVE YOU, NO ONE ELSE CAN--EXCEPT IT'S YOURSELF YOU'RE IN LOVE WITH.
OF COURSE, IF YOU KILL ME, YOU'LL GO TO PRISON FOR IT...YOU'LL BE RIGHT BACK WHERE YOU STARTED.
MAYBE... MAYBE NOT.
I'LL GO DOWN AS THE GUY WHO SHOT A WALL STREET CROOK. YOU THINK ANYBODY'S GONNA SEND ME TO PRISON IN THIS ENVIRONMENT?
HELL, IF IT GOES TO A JURY TRIAL, THEY'LL PROBABLY GIVE ME A MEDAL.
YOU TOOK A LIFE THAT WASN'T YOURS TO TAKE.
NOW I TAKE IT BACK.
BYE.

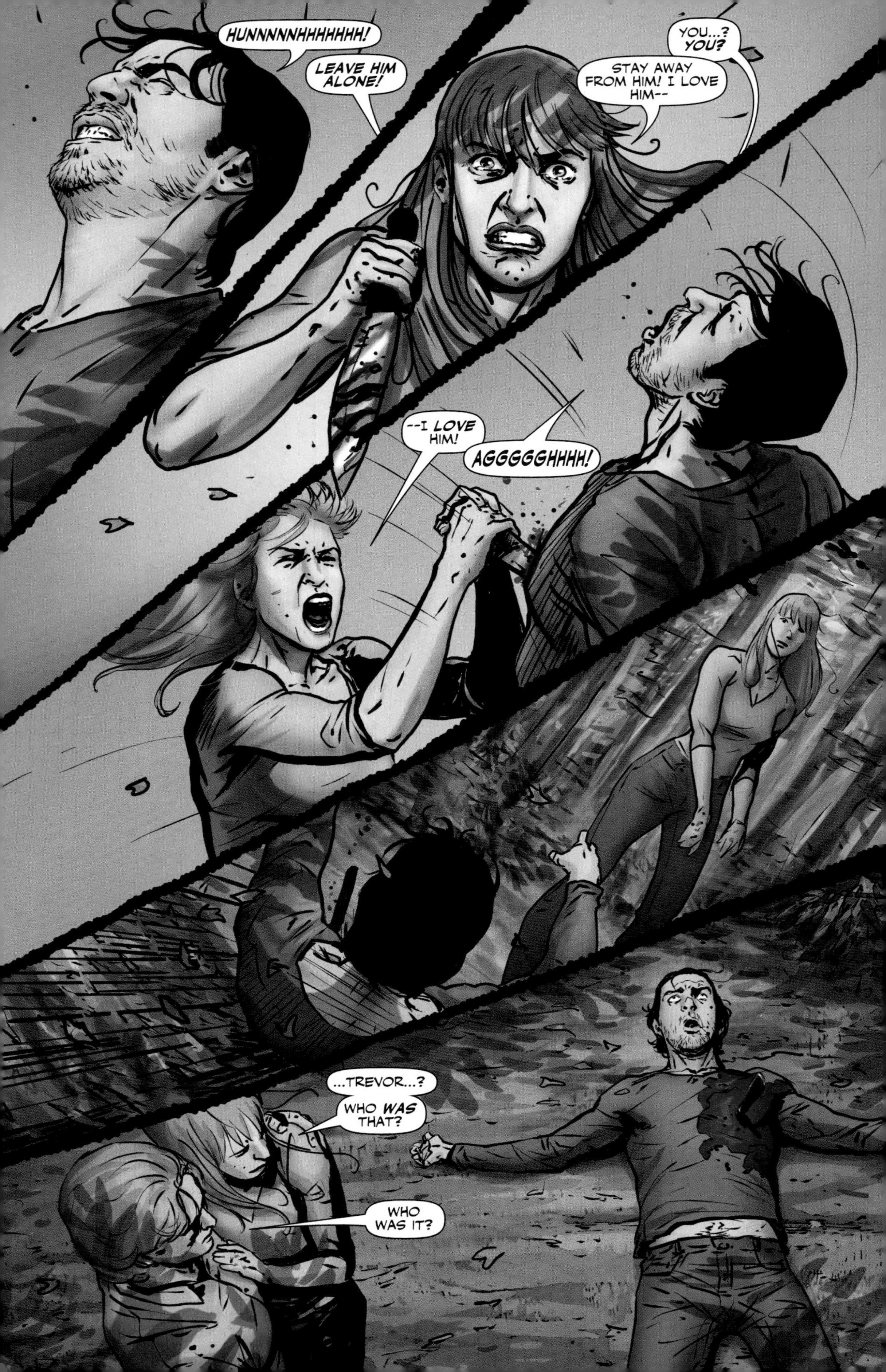
HUNNNNNHHHHHHH!
LEAVE HIM ALONE!
STAY AWAY FROM HIM! I LOVE HIM--
YOU...? YOU?
--I LOVE HIM!
AGGGGGHHHH!
...TREVOR...?
WHO WAS THAT?
WHO WAS IT?

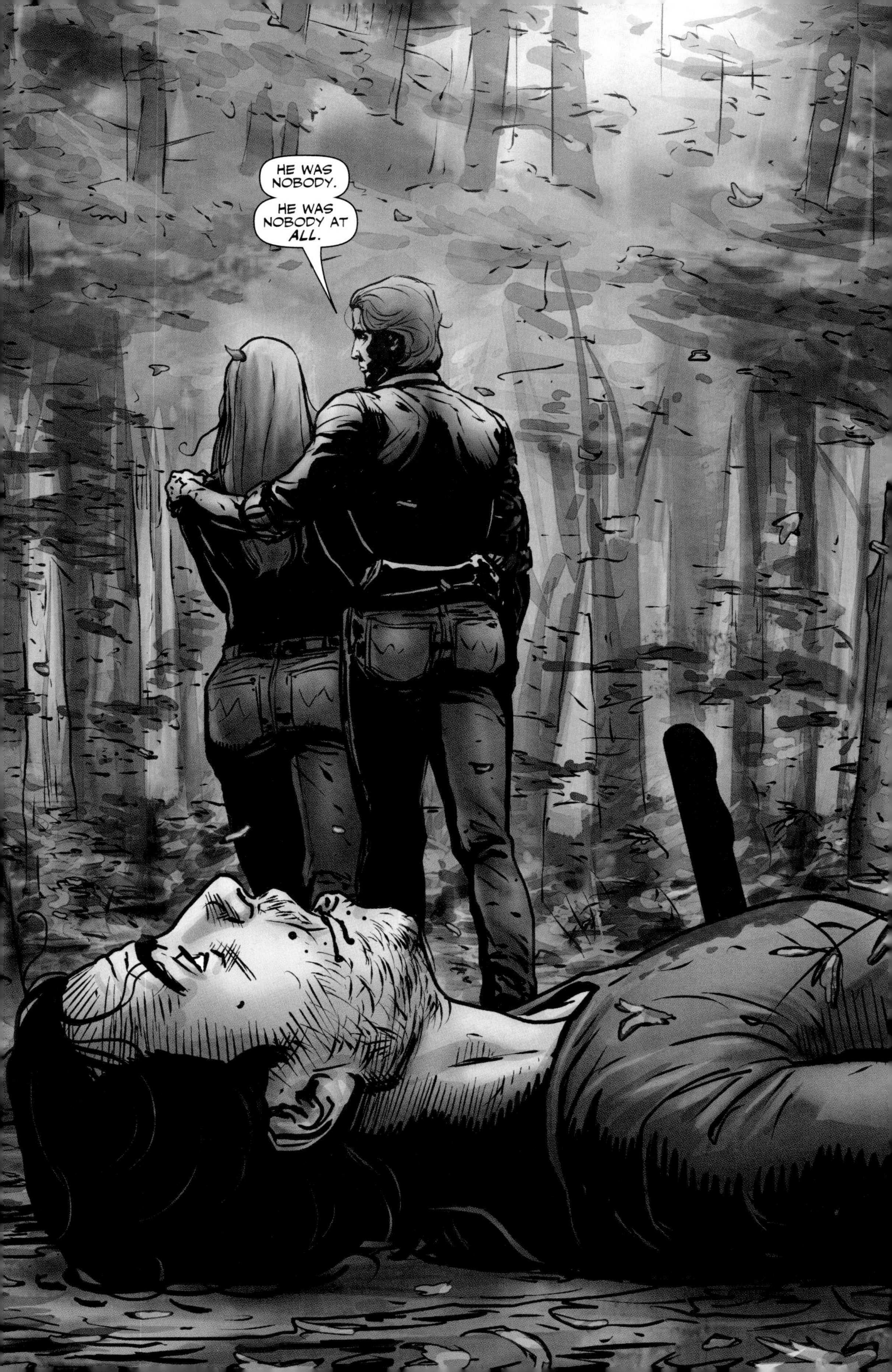
HE WAS NOBODY.
HE WAS NOBODY AT ALL.

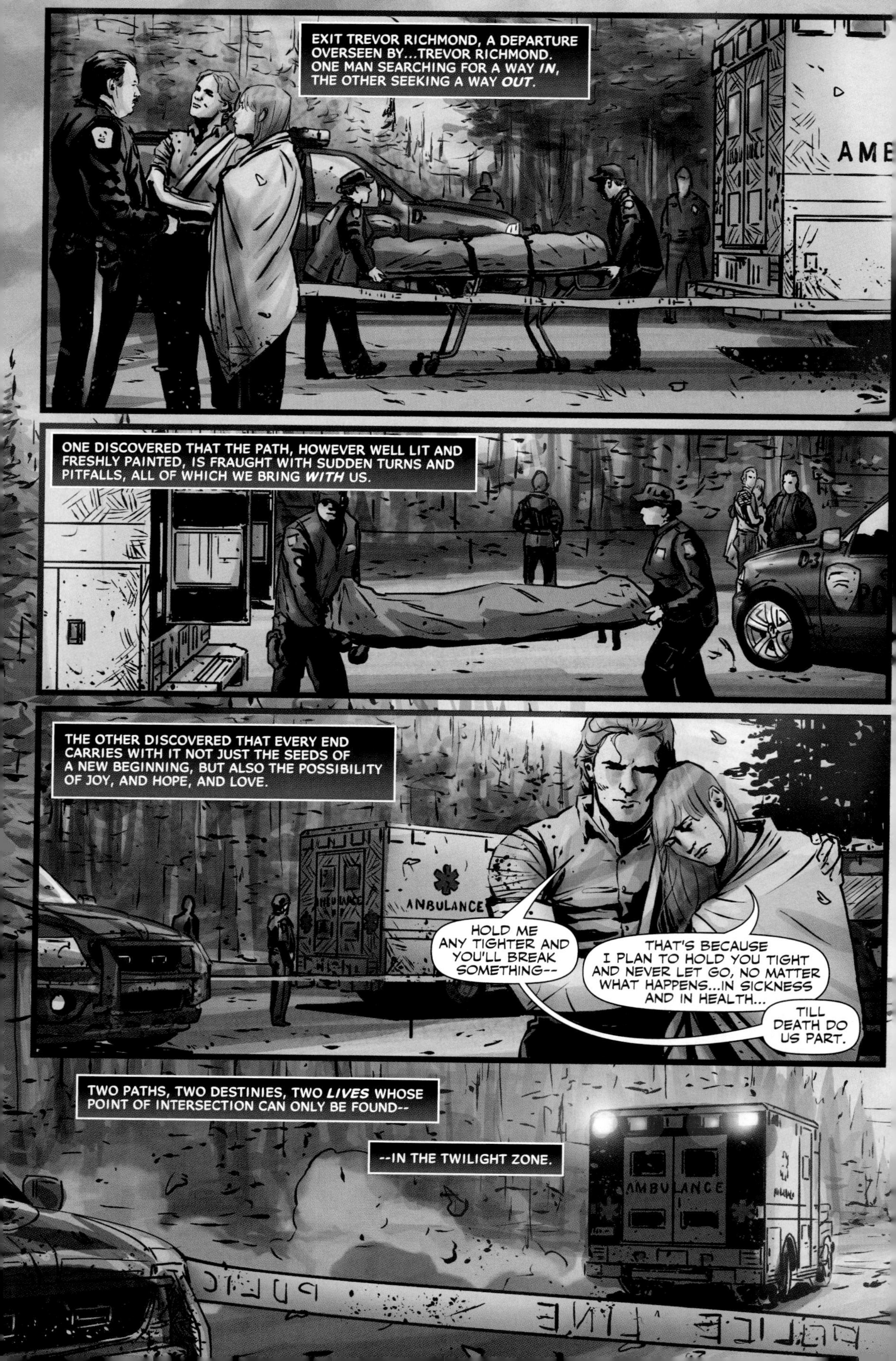
EXIT TREVOR RICHMOND, A DEPARTURE OVERSEEN BY...TREVOR RICHMOND. ONE MAN SEARCHING FOR A WAY *IN*, THE OTHER SEEKING A WAY *OUT*.
ONE DISCOVERED THAT THE PATH, HOWEVER WELL LIT AND FRESHLY PAINTED, IS FRAUGHT WITH SUDDEN TURNS AND PITFALLS, ALL OF WHICH WE BRING *WITH* US.
THE OTHER DISCOVERED THAT EVERY END CARRIES WITH IT NOT JUST THE SEEDS OF A NEW BEGINNING, BUT ALSO THE POSSIBILITY OF JOY, AND HOPE, AND LOVE.
AMBULANCE
HOLD ME ANY TIGHTER AND YOU'LL BREAK SOMETHING--
THAT'S BECAUSE I PLAN TO HOLD YOU TIGHT AND NEVER LET GO, NO MATTER WHAT HAPPENS...IN SICKNESS AND IN HEALTH...
TILL DEATH DO US PART.
TWO PATHS, TWO DESTINIES, TWO *LIVES* WHOSE POINT OF INTERSECTION CAN ONLY BE FOUND--
--IN THE TWILIGHT ZONE.
AMBULANCE

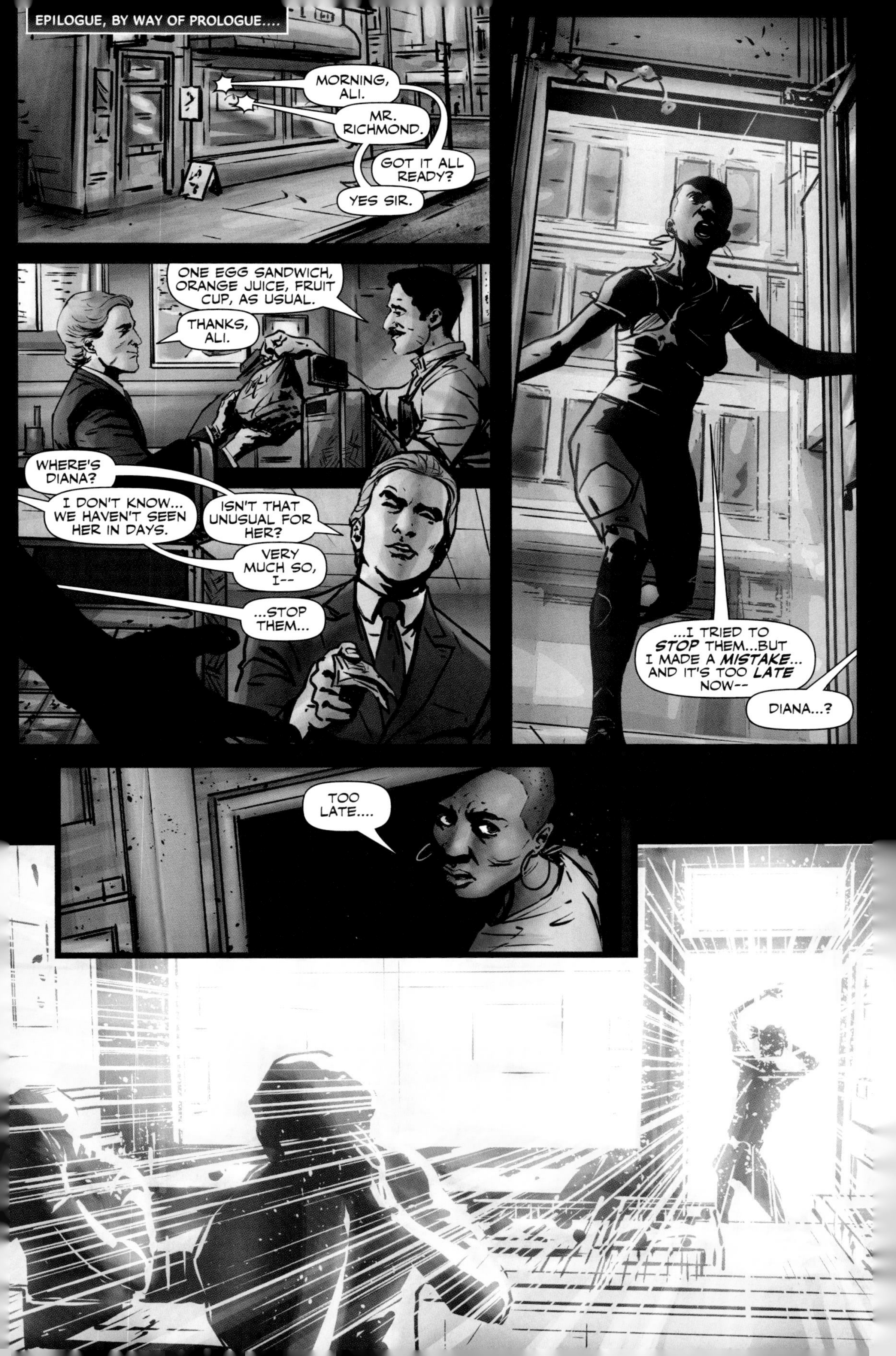
EPILOGUE, BY WAY OF PROLOGUE....
MORNING, ALI.
MR. RICHMOND.
GOT IT ALL READY?
YES SIR.
ONE EGG SANDWICH, ORANGE JUICE, FRUIT CUP, AS USUAL.
THANKS, ALI.
WHERE'S DIANA?
I DON'T KNOW... WE HAVEN'T SEEN HER IN DAYS.
ISN'T THAT UNUSUAL FOR HER?
VERY MUCH SO, I--
...STOP THEM...
...I TRIED TO STOP THEM...BUT I MADE A MISTAKE... AND IT'S TOO LATE NOW--
DIANA...?
TOO LATE....

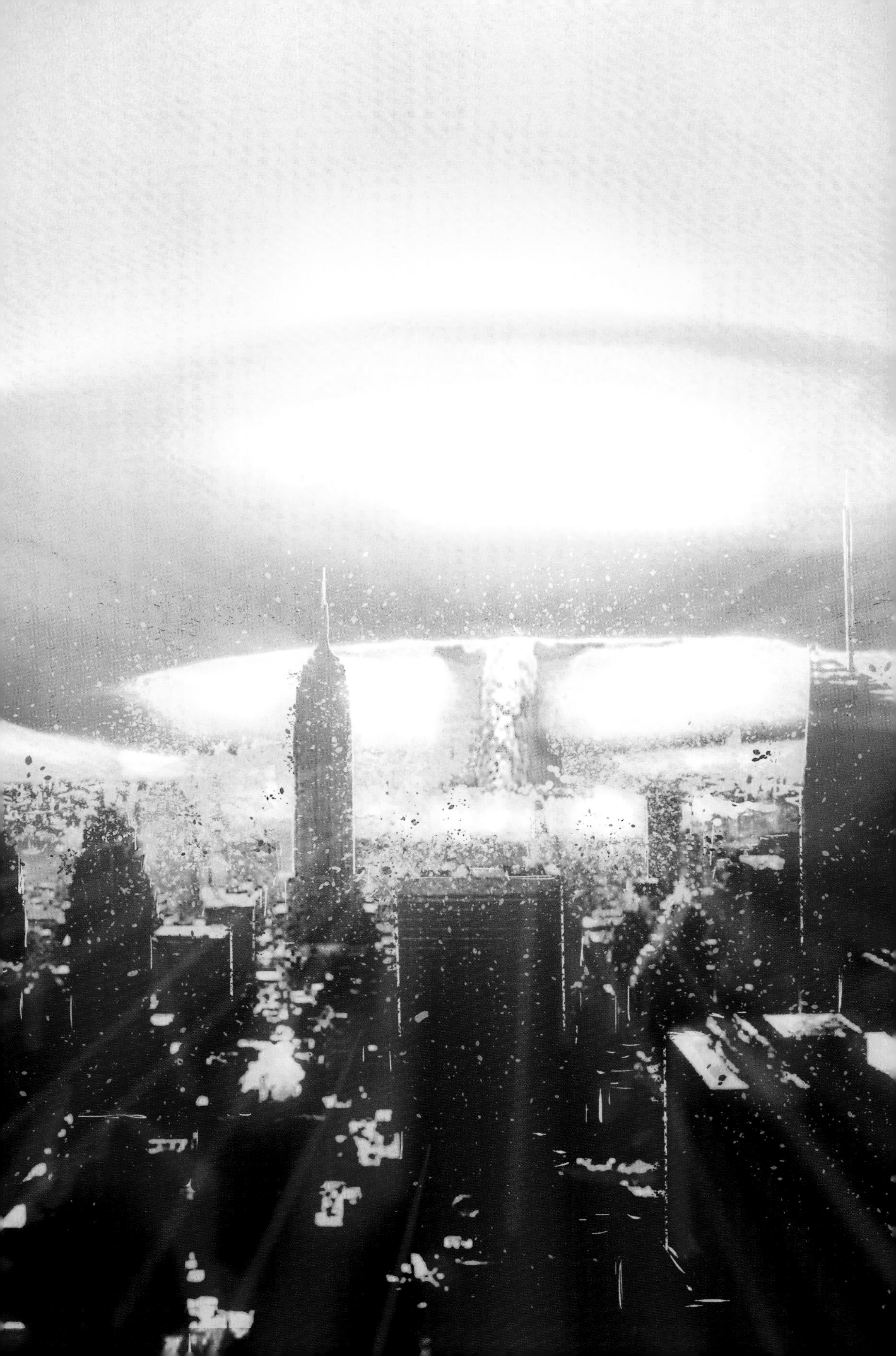

HUUUUCCCCHHHH--

A DREAM...
JUST A DREAM,
THAT'S ALL...

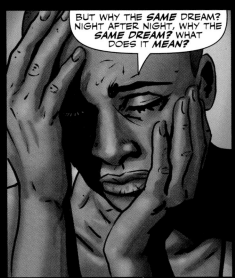

BUT WHY THE *SAME* DREAM?
NIGHT AFTER NIGHT, WHY THE
SAME DREAM? WHAT
DOES IT *MEAN?*

...AND PROLOGUE, BY WAY OF EPILOGUE.

Next:
Episode Two,
THE WAY IN

THE TWILIGHT ZONE
ISSUE ONE: "THE WAY OUT"
BY J. MICHAEL STRACZYNSKI

PAGE ONE

FULL PAGE
A panoramic view of New York City at dawn. Beautiful. Concrete chasms touched by red sunlight.

> CAPTION: *The voice of common wisdom tells us that the age of miracles and magic is dead; that the edges of the world are finite, circumscribed by a confluence of glass, concrete, and enlightened self-interest.*
> (second)
> *It tells us that we journey from dust to dust through the bargain-basement floor of a clockwork universe utterly oblivious to our existence... and that in the end, we all stand alone.*

TITLE at bottom of page.

PAGE TWO

PANEL ONE
One of those deli/restaurants so commonplace in Manhattan, little fast food shops that come to life with the dawn crowd, pushing out eggs and bagels and coffee and ¬pre-made fruit cups. A young named DIANA WESTBY, 20s, is handing a coffee (with lid) and a small brown paper bag to a well-dressed man named TREVOR RICHMOND, 30s, a touch too good looking.

> CAPTION: *The opposition offers into evidence an otherwise nondescript neighborhood on the West Side of Manhattan.*

> DIANA: Here you go, Mr. Richmond, the usual.

> TREVOR: Thanks, Diana.

PANEL TWO
He walks out of the restaurant down the street toward a glass walled expensive looking building.

> CAPTION: *A crossroads of secrets, dreams and desires whose longitude and latitude can only be found --*

PANEL THREE
Inside that building, a Wall Street investment firm, JASON BLACK, late 60s, looks out a window at the city. It's a downshot so we can see Trevor walking toward the building.

> CAPTION: *-- in the Twilight Zone.*

> CAPTION: "-- and even a conservative projection of revenue streams from our current investment slate promises a ten percent increase over last year's earnings."

PAGE THREE

PANEL ONE
A conference room where Trevor is talking to Jason and other members of the Board of Directors. Though seated, Jason is still looking out the window, his mind a million miles away.

TREVOR: The strategy of routing savings-based investment capital into a wide range of foreign companies manufacturing everything from clothing firms to construction projects and electronics --

PANEL TWO
Closer on Trevor, smug in his moment in the sun.

TREVOR: -- the strategy that this board in its wisdom hired me to IMPLEMENT --
(second)
-- has proven more successful than even I could have anticipated. And I anticipated a LOT.

PANEL THREE
Past Trevor to Jason, looking out.

TREVOR: So...are there any questions?
(second)
Mr. Black?
(third)
...Mr. Black...?

PANEL FOUR
Jason looks to him.

JASON: Hmm? Oh. No, no questions, Trevor. Well done. Anything else?

TREVOR: No, sir, I believe that covers it.

JASON: Then we'll consider this meeting adjourned.

PANEL FIVE
Trevor holds the door open for Jason as they leave. One board member looks to the other, unhappy. They confer in quiet tones.

BOARD 1: I don't like it. The Old Man's barely paying attention these days.

BOARD 2: I know. It's his COMPANY, but lately it's as if he's barely even HERE anymore.

PANEL SIX
Jason is heading toward his office, Trevor looking on. ROY CHAMBERS, a haggard looking man in his late 30s is standing outside Jason's office, by an assistant, waiting for him.

CAPTION: "And maybe he's not...maybe he's someplace more IMPORTANT...."

JASON: Mr. Chambers?

ROY: Yes, sir.

JASON: Please, step into my office.
(second)
Hold my calls, Betty.

PAGE FOUR

PANEL ONE
Follow Trevor as he goes past his own office, and looks to his assistant. A clock on the wall reads 9:15.

TREVOR: I'm going to lunch, Lori.

LORI: Lunch? But it's just --

TREVOR: Is there a problem, Lori?

LORI: No, sir, no problem at all.

PANEL TWO
He gets into a glass-walled elevator that gives a view of the city.

PANEL THREE
He looks at his cell phone as it BREEPS with a text message.

PANEL FOUR
The screen states PLEASE CONFIRM 10 A.M. MEETING WITH M. WYLDE. THIS WILL BE YOUR ONLY NOTIFICATION.

PANEL FIVE
He types CONFIRMED. EN ROUTE.

PANEL SIX
He looks out the city. Smiling. There's something vaguely unpleasant about it.

> CAPTION: "And why, precisely, do you wish to avail yourself of our services, Mr. Richmond?"

PAGE FIVE

PANEL ONE
The office of MARTIN WYLDE, 50s, avuncular, is old-world luxurious: lots of dark wood, brass, glass, antiques and comfortable wing-backed chairs. The two men sit looking at each other across a coffee table, a serving tray, and a range of competing agendas.

> TREVOR: I'm a man who likes challenges, Mr. Wylde. I've gone about as far as I can in my current situation, and I'd like to start fresh, start OVER with a new set of challenges.

> WYLDE: And a new name, a new identity --

> TREVOR: Of course.

> WYLDE: Mmmmm.

PANEL TWO
Martin studies Trevor the way a cat studies a particularly interesting mouse.

> WYLDE: Starting over in the way our firm can arrange is not something to be done out of boredom, only as a last resort. Surely there are new challenges still before you?

> TREVOR: Not really....

PANEL THREE
On Trevor. Fingers templed. Calm.

> TREVOR: My employer, Jason Black, is becoming less engaged with the company every day...Retreating into the past.
> (second)
> His son was robbed and murdered years ago and they never caught the men responsible. He's never gotten over it.

PANEL FOUR
We're peering through a window that looks into Jason's office. He's looking out at the street, hands folded behind his back. Roy Chambers is standing behind him, holding a folder.

> CAPTION: "Now that he's approaching death himself, that loss is pulling him down. He can't move forward and he won't let anyone else -- me, for instance -- step in to take over."

> JASON: Promise a dying man that you will go wherever the truth takes you, no matter where it leads.

> ROY: You have my word, Mr. Black.

PANEL FIVE
In the restaurant/diner we saw earlier. Diana is looking at a coin (we don't have to see the details of it). The cashier is watching her.

> CAPTION: "I'm drowning in routine. I even pick up the same egg sandwich every morning on my way to the office."

> CASHIER: What's that?

> DIANA: I don't know...a coin of some kind. Looks really old.

PAGE SIX

PANEL ONE
A peek inside Trevor's bedroom at night: he's sitting up in a curtained four-poster bed as a beautiful woman, NATALIE KYLE, stands before him at the foot of the bed, discreetly nude, her back to us.

> CAPTION: "What about love, Mr. Richmond? Is there any one special in your life?"

> CAPTION: "Yes. Natalie. Beautiful, vacuous Natalie. Hold her to your ear and you can hear the sea."

PANEL TWO
Back in the room with Wylde and Trevor.

> WYLDE: And all THAT is why you wish to use our rather special services.

> TREVOR: That's correct.

> WYLDE: Mmm.
> (second)
> Mmm.
> (third)
> No.

PANEL THREE
On Wylde. Dropping the hammer.

> WYLDE: We're very careful here to do our due diligence before accepting new clients...because very few tell us the REAL reason they need our help.
> (second)
> Let me tell you what we learned about YOU, Mr. Richmond.

PANEL FOUR
Trevor is behind the computer in his home, frowning at a series of emails (we don't need to read them).

> CAPTION: Through highly-paid contacts you've learned that the FBI is conducting an investigation into financial irregularities at your firm.
> (second)
> Millions of dollars embezzled from investors and shareholders, then transferred to Swiss bank accounts. YOUR accounts.

PANEL FIVE
Night at a construction site somewhere in South America. Trucks bearing lumber rumble in while others similarly loaded up rumble out.

CAPTION: "On construction projects in South America your agents purchase grade A lumber and swap it in the middle of the night for grade C lumber so you can pocket the difference, pouring still more money into your accounts."

PAGE SEVEN

PANEL ONE
A sweat shop somewhere in Asia.

> CAPTION: "You divert funds from quality clothes manufacturing firms you've acquired to second-rate sweat shops in Taiwan, once again keeping the difference for yourself."

PANEL TWO
Back with Wylie and Trevor, who is looking increasingly agitated.

> WYLDE: To conceal your illegal activities, you altered the firm's books to the point that almost all the profit on the company's ledgers is non-existent.
> (second)
> Once this is discovered, it will wipe out the life savings of most of your investors.

PANEL THREE
On Trevor, nervous, worried. Where is this going?

> WYLDE (O.S.): It's only a matter of time before an indictment arrives with your name on it. A good lawyer might drag things out for a while, but eventually you WILL end up in jail for a very, VERY long time.

PANEL FOUR
Back in Trevor's bedroom as before, but now we see a different view of that scene: Natalie is partially turned away, in shock and tears, as we see that Trevor is in bed with another woman.

> CAPTION: "As to Ms. Natalie Kyle, apparently that relationship is considerably more --
> (second)
> -- COMPLICATED --
> (third)
> -- than you describe."

PANEL FIVE
Back with the two of them as Wylde gets up and approaches a wall.

> TREVOR: So what do you plan to DO with all this information? Blackmail? Extortion?

> WYLDE: Don't be worried, Mr. Richmond. We only needed this in order to evaluate how we might best HELP you.

PANEL SIX
Wylde has touched a control and the wall is sliding back to reveal white light and stainless steel walls.

> WYLDE: Let me show you.

PANEL ONE
A marked contrast to the friendly, earth-toned office we saw earlier: stainless steel and glass and high-tech consoles and displays, manned by men and women in suits and white lab coats. Wylde leads Trevor through it.

> WYLDE: Our clients don't WANT to disappear, they HAVE to vanish. Tyrants and dictators, war criminals and torturers, deposed presidents and a growing number of people from the financial industry.
> (second)
> You don't REALLY think Kenneth Lay just HAPPENED to die just before he was to go to prison, do you?

PANEL TWO
They pause beside one of the banks of consoles and workers.

> WYLDE: This is where we create identities: work histories, diplomas, passports, birth certificates...a new life, free of obligation. Our firm GUARANTEES that no one will EVER come looking for you.

> TREVOR: But if anyone ever DOES, I can still be IDENTIFIED. I'm still ME.

> WYLDE: Actually, no, you're not.

PANEL THREE
Wylde holds up a glass tube containing a small pill.

> WYLDE: This remarkable pill cost BILLIONS to develop. It uses organic nanoparticles to rearrange you bit by bit from the inside out. Blood type, eye color, skin, even your fingerprints.
> (second)
> It's quite harmless, but by the end of the process, even your own MOTHER wouldn't be sure it was YOU.

PANEL FOUR
Favoring Trevor.

> TREVOR: And what exactly does this service COST?

> WYLDE: Why, it costs you EVERYTHING, Mr. Richmond. Every PENNY you've earned through your ACTIVITIES.

> TREVOR: Whoa, hold on --

PANEL FIVE
Favoring Wylde.

> WYLDE: Don't worry, we'll set aside an account so your needs are looked after for life. You will want for nothing.
> (second)
> You have only two choices: wait to be indicted and lose your money AND your freedom...or lose your money but still walk around a free man.

PANEL SIX
Wylde holds up the glass tube with the pill.

> WYLDE: So what'll it be, Mr. Richmond?

PANEL ONE
In Trevor's bathroom. Night. He's wearing pajama bottoms and no shirt. Holding the glass-encased pill in his hand.

PANEL TWO
He holds the container up to the light.

> CAPTION: "So what'll it be, Mr. Richmond?"

PANEL THREE
He swallows the pill.

PANEL FOUR
He comes out of the bathroom into the bedroom, where Natalie stands off a bit. Pensive. Unsure.

> TREVOR: Listen, Natalie, I know things haven't been great between us lately, but I want you to know --
> (second)
> -- that's all going to CHANGE, very soon.

> NATALIE: Do I have your PROMISE on that, Trevor?

PANEL FIVE
He holds her, and she can't see his smile, the one that says "I am SO out of here."

> TREVOR: I promise.

PAGE TEN
The panels on this page are meant to show the passage of time. Not a lot but enough....

PANEL ONE
Trevor is standing in the conference room, in front of a display showing corporate profits. Everyone in the room is looking at him except Jason, who is looking out the window.

> TREVOR: -- so we're looking at a five percent increase in fourth quarter profits based on projections from our partners in Korea and Brazil --

PANEL TWO
He's in his bathroom, nose practically up against the mirror, touching his face. Frowning.

> TREVOR: Still no change...c'mon, c'mon...we don't have all YEAR here....

PANEL THREE
In a fancy hotel bedroom with the other woman in his life (the one we saw Natalie turn from when she caught them). They're in bed and he's holding her. Giving her the same line.

> TREVOR: I know things haven't been great between us lately, Sandra, but I want you to know --
> (second)
> -- that's all going to CHANGE, very soon.

PANEL FOUR
Trevor's assistant stands at his desk, handing him some paperwork.

> TREVOR: So what's the problem?

> LORI: Well, it's just...transportation didn't put through the order because your signature on the manifest doesn't match what we have on file.

PANEL FIVE
Looking over his shoulder at the two versions of his signature. He's amazed, seeing the first traces of the change.

> TREVOR: Fascinating....

> LORI: Sir?

> TREVOR: Nothing...I'll fix this.

> LORI: Thanks. Oh, and don't forget --

PANEL SIX
He's in a dentist's chair as the dentist examines his teeth.

> CAPTION: "-- your appointment with the dentist for a cleaning at three o'clock."

DENTIST: So odd...as if the shape of your jaw is CHANGING on its own. We'll have to set a date to do x-rays, update your charts, because if I saw THIS without knowing it was YOU --
(second)
-- I'd swear it was the dental profile of someone else ENTIRELY.

PAGE ELEVEN

PANEL ONE
He's at the bank, his thumb pressed against a reader by the entrance to the safe deposit area as a clerk looks on.

> BANK CLERK: I'm sorry, Mr. Richmond, the system isn't recognizing your fingerprints. I'll have tech support check out the system. Meanwhile, if you could just give me your ID and key --

PANEL TWO
In his bathroom again, his back to us. He's on the phone, looking in the mirror.

> TREVOR: Lori, could you tell Mr. Black I won't be coming in today?

PANEL THREE
We've turned around to see that his hair color has started to change and his face looks a bit longer than it did before. As if his previous appearance is being sanded down, inch by inch.

> TREVOR: I'm a bit under the weather today... not quite feeling like myself.

PANEL FOUR
He's in bed. Daylight streams through parted curtains. He's sleeping on his front. A voice comes through the answering machine by the bed.

> VOICE ON MACHINE: Trev? Ben Thomas from accounting. I know you're still under the weather, but we just got an odd call from Jon Baxter at the Federal Exchange Commission. He wants to come in on Monday and check out our books. Do you know anything about this? Call me, I'll be home all weekend.

PANEL FIVE
Close on the back of Trevor's head, in bed. Night. There's another voice on the answering machine.

> VOICE ON MACHINE: Mr. Richmond...Martin Wylde. I'm sure the discomfort of these final changes has been consider able, but the good news is that you are ready for the final phase of our services.
> (second)
> From what my sources tell me, we're just in the nick of time.

PANEL SIX
On the closed door to the bedroom, under which we notice a thin rubber pipe exhaling gas into the room.

VOICE ON MACHINE (O.S.): The HISSING you should be hearing right about now is a harmless but effective GAS designed to help RELAX you through the final stage of your transition.

PAGE TWELVE

We can go a bit smeared on these images, since he's either barely conscious or unconscious...unless it gets in the way, then ignore that idea.

PANEL ONE
Face covered by an oxygen mask, Trevor is on a hospital-style gurney being wheeled down a long white hallway by staff in white surgical gowns.

> CAPTION: "You're almost done, Mr. Richmond...."

PANEL TWO
He's on a surgical bed in an operating theater. A nearby monitor shows an image of his body and the changes they plan to make.

> CAPTION: "...a name that will never again be identified with you after today."

> DOCTOR: Height?

> NURSE: Five foot nine.

> DOCTOR: All right, let's see if we can raise that to five ten. Can we get the implants in here?

PANEL THREE
A different medical room, a dentist-style room. A dentist sits beside an unconscious Trevor, drilling away, two different dental x-rays in front of him. A nurse looks on. SFX: fweeeEEEEEE fweeEEEEE

> DENTIST: Be sure to get the originals to Wylde. He'll need them for the alt.

> NURSE: Of course.

PANEL FOUR
Wylde looks on as one of his employees works at a computer terminal.

> WYLDE: You've got access to all of it? Stocks, bonds, savings, checking?

> EMPLOYEE: Yes, sir. Transferring to our accounts now.

> WYLDE: Good. Once you set up his new accounts, funnel in enough to look after all his basic requirements. Nothing fancy, but enough.

> EMPLOYEE: Yes, sir.

PANEL FIVE
Wylde is heading out of the room.

> WYLDE: And be sure to leave enough behind for the alt. That's important.

> EMPLOYEE (O.S.): Yes, sir.

> CAPTION: "Which brings us to the question on the minds of everyone on Wall Street today --
> (second)
> -- WHERE is Trevor Richmond?"

PAGE THIRTEEN

PANEL ONE
We're in Jason Black's office. Two of his board members are standing or crouching beside him, trying to get through to him. The TV is on in the background.

TELEVISION: By all accounts Richmond hasn't been seen since several days before the grand jury indictments were unsealed in this latest Wall Street scandal.

BOARD 1: Mr. Black, we HAVE to get in front of this. You HAVE to issue a statement.

JASON: Doesn't matter...nothing matters....

PANEL TWO
Another angle on the scene.

BOARD 2: Sir, if we don't get aggressive with this situation, the feds could decide we're INVOLVED. The indictments name Trevor AND persons A through X --

BOARD 1: -- leaving room for ANY of us to be indicted if he doesn't show up and this goes badly...even you.

PANEL THREE
Jason looks out the door to his assistant.

JASON: Betty, any word from Mr. Chambers?

BETTY: No sir, not in the last several days.

PANEL FOUR
Two dark-suited FBI agents appear in the doorway, holding up their ID and badges.

BETTY: But these gentlemen said they'd like to have a word with you.

PANEL FIVE
Back on Jason, the board members behind him. His expression is shattered, sad...lost.

JASON: Ben?

BOARD 1: Yes sir?

JASON: You may want to call down to Legal Affairs, I think we're going to need some lawyers up here.

CAPTION: "So Mr. Richmond came here regularly?"

PAGE FOURTEEN

PANEL ONE
In the deli/restaurant. One of the other servers is talking to an FBI agent. There's no sign of Diana.

SERVER: Yes sir, every morning at eight thirty, just like clockwork.

FBI AGENT: Did you wait on him personally?

SERVER: No, that was Diana, she was kind of his favorite.

FBI AGENT: Is she here now?

PANEL TWO
Another angle on the conversation.

SERVER: No, we haven't seen her since day before yesterday.

FBI AGENT: Any chance of a connection?

SERVER: Between her and him? Nah. She's not his type and he's not hers.

PANEL THREE
The FBI agent is looking in a door at the woman Trevor was fooling around with.

CAPTION: "He probably goes for those high society types, all blonde and high heels."

WOMAN: No, I haven't seen the sonofabitch in DAYS.

PANEL FOUR
Other agents are interviewing Natalie, who looks devastated.

FBI AGENT: So he never gave you any indication that he was going to leave town?

NATALIE: No...he said things were going to get BETTER between us, he --
(second)
-- he PROMISED me.

PANEL FIVE
Close on her face as she looks out a window, tears in her eyes.

NATALIE: (small font) He said he was going to CHANGE....

PAGE FIFTEEN

PANEL ONE
Afternoon. A nondescript apartment building somewhere on the east side of New York. Not bad, not great, just very average.

CAPTION: "...PROMISED me he would CHANGE."

PANEL TWO
Inside the apartment. Again, very middle of the road. Unimpressive, but not bad. Simple. Sparse. A figure is on the bed, on the made bedspread, dressed and gradually waking up.

TREVOR: Oh, man...everything hurts....

PANEL THREE
He gets up and bangs his knee on the bedside nightstand, unfamiliar with his setting.

TREVOR: Ow! Son of a...who put THAT there? Where --

PANEL FOUR
Still cheating him in the shadows. He looks around.

TREVOR: -- where the hell AM I?

PANEL FIVE
He picks up a driver's license and other ID cards on the table. We may or may not be able to make out details, but if we do, the ID reads THOMAS RILEY.

TREVOR: Wait...I remember now, I --

PANEL SIX
He rushes into the bathroom.

TREVOR: -- I remember!

PAGE SIXTEEN

FULL PAGE

Coming from the side so we see both Trevor and his reflection in the mirror looking at each other. He's touching his face in astonishment. Here's what we see: his skeletal structure inside is still what it was, so the same shape is there, but the rest is very different. If you know he looked a certain way before this you might be able to pick out some elements that seemed familiar, but otherwise...you'd think this was a completely different person.

> TREVOR: It worked --
> (second)
> -- holy crap --
> (third)
> -- IT WORKED!

SFX from OS: *ring-ring...ring-ring....*

PAGE SEVENTEEN

PANEL ONE

He runs into the room where the land line phone is ringing. Ring-ring...ring-ring....

PANEL TWO

He has the phone to his ear.

> TREVOR: Hello?

> PHONE VOICE: Welcome to your new life, Thomas.

> TREVOR: Thomas?

> PHONE VOICE: Thomas Riley. Puckish, I suppose, but I gave you the same initials in case you loved the look in a monogram.

PANEL THREE

On Wylie in his office. On the phone. Sitting comfortably behind his desk.

> WYLDE: The dossier on your new persona is in the top drawer of your dresser. Memorize it. You'll also find clothes and shoes all sized to fit, along with a checkbook. We'll replenish the account as you need additional funds, but try not to go too crazy.

PANEL FOUR

Back with Trevor as he looks in the closet, revealing rows of clothes on the hangers.

> TREVOR: These look used --

> PHONE VOICE: A careful illusion. Nothing more suspicious than someone who appears out of nowhere with an all new wardrobe.

PANEL FIVE

Closer on Trevor.

> PHONE VOICE: Since you've been out of the loop for a while, you should know that the hammer has fallen, as

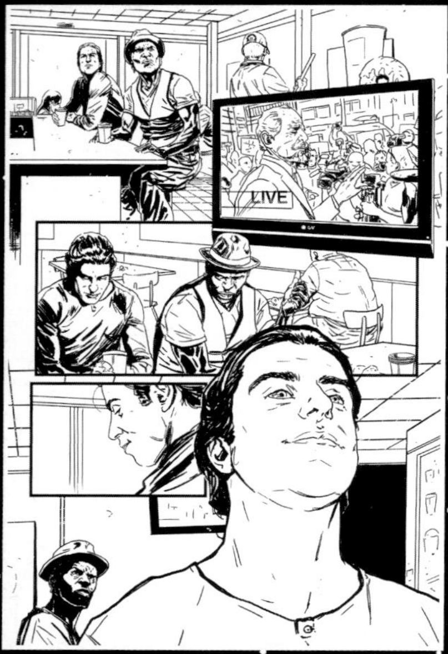
LIVE

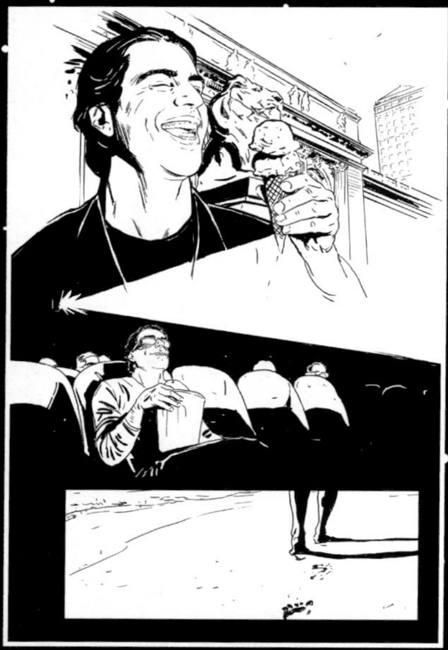

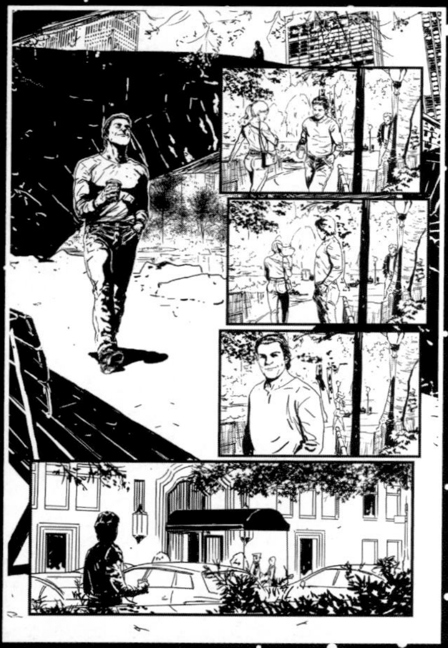

predicted. But because of your foresight, it's going to hit everyone BUT you. You should be most proud.
(second)
That said: never contact us again except in an emergency. Goodbye, Mr. Riley.

SFX: Click!

PANEL SIX
Trevor raises his arms in triumph.

TREVOR: Yes! I did it! I got away with it!
(second)
YES!

CAPTION: "As aftershocks of the latest Wall Street scandal continue to ripple out across the financial community."

PAGE EIGHTEEN

PANEL ONE
Trevor is in a coffee shop, having a latte. The TV is on in the corner. The barrista at the coffee machine is keeping an eye on it. There are a few other customers in the place, but it's not crowded. Trevor is also watching the screen, vaguely amused by the whole thing...now that he's not part of it.

On the screen, reporters are crowded around the entrance to his former company.

TELEVISION: In one of the biggest scandals in recent years, tens of millions of dollars have been diverted from the accounts of investors and shareholders for personal gain.

PANEL TWO
Tighter on the TV as Jason Black works to get past the crowd of reporters and angry customers.

TELEVISION: CEO Jason Black spent six hours today being interviewed by agents from the FBI and representatives of the FEC in an attempt to determine what happened, how, and who is to blame.

BARRISTA (O.S.): If you ask me they ought to ¬perp-walk those guys out of their fancy offices right into jail.

PANEL THREE
Widen back out to include Trevor and the barrista.

BARRISTA: Can't WAIT to see these guys get what's coming to them.

TREVOR: Then you're going to have a long wait ahead of you.

PANEL FOUR
Favoring Trevor.

TREVOR: The legal system doesn't work the same way for people at the TOP as it does for --
(second)
-- well, for everyone ELSE. For the people with POWER, for the people who MATTER...there's ALWAYS a way OUT.

PANEL FIVE
He heads out. Smiling.

      TREVOR: You just need to know where to look for it.

PAGE NINETEEN

FULL PAGE
A montage of images of Trevor enjoying himself in his new life: ice cream outside the New York Library, sitting in a movie theater, taking a walk along the shore...happy.

      CAPTION: Growing up I always heard that the fruit that tastes sweetest is the one you steal from the store.
(second)
Never realized until now how true that it.
(third)
I'm free.
(fourth)
I never have to worry about anything ever again. I can DO what I want, BE what I want, no obligations. A fresh start.
(fifth)
I'm FREE.
(sixth)
Imagine that....

PAGE TWENTY

PANEL ONE
Trevor is walking through Central Park at night. Smiling as he sips coffee.

PANEL TWO
He looks over as a lovely woman passes. We should notice Roy Chambers standing alone in the shadows. Not much detail, just enough to see his face and know it's him.

      TREVOR: Beautiful night.

      LOVELY WOMAN: Yes, it is, isn't it?

PANEL THREE
He looks to her as she walks away. Watching her ass. We still notice Roy back there.

      TREVOR: It sure is...

PANEL FOUR
He continues away, as we notice...just in the background... that Roy is no longer in the park. He's just disappeared. We don't play this up, it's "subjective camera" for lack of a better term...but if we go back at a later date readers can notice that he simply vanished.

      TREVOR: ...and then some.

PANEL FIVE
He's passing one of the high-price buildings that line the street across from Central Park as he hears --

      VOICE FROM OS: -- please, you can't do this --

PAGE TWENTY-ONE

PANEL ONE
Natalie is talking with the doorman.

      DOORMAN: Sorry, Ms. Kyle, but the rent's gone unpaid and with all that's going on --

      NATALIE: Please, all my things are in there. If you can just unlock --

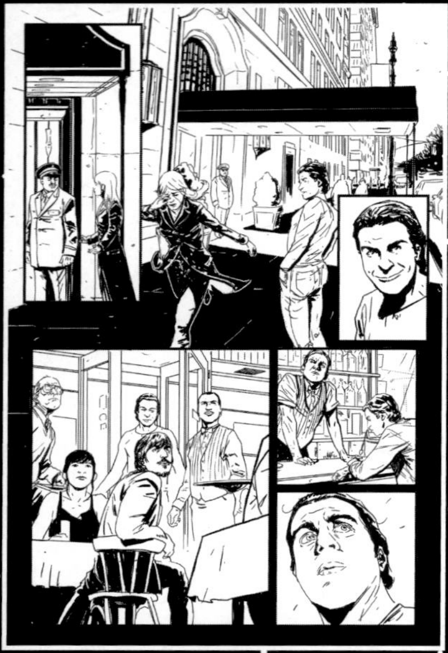

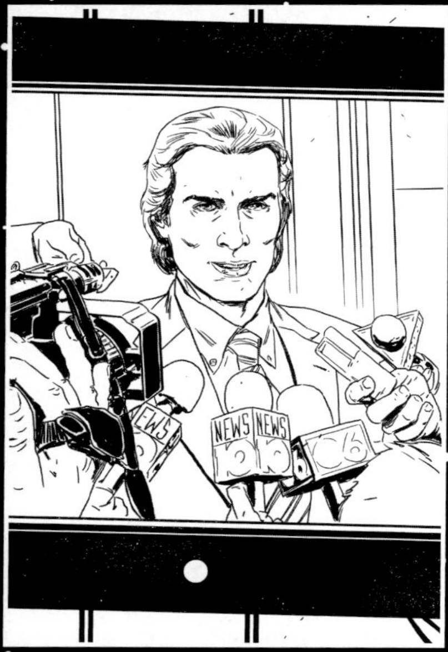
NEWS
NEWS

DOORMAN: I'm sorry, there's nothing I can do.

PANEL TWO
She rushes away, fighting tears, going right past him.

PANEL THREE
He smiles as he watches her go.

TREVOR: No idea...walked right past me --

PANEL FOUR
He walks into a bar. A crowd has gathered in front of the TV. Even the bartender is watching the set.

TREVOR: Hey...can a guy get a beer in here?

BARTENDER: In a sec --

TREVOR: What's on the TV? Somebody get shot?

PANEL FIVE
Trevor makes his way to the bar.

BARTENDER: Better...that asshole just surrendered himself.

TREVOR: WHAT asshole?

PANEL SIX
CLOSE on Trevor as he sees what's on the screen. We don't see it yet. Shock and astonishment and disbelief.

TREVOR: No...it CAN'T be --

VOICE FROM OS: I come here today to try and do the right thing.

PAGE TWENTY-TWO

FULL PAGE
Someone wearing Trevor Richmond's face, and clothes, stands on the steps of his company, surrounded by onlookers. (This isn't a TV image, we're here.)

TREVOR 2: My name is Trevor Richmond --
(second)
-- and there's something important that I need to tell all of you.

TO BE CONTINUED....

CHARACTER DESIGNS
BY GUIU VILANOVA

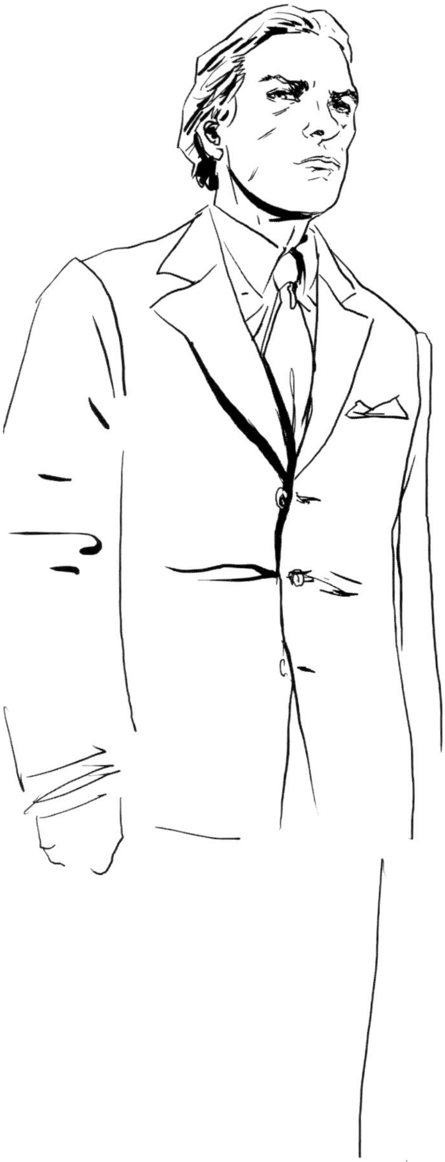

Trevor Richmond

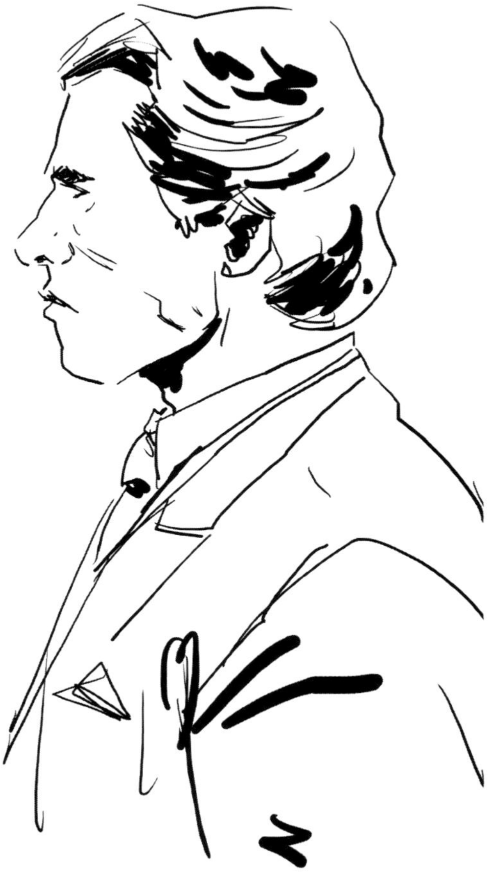

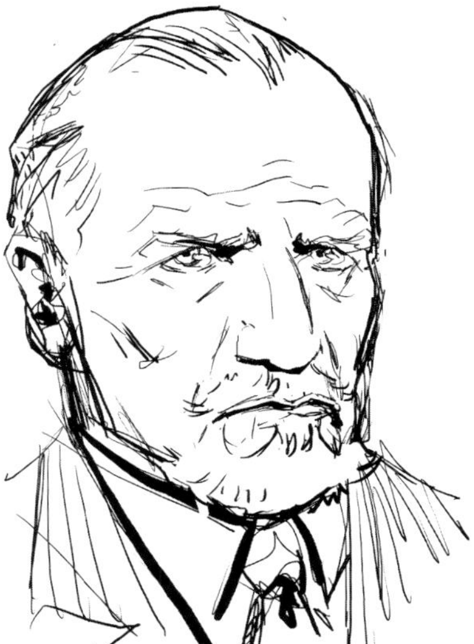

Jason Black

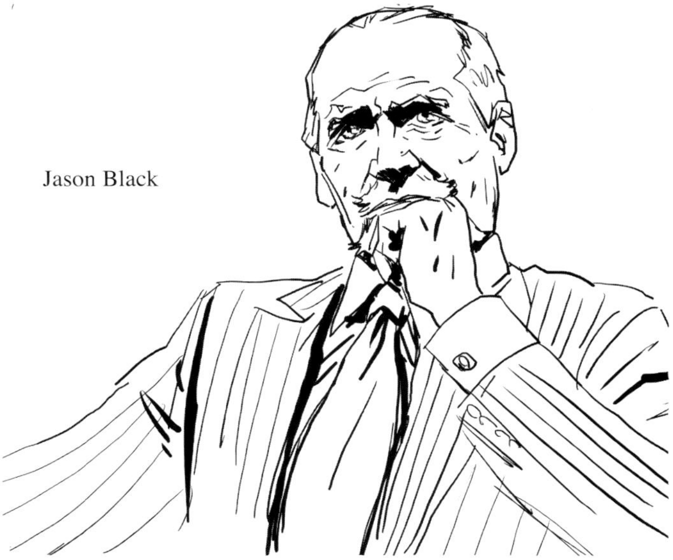

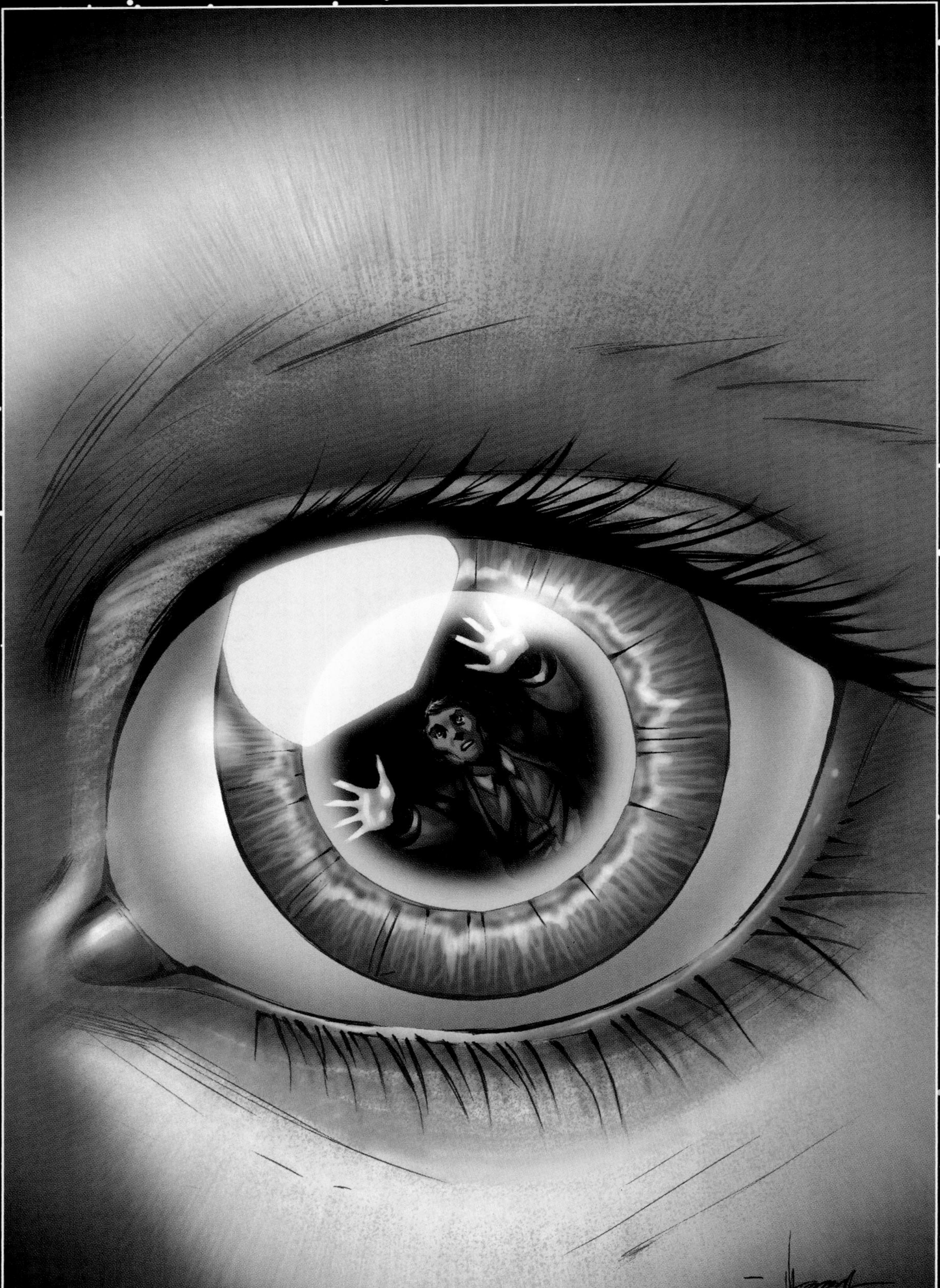
LUIS GUERRERO

ISSUE #1 CARDS, COMICS, AND COLLECTIBLES EXCLUSIVE COVER
art by ALÉ GARZA colors by LUIS GUERRERO

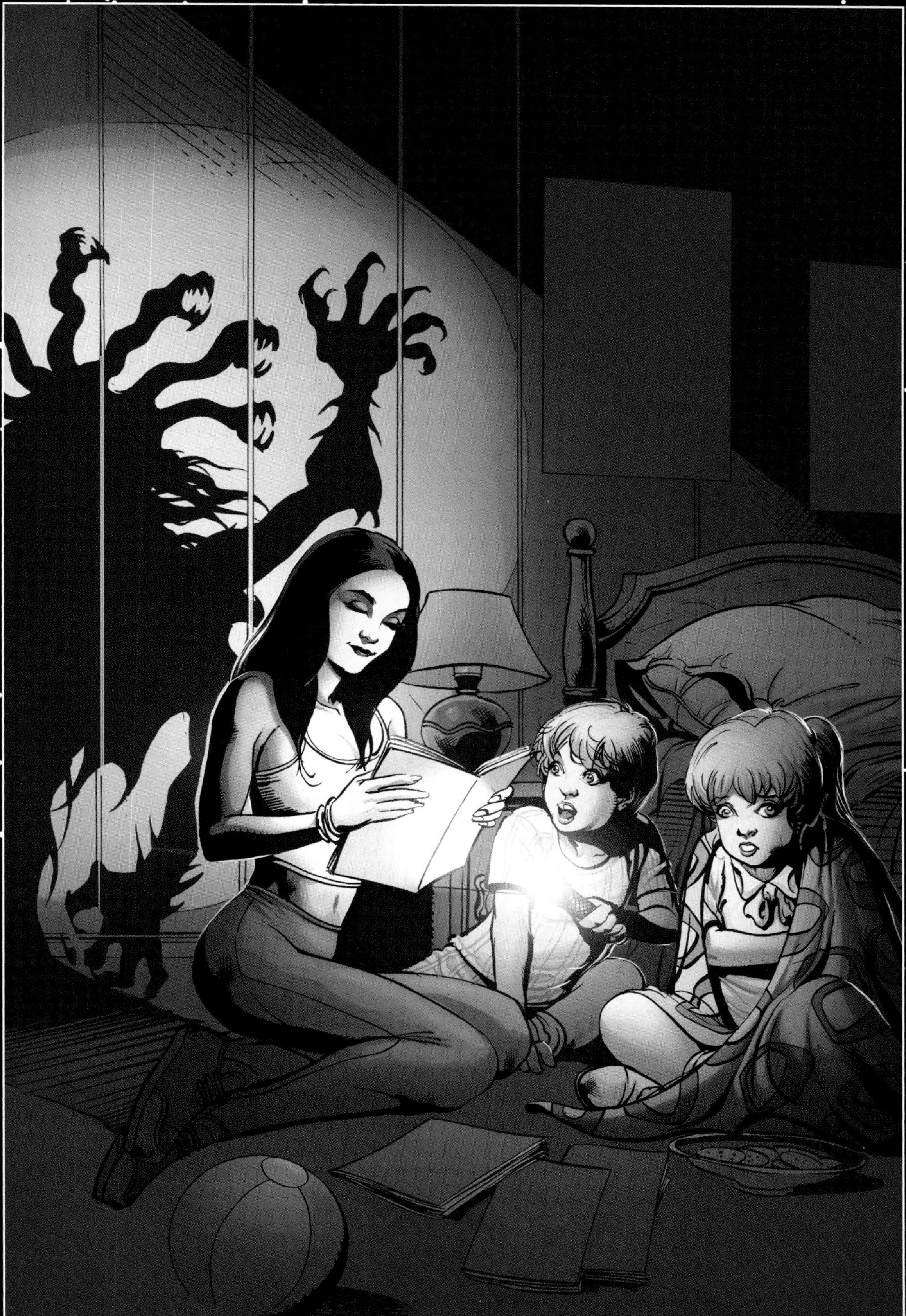

ISSUE #1 DISCOUNT COMIC BOOK SERVICE EXCLUSIVE COVER
art by ROBERTO CASTRO colors by ADRIANO LUCAS

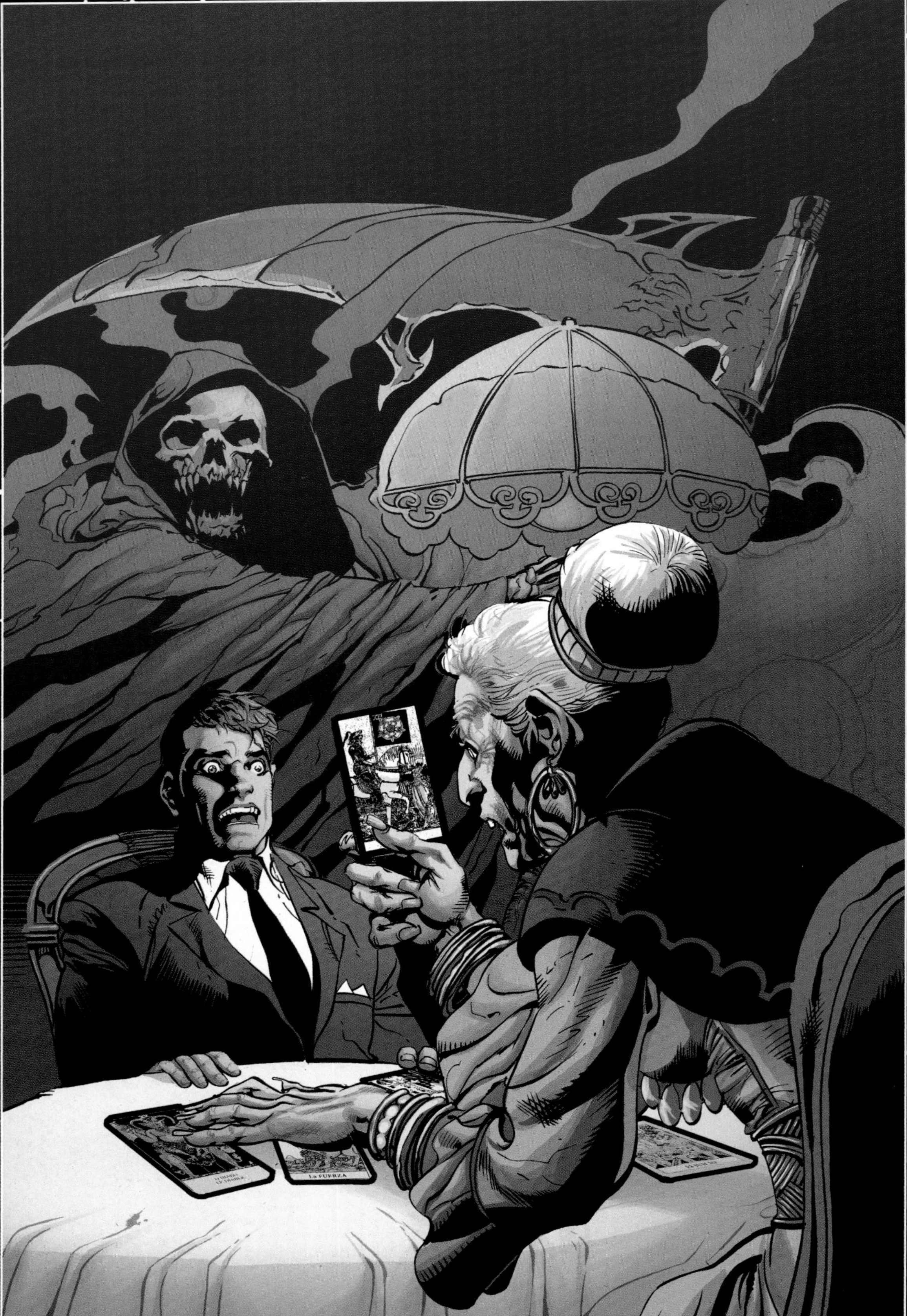
La FUERZA

ISSUE #1 FAT JACK'S COMICRYPT EXCLUSIVE COVER
art by ROBERTO CASTRO colors by ADRIANO LUCAS

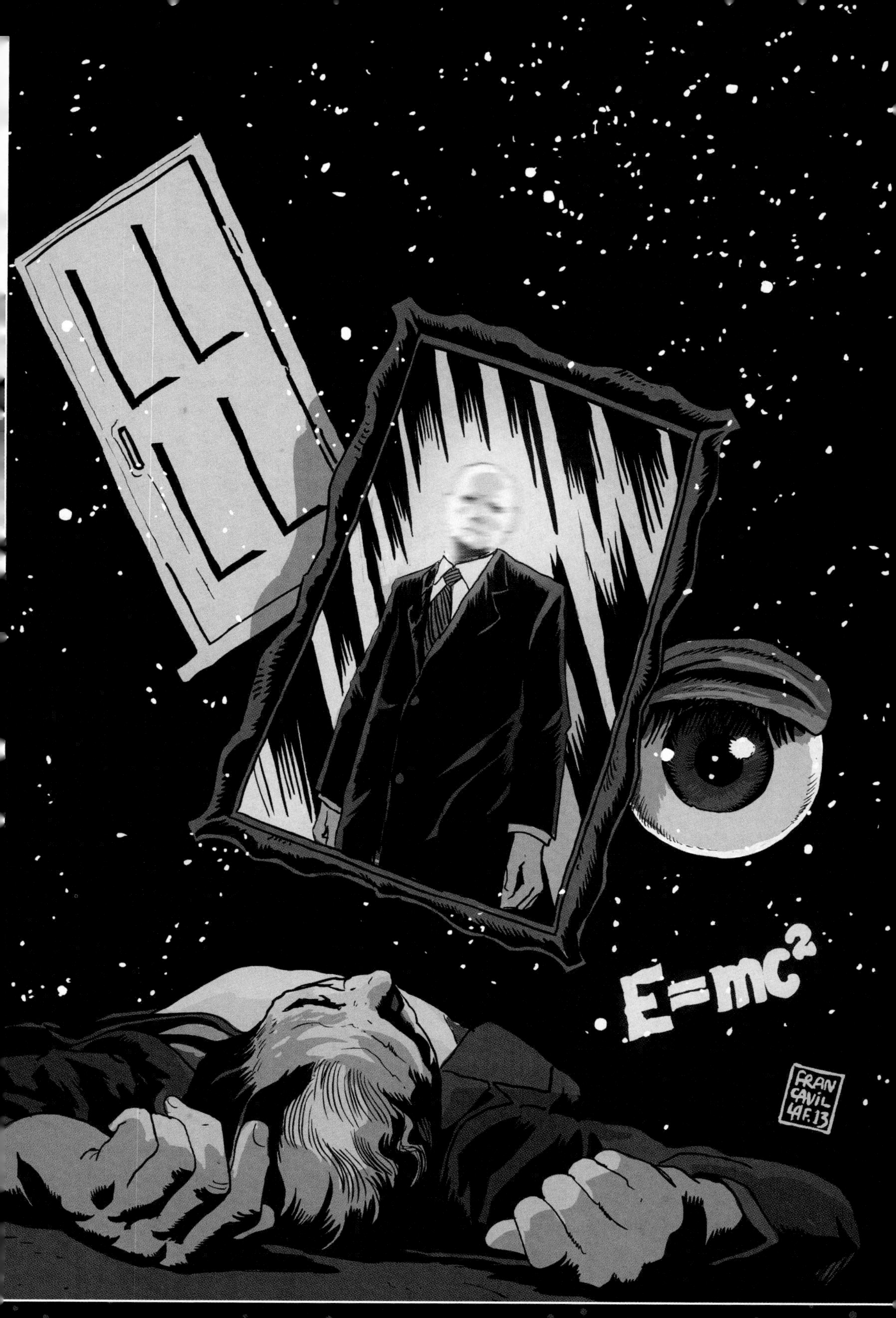
E=mc²
FRAN CAVIL LA F.13

ISSUE #1 MIDTOWN COMICS EXCLUSIVE COVER
art by FRANCESCO FRANCAVILLA

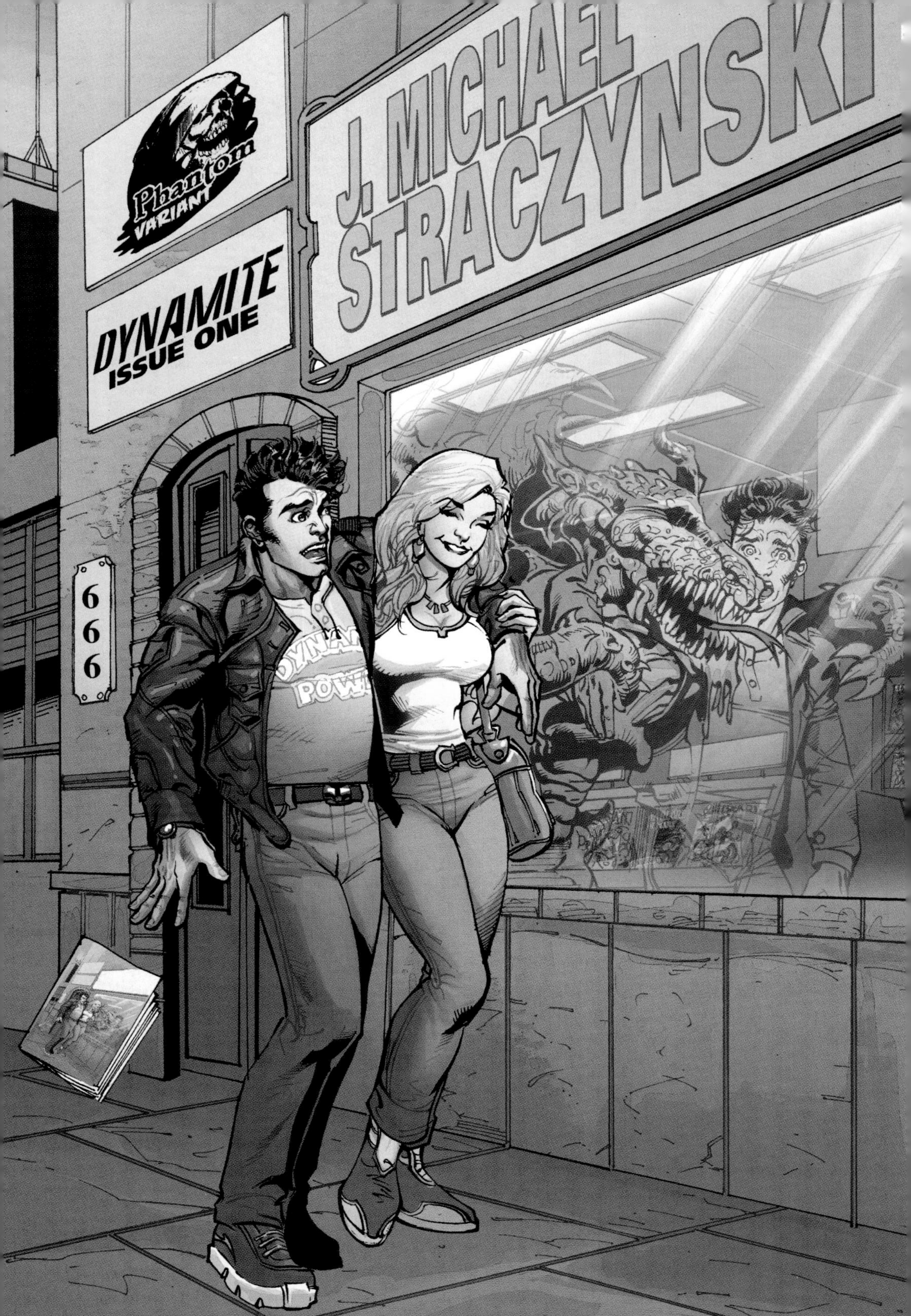
Phantom
VARIANT
DYNAMITE
ISSUE ONE
J. MICHAEL
STRACZYNSKI
666

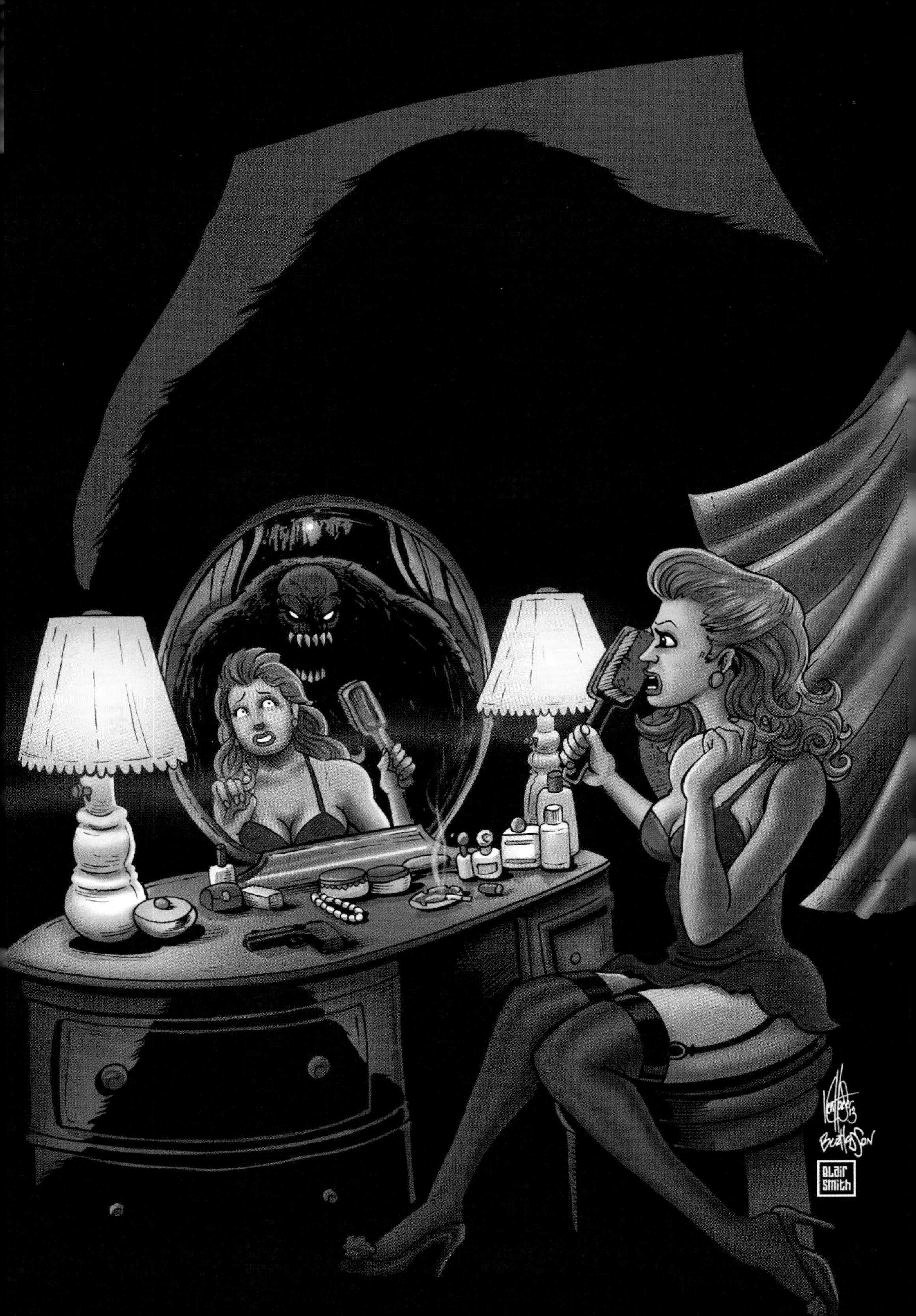
BLAIR SMITH

LOOK FOR THESE DYNAMITE GREATEST HITS!

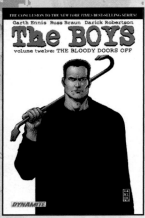

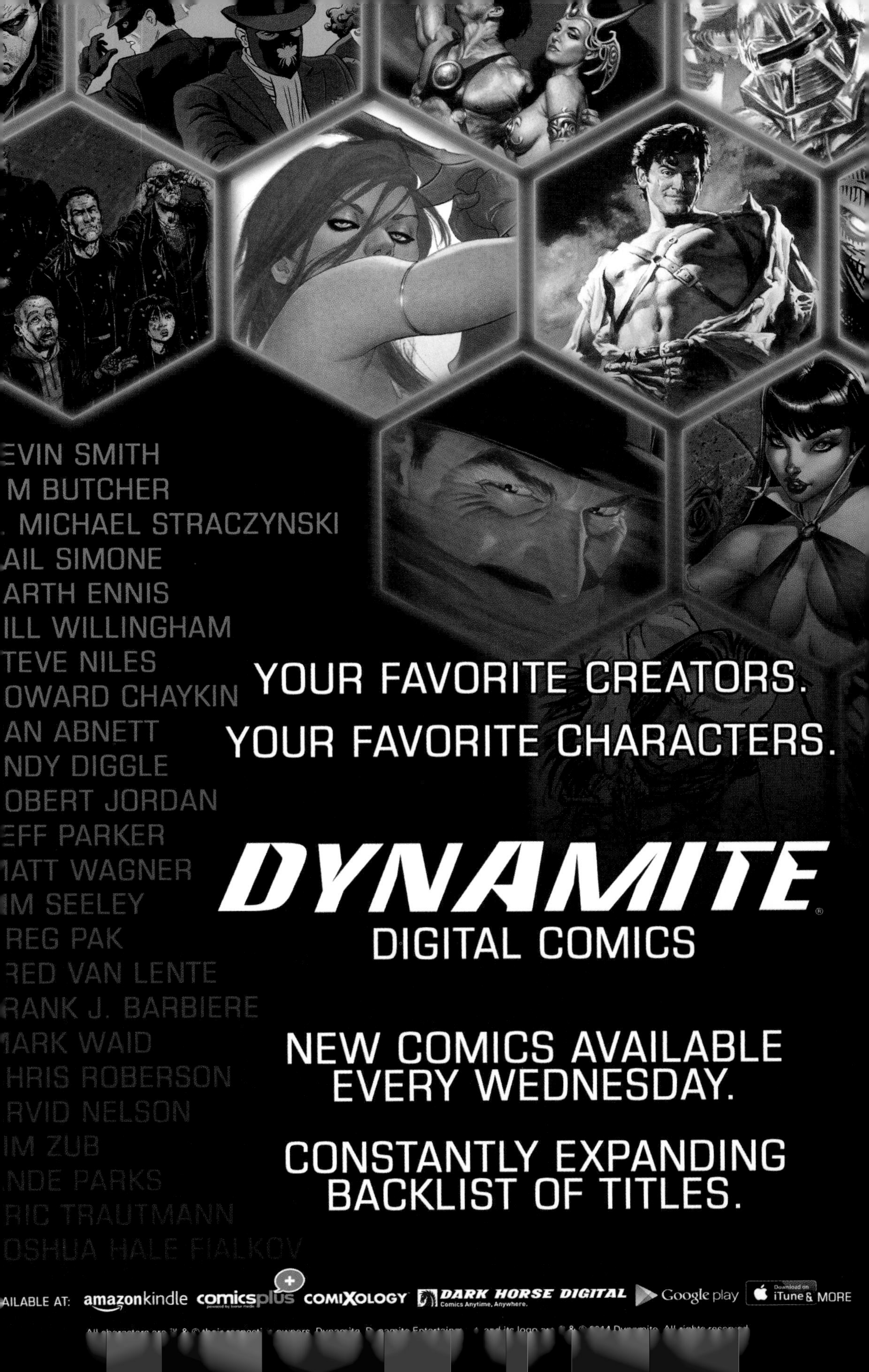

EVIN SMITH
M BUTCHER
MICHAEL STRACZYNSKI
AIL SIMONE
ARTH ENNIS
ILL WILLINGHAM
TEVE NILES
OWARD CHAYKIN
AN ABNETT
NDY DIGGLE
OBERT JORDAN
EFF PARKER
ATT WAGNER
IM SEELEY
REG PAK
RED VAN LENTE
RANK J. BARBIERE
ARK WAID
HRIS ROBERSON
RVID NELSON
IM ZUB
NDE PARKS
RIC TRAUTMANN
OSHUA HALE FIALKOV
YOUR FAVORITE CREATORS.
YOUR FAVORITE CHARACTERS.
DYNAMITE®
DIGITAL COMICS
NEW COMICS AVAILABLE EVERY WEDNESDAY.
CONSTANTLY EXPANDING BACKLIST OF TITLES.
AILABLE AT: amazonkindle comicsplus comiXology DARK HORSE DIGITAL Google play iTunes & MORE